WHAT CHEER

This word is the common seaman's salutation, "What cheer," now thoroughly naturalized into Cree . . . The expression, *"what cheer?"* has been adopted by the Indians, and is used both at *meeting* and at *parting,* answering in the former case to "how do you do?" and in the latter to "good bye." It is generally doubled, "what cheer? what cheer." From these words also is derived the verb *whatcheāmāo,* he "what cheers" him, that is, "salutes" him.

Watkins' Dictionary of the Cree Language, 1865

When, on Slate Rock, a footing was found,
*   The Abby Origines were sitting around;*
And Roger, thinking he'd like to sit down,
*   He quietly asked, "What Cheer?"*
From Miller's *"The Settlement of Rhode Island"*

Aye, aye, my boy,
What cheer, what cheer?

SIR W. S. GILBERT

"Avast!" says he, "Belay! What cheer!
How comes this little wessel here?
Come, tumble up your crew," says he,
"And navigate a bit with me!"

Says Captain Pitch, "I can't refuse
To join you on a friendly cruise;
But you'll oblige me, Captain Tar,
By not a-taking of me far."

CHARLES E. CARRYL

Books by DAVID MCCORD

Essays & Sketches:

ODDLY ENOUGH

STIRABOUT

ONCE AND FOR ALL

H.T.P.—PORTRAIT OF A CRITIC

Poetry & Verse:

FLOODGATE

THE CROWS

BAY WINDOW BALLADS

OXFORD NEARLY VISITED

TWELVE VERSES FROM XII NIGHT

AND WHAT'S MORE

ON OCCASION

WHAT CHEER

What Cheer

AN ANTHOLOGY OF

AMERICAN AND BRITISH

HUMOROUS AND WITTY VERSE

GATHERED, SIFTED, AND SALTED,

WITH AN INTRODUCTION BY

David McCord

COWARD-McCANN INC *NEW YORK*

Designed by Robert Josephy

J. N. W.

To Jim:
One book that is for him
Who shared so much so long
In weather, word, and song.

CONTENTS

Part Two

INTRODUCTION

In a collection where the reader has so wide a choice of anything and everything as here, I suppose he ought also to have the choice of at least a dozen introductions. Unfortunately, there is room for only one; and now that the labor of gathering, sifting, admiring, accepting, rejecting, regretting, arranging, rearranging, and re-admiring these many items is definitely over, a depleted editor has energy but for one. This is it.

I

Much might be said in behalf of laughter, yet I shall say little. In a world late at war, none but an idiot is likely to argue the worth of a top-drawer laugh, or even one of junior grade. Possess it while you can.

Abiding faith in laughter was the incentive for the making of this book. Fresh, saline, and cleansing as the sea, laughter is a basic commodity, an old affair in the world, an abstraction and reaction about which few will quarrel. So this book is based on nothing less —on the laughter of humor, something audible and contagious; on the laughter of wit, something swift and sudden in the queer little reflex tightening about the eyes. A large but simple collection, it includes, simply enough, what to me is the happiest of available wit and humor in American and British verse from any sensible date you want to name up to the vivid present. Territorially, it covers the United States and Great Britain—touching Scotland, Ireland, Canada, Australia, and South Africa. A lot of ground, a lot of laughter; a lot of authors, a lot of anonymity; a lot of divergence, a lot of correlation.

A few things need explanation. This is *not* a collection of "light verse" as such. I want to make that quite clear. A great deal of light verse is little more than a facile and charming exercise in the technique of rhyme and meter. Locker-Lampson, Austin Dobson, and Oliver Herford, for example, excelled in it. It pleases the eye and ear, reads well aloud, is polished as a pipkin—but is not necessarily funny or witty. Perhaps *bright* is the word. On the other hand, humorous and witty verse *is* light verse at its transcendent best. One has only to listen. The effect is like Spring.

> And if in Queens or Como
> I hear you singing, say!
> I'll sniff the sweet arom-o
> And breathe another day.

On this jaunty assumption, the editor set the qualifying conditions for admission to *What Cheer*. He set them as high as he could reach, and his neck is a little stiff from looking up. But nothing has slipped in out of favoritism or friendship or by request. The test has been: Is it funny? Is it witty? Nor has *yes, yes* to that afforded sufficient answer in itself. The verse had to be well turned and technically sound, so far as I could judge it. We are living in a day of sloppy writing, but you will discover, I hope and believe, nothing of the astigmatic in these pages. It was all in focus when last I bade it good-by.

One can hold up an egg to a candle to see if it is a good egg—if I may re-silver a phrase. One can do something of the sort with a piece of light verse, for unlike poetry there is no poor light verse: it is either good or bad, and the technique largely decides it. But there is no such test for the embyro of humor. Even the best of it seems to shift balance with the notional mood and perceptions of the reader. I am painfully aware of this abstruse and humorless fact. Thus, in assembling *What Cheer,* there was nothing to go by but brazen confidence in single judgment and in the impish impulse which makes any reader want to share with the next fellow what has just amused him.

But if humor and wit are treacherous and volatile goods, they are issued in no standard package. Their staccato, rhythmic expression in this anthology is to me endlessly and refreshingly new. This is a book of final differences, therefore, and not of mirrored similarities. I can put that in another perspective by quoting the words of a New England spinster on a Cape Cod train fifty years ago: "There's Sister Sarah, now. Her'n me ain't no more alike than's if 'twant us. She's just's diff'rent as I be, t'other way." So it is. And if people are friends in spots, as George Santayana (not Emerson) says, there are plenty of spots in which you and these verses are likely to become friends. The first nervous glance ought to tell you that.

II

There were difficulties and problems. The self-proposed range was broad in time and large in geography. It grew, if anything, broader and larger before *finis* could be said. How to relate the old with the new: the breezily American with the relaxed English, the period piece with the figure of jive, Australian slang with Mansota Norsk, the serenely classic with the animate colloquial? Or familiar with unfamiliar, seasoned with unseasoned, the old favorite with the young experimental? In what proportion? With what emphasis? For what audience? Most anthologies, it seems to me, jog on the chronological footpath way; some of them amœbae-like, divide and sub-divide into easy categories of satire, love, and antimacassars. But the chronological makes for the dullest of gambits, and the departmental jellies almost always into sections too

wide and too deep. I have to sit down in the middle
of my satire. I have to breathe; I have to digest. So I
early resolved that small and comfortable divisions
were what I wanted—each of them like an old chair,
easy to slip into; each with its own peculiar grace,
each with an inviting title, each with a likely subject
for someone. Furthermore, I would not permit the
categories to dictate; I would first see what my haulage
was and then worry about distribution. Once, many
years ago in Geneva, I saw this French sign in the window of a little bird shop: *Mélange Surchoix pour Bons
Chanteurs*—Super-Super-Mixture for Good Singers. I
would mix thoroughly in each section the verses that
went into it: time, place, voice, tone, size, shape—dis-
parate particles dispassionately shuffled. *Mélange surchoix!*

A labor of delight, I must confess—full of strange re-
wards and oblique surprises. It has meant the ransack-
ing of a larger segment of literature than one might at
first suppose. Even the circumstance of lifelong interest in the subject proved to be of not much more practical value than stimulus. I thought it unsafe, for instance, not to reread all of Bret Harte, Kipling,
Stephen, Holmes, Chesterton, Belloc, Gilbert, A. P.
Herbert, Hoffenstein, Squire, Quiller-Couch, Don
Marquis, Drummond, T. A. Daly, and dozens of others. It seemed only fair and sound to give such writers
fresh representation where that was possible, or at
least to re-satisfy oneself that the familiar choices from
their work had been the right ones right along. (Often
they were.) Certain American wits like Keith Preston,
Bert Leston Taylor, Leonard Bacon, and Christopher
Morley have never been too favored by anthologists in
this field, or across the fence in the loamier topsoil of
light verse. Several of the best things in the following
pages are signed with their names. First-flight British
Calverleys like Dum-Dum, Frank Sidgwick, Patrick

Barrington, and the late Sir Walter Raleigh, I venture
the opinion, are virtually unknown to any considerable American audience. Or known but for one thing,
as Sidgwick for his parody, "An Antient Poem" (not
present) and Raleigh for his famous "Wishes of an
Elderly Man" (present). The Canadian Wilson Mac-
Donald deserves a better hearing among those familiar
with the flavory old Province of Quebec from which
his contemporary *voyageurs* are drawn. The late C. J.
Dennis of Australia has never before, to my knowledge, appeared in any American anthology of this sort.
His countryman, Ernest G. Moll (a poet of strength),
should be better known to us, and some of his lighter
side is represented here. I am particularly glad to have
these verses from the courageous land Down Under.

Then what of the poets themselves—both British
and American—who have turned in a fateful hour
from the serious to the humorous? Such intramural
writing is frequently better than all but the best of the
marketed article. So you will find in this company
some odd yet characteristic verses not only by Hardy,
Housman, Rupert Brooke, and Edwin Arlington Robinson, but others by Frost, Masefield, de la Mare, Gogarty, L. A. G. Strong, James Stephens, Ralph Hodgson,
and Robert Hillyer. Back of them, of course, I have
drawn (though sparingly) against the familiar cache of
humor in the work of Coleridge, Hood, Pope, Cowper,
Burns, and a few more of the ripe old boys. Of new
and unknown names in verse, it pleases the editor to
claim at least fourteen, including the anthropologist
Earnest A. Hooton, whose very few published rhymes
have hitherto been modestly trapped in the footnotes
of his own scientific books. As to the elder great masters—Lear, Carroll, Calverley, and who else?—I have
tried to temper enthusiasm with proportion.

A few chance ventures disappointed. Reading Hen-
ley through yielded but one double ballade—and not

funny enough when weighed on the scales in the presence of contending material. Upturning nothing useful in W. H. Davies, a rather serious poet, was no surprise; but nothing in Sandburg, yes. Wherever hidden humor was suspected, it was sought. A zero for H. C. Bunner, though, will surely seem incredible to some; but Bunner for me remains a writer of delicate sentiment and light (not humorous) rhyme. His famous "Home Sweet Home with Variations" might be here, but it dates and creaks a little now, and is in enough anthologies not to miss the patronage of one more. Praed's lovers will want other Praed—but again, in my judgment, this minor master belongs wholly in the light category. For all deplorable gaps I am truly sorry. No one knows better than an editor how frighteningly close to his back yard is the vast and pathless estate of ignorance.

Among individual verses, excluding limericks and epitaphs, fewer than one hundred old favorites passed through the gilded portals. What reason to leave them out? What argument to include them? If time has been kind to their vitamin content and they have clearly retained the red corpuscles of amusement, there was no denying them entrance: "A Ternarie of Littles," "The Owl and the Pussy-Cat," "Gemini and Virgo," "Canopus," "Antigonish," "Plain Language from Truthful James," "Tobacco," "Lay of Ancient Rome," "Résumé," "A Letter of Advice," "The Walloping Window-blind," "The Modern Hiawatha," "On the Antiquity of Microbes," "When Moonlike Ore the Hazure Seas." . . .

A slice of America itself is in this book, and a wedge of the British Isles. But not quite fifty-fifty. Humorous verse has flourished longer in England than with us. For many years we were too busy requiting Indians, colonizing, moving west, building cities, learning to read—and growing up—to cultivate it as an art. You find calico humor, of course, in our frontier ballads; but ballads out of their setting are apt to be long, monotonous, and uneven—skeletons for the scholar rather than flesh and blood for posterity. *Tuneful* is the banjo word for folk-song. "Casey Jones" and all his pals of two opposed sexes are stationed in enough books not to be missed here with these jolly Jack Points where they do not actually belong. But the *sense* of balladry is in many of the verses present. American names so desperately dear to Stephen Benét are strewn like New Hampshire boulders through "The American Traveller," "Pan in Vermont," "Étude Géographique," and "The Maiden of Passama-quoddy"; and their presence elsewhere tends to out-syllable the Bootles, Hulls, and Tattenham Corners of England in such verses as "The Spectre," "Come to Britain," and "The Famous Ballad of the Jubilee Cup." Kid March in the ring while Idbury Bells are rung. . . .

III

A book, unlike a ship, is never launched into a fully predictable medium. The ship slides down the ways, with the blessing of champagne and band music, into a sea of water. A book emerges, to the tiny dry piping of its publisher, into a world of conflicting taste and opinion. It is cheering to reflect, therefore, that at this strange immediate moment rhyme is more on the tongues of men and women than one would think. The armed services, the headline writer; the sound-track on sports, travel features, and such in the movies; some of the national advertisers, and certain radio programs are fooling with funny and not-so-funny verses daily. The younger generation, with a jukebox fondness for expressions like *beat feet*,[1] *zoot-suit, drape*

[1] How De Quincey hated "a book bearing on its backbone the harsh title 'Burke's Works'!" But Swinburne could swing it. See his half-title verse to *Bowlines & Seascapes*.

shape, thriller-diller, razzle-dazzle, quiver-giver, fender-bender, slick chick; What's buzzin', cousin?; What keeps this noggin joggin', or this chicken tickin'?; In a word, bird; Do you dig me, Pygmy?; and such bargain jargon is fully aware of it. The super-duper paratrooper hit the silk along with thousands of other white dandelions floating to the earth in the second World War. An *AP* Wirephoto of a warning in rhyme on the road to Bizerte read:

> Don't bunch up
> You silly Gookus;
> They still have 88's
> And Stukas.

A *UP* dispatch from Hove, England, October 2, 1941, reported that "this verse was chalked on the walls of the Hove railway station today":

> Gather ye rosebuds while ye may
> For time brings only sorrow;
> Girls you might have kissed today
> May wear gas masks tomorrow.

One of the most famous epigrammatic lines to emerge from the War to date is, of course,

> Sighted sub sank same.

It isn't verse, it doesn't rhyme; it merely alliterates. Yet the *feeling* for verse is there; and the balance, rhythm, and laconic humor of it stop you, plain as a pikestaff.

Now the do-you-dig-me-pygmy school flourishes most concisely in the sound-track industry. For example, in a film showing the training of one of the big Coast crews, the coxswain puts it up to thirty-six, and the sound-track says:

> How'd you like a coke, stroke?

and everybody laughs. Everybody laughs again—we
may suppose—when the voice says

> On your hide: *slide!*

This use of what I call *juxtarime* may yet amount to
a national disease. Some of it is cheap, some of it inspired; but I have never heard one quite so good as
the dainty aside of a State-of-Maine man who years
ago, to my knowledge, referred to his indolent boy as

> My son, Emmet,
> God demmit!

Another thing, and less temporal. From the days of
our counting-out rhymes, fragments of funny verse
have stuck in the minds of most of us—stowed away
topside, perhaps, and forgotten.

> Oh, what is the use
> Of chewing tobacco,
> And spitting the juice?

Or

> Lips that touch wine jelly
> Will never touch mine, Nellie.

Perhaps a Macaulay schoolboy wrote the next one,
though it is possibly too good for that. I quote it to
prove that high polish and sheen are not the last
desideratum in the art. "How true," as Morris Bishop
says; "how true!"

> As I was laying on the green,
> A small English book I seen,
> Carlyle's *Essay on Burns* was the edition,
> So I left it laying in the same position.

Deepest down in us, possibly, is the half-developed
creative faculty which once in a long while comes wonderfully to our command to help us turn some measly

bit of prose into what might be or become a single line of laughable verse. Have you never done something akin to what Doctor Johnson is doing here?

> "Johnson was present when a tragedy was read, in which there occurred this line:
>> Who rules o'er freemen should himself be free.
> "The company having admired it much, 'I cannot agree with you [said Johnson]; it might as well be said,
>> Who drives fat oxen should himself be fat.'"

IV

Parody for the moment is out of fashion. It may be that there is nothing new or good enough to invite the art of writing "nonsense for the nonce"—to misappropriate the words of Byron. The last double lustrum of verse-parody perished somewhere in the twenties—a harder death in England than here at home. One day it will surely revive. If "a not wholly admirable art," as Sir J. C. Squire allowed twenty-eight years ago in the dedication to his *Tricks of the Trade,* let us remember that a sturdy and impressive band has flown its clown-white standard since before the time of Euboeus. *Alice* would not be much of a book without it, would it now?

I have tried to deal sternly with it here, yet there was enough left over after the fifth screening to fill a section. Of course, not all of the parodies chosen could be so isolated. Where the subject controlled, it seemed wisest to put those stanzas elsewhere. For example, E. B. White's "A Classic Waits for Me" belongs in *Life & Letters*—where you will find it, cornfed and silky-coated. Corey Ford's quite remarkable literary prize fight (March vs. Frost) seeks a trickier sort of company. "A Pipe of Tobacco" obviously goes with the other clear Havanas; Harold A. Larrabee's disturbing

effort, "The Very Model of a Modern College President," has a one-way ticket for *College & Curriculum;*
A. P. Herbert's Shakespearean "Recipe" joins the right
wing of *Grapejuice & Mr. Collins.* So, as a matter of
fact, with some other things in other categories: Edward Lear's beloved self-portrait is with *Acquaint-
ances* and not under *Incense & Nonsense,* where it well
could be. But mostly—mostly—the peach is on the
peach tree and the melon on the ground.

Of dialect I was even more frightened. But there
was plainly enough good stuff available to tell me that
I could not jettison it all. Lowell seemed too much
like Keats' stretched metre to yield a short burst for
my purpose. Dialect doesn't age well. But this little
roundup of relatively recent things amuses me, and it
may well amuse the reader. Try MacDonald. And how
could one as yet pass by "Mia Carlotta"? The French
Quebec material I segregated under *Habitant.* Perhaps only the fishermen will turn to it (though it is
not about fishing)—but then who better?

Presence of Drummond's "The Wreck of the 'Julie
Plante,'" a veteran of American anthologies if there
ever was one, reminds me that often it was impossible
to find more than a single choice among my authors.
"M'sieu Smit'," also by Drummond, was his only other
possibility; but "M'sieu Smit'" is much longer than
his name, and he is present in a slightly cut version in
Morris Bishop's *A Treasury of British Humor.* There
were only two choices for this collection from Jan
Struther's *The Glass-Blower and Other Poems.* I later
found them both in F.P.A.'s *Innocent Merriment;* had
circumstances permitted, I should have used one.

Curiously enough, there came to light no really
funny verses about golf, baseball—sports in general,
for that matter—or dogs. Very little on cats, either.
The golf supply, in particular, seemed outmoded and
outplayed. So there is no sports section as such, though

Q's "The Famous Ballad of the Jubilee Cup" is almost
a sports section in itself. I have stabled it with my
string of piebald ponies *(Bridlewise)*, and it seems
quite comfortable there. In another area: but little on
art; relatively nothing on the theatre. Again, though
not quite so curiously: In reading proof I first observed that the majority of the verses under *Romance*
are by Englishmen—and one Irishman; the American
counterpart is lodged with the wicked skeptics in *The
Malicious Male* and *The Unfair Sex*. And we used to
be called a sentimental nation!

For one's money, I daresay that the nearly seventy
epitaphs under *Tombstone & Twilight* are best likely
to reward the widest reading. Anyway, they are short
and not difficult to commit to memory.

> Here lies the body of Mary Anne Lowder,
> She burst while drinking a Seidlitz powder.
> Called from this world to her heavenly rest,
> She should have waited till it effervesced.

As to that, most good humorous or witty verse is short,
and there are relatively few long pieces in this book.
Only "The Up-Set" and Q's "Ballad" come to seven
or more pages—or anything like it.

V

The final text, when all assembled, suggested without
much uncertainty some thirty-one sections. Perhaps
there were one or two others, but eventually they were
absorbed by lateral osmosis into the larger units. Most
of these sections confine themselves to a single subject:
eating, drinking, childhood, characters, places, the sea,
tricky verse, etc. A few coalesced—such as brief satire
and epigrams, history and science. Tobacco and fishing are natural twins, and there was no doubt about
grouping *them* together. Tobacco verses come a dime

a dozen. As to fishing: like any fly fisherman, I began my search thinking, "I'll hae a wheen o' troots ere nicht." But I didna hae 'em. Still, to land "Master and Man" unexpectedly from the deep pool of Henry Newbolt's collected poems sent me back to camp happy and well rewarded.

The limerick, being a very special form in itself, and plentiful in season, is entitled to a separate enclosure, and gets it. Other special verse forms, however, such as the ballade, triolet, sonnet (for there *are* some funny sonnets), the chant royal, and all these fancy French and foreign things, are dispersed according to subject and not according to structure. A number of verses concern war—a few of them hot from the smoke of the fight as then unfinished. But it has seemed wiser to arrange them according to individual character rather than to give them collectively a battle title. Excellent among these are the now famous "Message to General Montgomery" and "Ludmilla." Three other good war verses came from Italy via the *Stars and Stripes*. I wish something had turned up from the Pacific—as it will one day.

VI

The mechanics of the whole collection are as simple as a T square. You may read and run—or run first. I think I have not forgotten that all verse must meet the eye as well as the ear, and that it may also have to meet the mind. Now there is nothing more discouraging than a good stanza tangled up in footnotes. The bloody assassin of poetry studied in school is largely the freckled face of the textbook page on which it is printed. "Lycidas" with footnotes looks like the blueprint for a slalom course. Away with Persian apparatus! The pinch of notes salted the length of the following text is virtually invisible. All glossaries, asides, comment, observations, comparisons, references, appraisal, collateral evidence, and quotations which the editor was feebly unable to resist repose in a single section entitled *After All*. If you are fascinated by "Antigonish," for instance, you will find by turning there to the corresponding paragraph a word on the verse by the author himself. Mr. Hemminger (as interviewed) explains the origin of "Tobacco is a dirty weed"; Mr. Ybarra reflects on his "Lay of Ancient Rome"; Harry Graham's "Little Willie" is modernized for England at war, and so on. . . . It would neither be fair nor intelligent to include two selections by C. J. Dennis without his personal glossary—and that's where the glossary is. "Waltzing Matilda," familiar enough to Americans as a radio song, is also (and primarily) an exciting piece of verse, with a queer little humor and a tuckerbag history. But by and large, *After All* should be enjoyed as another section of verse—albeit fragmentary and allusive. Some of the best things of this book are in it. It is, in a way, a little book in itself.

A word on editing. No book is editor-proof or proof-reader-proof, but the greatest pains have been taken to make this collection as accurate as humanly possible. The editor alone is responsible for the work (and the works) from first selection to final index. Not the least part of anything but typing has been delegated. So many anthologies lately have been made from other anthologies that by now some strange-looking verses are in the public domain. Quite a lot of them typographically resemble an old pair of darned socks—undarned would be nearer the truth. One famous item in a current popular low-priced collection has no less than five important words wrong in its twenty brief lines. This is a regrettable disservice to an author no longer alive to defend his rights. Why not consult the original? People don't go about putting juicy wet accents of blue and red oil on well-known pictures by reputable painters. They wouldn't dream of it! Yet some editors have no comparable respect for the considered words of a poet, let alone for his disposal of them and his dreamy sense of punctuation.

In *What Cheer* I have assiduously tried to use authoritative editions wherever feasible. Occasionally a small correction has been made where something obviously slipped in the original: as *corncake* for *corncrake* in de la Mare's "The Spectre" in the American edition of his *Stuff and Nonsense*. A few untidy little messes of commas and semi-colons here and there have been mopped up. I have endeavored to retain English spelling wherever characteristic: colour, harbour, honour, enamour, kerb, grey, despatch, etc. Single quotation marks in general have been adhered to for English verses; double for American. Asterisks, as in Dum-Dum's "Circumstance without Pomp" and Graham's "Presence of Mind," were put there by the author himself; dots (. . . .) are the editor's handiwork and indicate omission on his part. In a very few cases, some obvious inconsistencies in dialect verse have been corrected. Proofreading dialect, incidentally, is an easy short cut over the hill to the lunatic asylum. At best it resembles driving slowly over a stretch of highway under repair, and the only reward lies in regaining the swift, smooth levels of verse of normal speech in the galleys beyond. Very fortunately the lay reader doesn't have to spell it out. And I am sure there are no luke-warm admirers of dialect rhyme. One either likes it or hates it. I know a few people who really like it.

VII

Wide as the reach of subject and circumstance which produced, across two hemispheres and several centuries, these hundreds of verses, even wider is their range of expression between a) elemental humor and b) the razor edge of wit. How wide, a serendipitist could not guess until this moment. But no anthology was ever meant to be swallowed at a sitting, and the reader (I hope) will quickly find his happiest level and proceed at his own pace. He may (you may) wonder now and then exactly what took my fancy in this and that, and just why I think it is amusing. In every case, I could give you a cheerful and astonishing answer, though it might not satisfy. Sometimes it was merely the viewpoint, the approach, or the turn of a phrase that won me. Anybody can see that Chesterton's "Elegy in a Country Churchyard" is witty, though—or perhaps because—the wit lies wholly in the last two contrasting lines. But some things are witty by indirection, and some things are comic simply by being unexpected. Analysis can kill; I put my trust in reaction. A twinkle is often better than a hundred watts of Mazda. I am thinking in particular of "Retrospect" by Roy Davis—and not just because I am a fisherman.

Perhaps an editor's choice of a dozen favorites will help the lone adventurer who has pressed this far into a totally new and unexplored tundra, and revive his doubting spirits. Only a dozen; but they differ widely, each from the other. If all are failures, then this book is definitely not for him. Perhaps a treatise on fungus or an old book of sermons . . . At any rate here are the dozen, with page references for easy examination. They are not arranged in any special order. Rinse the mouth with black coffee between sips.

VIII

Finally, an affectionate word on the craft itself.
There is no denying the fact that verse written solely
to amuse is at a disadvantage on the critical scale. Perhaps because it lays no serious claim to distinction it
is not presumed to be distinguished. And yet it often
is. "Lady Jane," for example, for all its wonderful
humor and sheen of surface-tension—for all its pro-
fessed artificiality—remains a very simple and touching
verse at heart; and many must remember it, and prefer
to remember it, above a slew of serious poems which
pass (and have long passed) for the real thing.

The gift of wit is a rare talent in itself; and if not
bitter or misused, as Pope had a way of misusing it,
capable almost on its own of high flights into art.
Many verses in this collection are superior in technique, freshness, and subtlety to many first-rate lyrics,
covering many periods, in the serious anthologies.
There is good reason for this. For one thing, as A. P.
Herbert has pointed out, the standards of light verse
in general are high and they are held high. For another, certain definitions and limitations—equally in-
escapable—compel respect for those standards. An idea,
a situation, a sense of playfulness *has* to be communicated. There is no halfway about that. Fashion, which
always has a hand in the higher art of poetry, is cau-
tious and slow to move in this small field. Writers
know instinctively that the devious, the labyrinthic,

is fatal to wit, fatal to humor. There is no substitute as yet for discipline, drill, and patience. I can think of a good deal of contemporary poetry, the reading of which is like swimming on your back under water and looking up at an uncomfortable sky. That may be all right, but not so with the things in this book. Ephemeral as many of them appear to be and are, they have an intrinsic strength and firmness, and the gossamer threads which bind them together have been well tarred. "A low kind of art?" asked the great George Saintsbury in *A History of English Prosody*. "That does not seem a necessary subject of discussion. The point is that it is the very highest kind of its own art; and that is all that we have to do with. An easy kind of art? Go thou and do likewise."

Well, most of these contributors, I think, have gone and done it. And when a verse looms up with the grace and ease and disarming inevitability of "The Anatomy of Humor," "Message to General Montgomery," or "Wishes of an Elderly Man," I have a queer, proud feeling of reverence for it. The perfect thing in a perfect mold.

> Since Leda's egg swans strive
> to innovate no curvature on that . . .

You are now on your own.

DAVID McCORD

Part One

ACQUAINTANCES

For all is not Bass that is bottled,
And all is not pork that is pie.
RICHARD LE GALLIENNE

Many men of many minds,
Many fish of many kinds.
ANONYMOUS

A creature of appearances, is he not?
PLATO

Circumstance without Pomp

The gale had passed, but chilling was the air,
  A simple tramp came wand'ring o'er the hill—
A man of peaceful habit, free from care,
  Save that he felt a trifle wet and chill.

Calmly, with equal mind but broken shoe,
  Onward he moved, until at length he stood
Where an adjacent haystack met his view
  (A crop both scarce and dear, but very good).

This he regarded in a casual way,
  Then, finding warmth his prevalent desire,
Drew forth a match and lit the ready hay,
  And in a moment had a first-class fire.

And there he basked upon the leeward side,
  Till the rude farmer came and raised a storm,
To whose unseemly protests he replied,
  Mildly, that he had done it 'for a warm.'

*   *   *   *

A simple tramp. Perchance a simple tale,
  But what a greatness! Surely we have here
A calm, cool mind that knows not how to fail,
  A steady brain that sees its purpose clear;

An elemental soul that gives no heed
  To right or wrong—surmounts without a pause
The disproportionate vastness of his deed,
  Nor care the 2d. that he lacks for laws.

What is a stack? A barn, a homestead roof—
  Whole villages shall flare at his commands;
Great towns and cities shall be nowise proof
  If such an one aspire to warm his hands.

Does he need victual? Is he void of trust?
  Poultry and flocks his instant need shall slake;
Ten thousand fatted beeves shall bite the dust
  Ere he go lacking in a modest steak.

Oh, see him! 'Tis a sight to stir the heart,
  Serene of purpose, ready, swift, and bold,
The kingly impulse of a BUONAPARTE
  Were less than his, if he is feeling cold.

Yet did men hail him as a demigod,
  And raise him up? Ah, no. I grieve to state
That this high soul is languishing in quod,
  With three months' hard, for daring to be great.

                                        DUM-DUM

How Pleasant to Know Mr. Lear

"How pleasant to know Mr. Lear!"
  Who has written such volumes of stuff!
Some think him ill-tempered and queer,
  But a few think him pleasant enough.

His mind is concrete and fastidious,
  His nose is remarkably big;
His visage is more or less hideous,
  His beard it resembles a wig.

He has ears, and two eyes, and ten fingers,
  Leastways if you reckon two thumbs;
Long ago he was one of the singers,
  But now he is one of the dumbs.

He sits in a beautiful parlour,
  With hundreds of books on the wall;
He drinks a great deal of Marsala,
  But never gets tipsy at all.

He has many friends, lay men and clerical,
   Old Foss is the name of his cat;
His body is perfectly spherical,
   He weareth a runcible hat.

When he walks in a waterproof white,
   The children run after him so!
Calling out, "He's come out in his night
   gown, that crazy old Englishman, oh!"

He weeps by the side of the ocean,
   He weeps on the top of the hill;
He purchases pancakes and lotion,
   And chocolate shrimps from the mill.

He reads, but he cannot speak, Spanish,
   He cannot abide ginger beer:
Ere the days of his pilgrimage vanish,
   How pleasant to know Mr. Lear!

EDWARD LEAR

Brown's Descent
or, the Willy-Nilly Slide

Brown lived at such a lofty farm
   That everyone for miles could see
His lantern when he did his chores
   In winter after half-past three.

And many must have seen him make
   His wild descent from there one night,
'Cross lots, 'cross walls, 'cross everything,
   Describing rings of lantern light.

Between the house and barn the gale
   Got him by something he had on
And blew him out on the icy crust
   That cased the world, and he was gone!

Walls were all buried, trees were few:
   He saw no stay unless he stove
A hole in somewhere with his heel.
   But though repeatedly he strove

And stamped and said things to himself,
   And sometimes something seemed to yield,
He gained no foothold, but pursued
   His journey down from field to field.

Sometimes he came with arms outspread
   Like wings, revolving in the scene
Upon his longer axis, and
   With no small dignity of mien.

Faster or slower as he chanced,
   Sitting or standing as he chose,
According as he feared to risk
   His neck, or thought to spare his clothes,

He never let the lantern drop.
   And some exclaimed who saw afar
The figures he described with it,
   "I wonder what those signals are

"Brown makes at such an hour of night!
   He's celebrating something strange.
I wonder if he's sold his farm,
   Or been made Master of the Grange."

He reeled, he lurched, he bobbed, he checked;
   He fell and made the lantern rattle
(But saved the light from going out).
   So half-way down he fought the battle,

Incredulous of his own bad luck.
   And then becoming reconciled
To everything, he gave it up
   And came down like a coasting child.

"Well—I—be—" that was all he said,
  As standing in the river road,
He looked back up the slippery slope
  (Two miles it was) to his abode.

Sometimes as an authority
  On motor-cars, I'm asked if I
Should say our stock was petered out,
  And this is my sincere reply:

Yankees are what they always were.
  Don't think Brown ever gave up hope
Of getting home again because
  He couldn't climb that slippery slope;

Or even thought of standing there
  Until the January thaw
Should take the polish off the crust.
  He bowed with grace to natural law,

Then circumvented it on foot.
  He jogged the lantern saying, "Ile's
'Bout out!" then took the long way home
  By road, a matter of several miles.

ROBERT FROST

Old Dan'l

Out of his cottage to the sun
Bent double comes old Dan'l,
His chest all over cotton wool,
His back all over flannel.

'Winter will finish him,' they've said
Each winter now for ten:
But come the first warm day of Spring
Old Dan'l's out again.

L. A. G. STRONG

There is Hallelujah Hannah

There is Hallelujah Hannah
  Walking backwards down the lane,
And I hear the loud Hosanna
  Of regenerated Jane;
And Lieutenant Isabella
  In the centre of them comes,
Dealing blows with her umbrella
  On the trumpets and the drums.

A. E. HOUSMAN

Miniver Cheevy

Miniver Cheevy, child of scorn,
  Grew lean while he assailed the seasons;
He wept that he was ever born,
  And he had reasons.

Miniver loved the days of old
  When swords were bright and steeds were prancing;
The vision of a warrior bold
  Would set him dancing.

Miniver sighed for what was not,
  And dreamed, and rested from his labors;
He dreamed of Thebes and Camelot,
  And Priam's neighbors.

Miniver mourned the ripe renown
  That made so many a name so fragrant;
He mourned Romance, now on the town,
  And Art, a vagrant.

Miniver loved the Medici,
  Albeit he had never seen one;
He would have sinned incessantly
  Could he have been one.

Miniver cursed the commonplace
  And eyed a khaki suit with loathing;
He missed the mediaeval grace
  Of iron clothing.

Miniver scorned the gold he sought,
  But sore annoyed was he without it;
Miniver thought, and thought, and thought,
  And thought about it.

Miniver Cheevy, born too late,
  Scratched his head and kept on thinking;
Miniver coughed, and called it fate,
  And kept on drinking.

EDWIN ARLINGTON ROBINSON

An Original Cuss

A real original, I think,
  My friend Bill can be termed;
A smoker, not inveterate,
  A drinker, not confirmed,

A hail fellow, but not well met,
  A realtor, but no Babbitt;
I never knew a cuss like Bill
  For cutting loose from habit.

KEITH PRESTON

Plain Language from Truthful James

Which I wish to remark,
  And my language is plain,
That for ways that are dark
  And for tricks that are vain,
The heathen Chinee is peculiar,
  Which the same I would rise to explain.

Ah Sin was his name;
    And I shall not deny,
In regard to the same,
    What that name might imply;
But his smile it was pensive and childlike,
    As I frequent remarked to Bill Nye.

It was August the third,
    And quite soft was the skies;
Which it might be inferred
    That Ah Sin was likewise;
Yet he played it that day upon William
    And me in a way I despise.

Which we had a small game,
    And Ah Sin took a hand:
It was euchre. The same
    He did not understand;
But he smiled as he sat by the table.
    With the smile that was childlike and bland.

Yet the cards they were stocked
    In a way that I grieve,
And my feelings were shocked
    At the state of Nye's sleeve,
Which was stuffed full of aces and bowers,
    And the same with intent to deceive.

But the hands that were played
    By that heathen Chinee,
And the points that he made,
    Were quite frightful to see;
Till at last he put down a right bower,
    Which the same Nye had dealt unto me.

Then I looked up at Nye,
    And he gazed upon me;
And he rose with a sigh,

And said, "Can this be?
We are ruined by Chinese cheap labor,"
    And he went for that heathen Chinee.

In the scene that ensued
    I did not take a hand;
But the floor it was strewed
    Like the leaves on the strand,
With the cards that Ah Sin had been hiding,
    In the game "he did not understand."

In his sleeves, which were long,
    He had twenty-four jacks,
Which was coming it strong,
    Yet I state but the facts;
And we found on his nails, which were taper,
    What is frequent in tapers—that's wax.

Which is why I remark,
    And my language is plain,
That for ways that are dark
    And for tricks that are vain,
The heathen Chinee is peculiar,
    Which the same I am free to maintain.

BRET HARTE

"Jim"

Say there! P'r'aps
    Some on you chaps
    Might know Jim Wild?
Well,—no offence:
Thar ain't no sense
    In gittin' riled!

Jim was my chum
    Up on the Bar:
That's why I come

Down from up yar,
Lookin' for Jim.
Thank ye, sir! *You*
Ain't of that crew,—
　Blest if you are!

Money?—Not much:
　That ain't my kind;
I ain't no such,
　Rum?—I don't mind,
Seein' it's you.

Well, this yer Jim,—
Did you know him?
Jess' 'bout your size;
Same kind of eyes,—
Well, that is strange:
　Why, it's two year
　Since he came here,
Sick, for a change.

Well, here's to us:
　　Eh?
The h— you say!
　　Dead?—
That little cuss?

What makes you star,
You over thar?
Can't a man drop
's glass in yer shop
But you must r'ar?
　It wouldn't take
　D— much to break
You and your bar.
　　Dead!
Poor—little—Jim!
—Why, thar was me,

Jones, and Bob Lee,
Harry and Ben,—
No-account men:
Then to take *him!*

Well, thar— Good-by,—
No more, sir,—I—
    Eh?
What's that you say?—
Why, dern it!—sho!—
No? Yes! By Joe!
        Sold!
Sold! Why, you limb,
You ornery,
        Derned old
Long-legged Jim!

BRET HARTE

Waltzing Matilda

Once a jolly swagman [1] camped by a billabong
Under the shade of a coolibah tree.
And he sang as he watched and waited till his billy
    boiled:
"You'll come a-waltzing, Matilda, with me!"

Chorus:

Waltzing, Matilda, waltzing, Matilda,
You'll come a-waltzing, Matilda, with me.
And he sang as he watched and waited till his billy
    boiled,
"You'll come a-waltzing, Matilda, with me!"

Down came a jumbuck to drink at the billabong,
Up jumped the swagman and grabbed him with glee,
And he sang as he stowed that jumbuck in his tucker
    bag:
"You'll come a-waltzing, Matilda, with me!"

[1] For some talk about this verse, see *After All.*

Chorus:

Waltzing, Matilda, waltzing, Matilda,
You'll come a-waltzing, Matilda, with me.
And he sang as he stowed that jumbuck in his tucker
     bag:
"You'll come a-waltzing, Matilda, with me!"

Up rode the squatter mounted on his thoroughbred,
Down came the troopers, one, two, three,
And his, "Where's that jolly jumbuck you've got in
     your tucker bag?"
"You'll come a-waltzing, Matilda, with me!"

Chorus:

Waltzing, Matilda, waltzing, Matilda,
You'll come a-waltzing, Matilda, with me.
And his, "Where's that jolly jumbuck you've got in
     your tucker bag?"
"You'll come a-waltzing, Matilda, with me!"

Up jumped the swagman, sprang into the billabong.
"You'll never catch me alive," said he.
And his ghost may be heard as you pass by that billa-
     bong:
"You'll come a-waltzing, Matilda, with me!"

Chorus:

Waltzing, Matilda, waltzing, Matilda,
You'll come a-waltzing, Matilda, with me.
And his ghost may be heard as you pass by that billa-
     bong:
"You'll come a-waltzing, Matilda, with me!"

A. B. PATERSON

And/Or

The Government gave Simeon Clay
Terrific headaches by the way
It made him fill out numerous blanks
Without a single word of thanks.
It even threatened, stern and grim,
To fine and/or imprison him
If he omitted to compile
The schedules which it loved to file.

Clay looked around, saw it was worse
And ever harder on the purse
In England, Finland, Yap, Siam,
The Argentine, and parts of Guam.
So off he went, a week ago,
To turn into an Eskimo,
Far in the North where cross officials
Will shriek in vain for his initials,
And where he will ignore their wishes
And live on ice and little fishes.

CLARENCE DAY

Sam

*At Brisbane
he meets an
old Chum
who has
contrived to
get a place
among the
Pilgrims.*

Propped on the bar,
His dial a-grin,
He shouted, "You thar,
Come on right in!
Togged up, a dude
In khaki, like me—
Didn't know you'd
Come on *this* spree.

"Eh? You do not
Know who I am?
I'm old Sam Stott,
Pious old Sam!—

But the Sam you
Knew's off the slate:
He's fifty-two—
I'm thirty-eight.

"Savvy, old chap?
I fixed it all.
(Let's have a lap;
This is my call.)
I am, I guess,
Two men in one:
I'm old Stott, yes,
And young Sam Dunn.

"Soon as I knew
War was the ticket,
I humped my blue—
I couldn't stick it
Out back; this scrum
Warn't to be missed;
So off I come
Here, to enlist.

"Told the young jay
Date o' my birth:
Forty next May,
Born down in Perth.
So I slid through,
Safe as a rock,
Till I come to
Deal with the doc.

"That doc's no card
To fondle the sick;
Pokes with a hard
Fist like a brick;
Biffs me—I stood
Stripped 'fore he'd start—

Says, *'You're* no good,
Y' want a new heart!'

"Gosh! but that squirt
Fair made me dizzy;
His 'Put on yer shirt,
Meander, I'm busy,'
Stunned me complete;
Next thing I knows on,
I'm in the street,
Chucked, wi' my clo'es on.

"That had me bust,
That did me down;
I went an' just
Painted the town,
Dreamed, while I sat
Blind in this pub,
I'd flattened that
Doc with a club.

"Then, when I stood
Pretty near broke,
Thinks I, 'No good
Playin' the moke;
I could arrive at
Th' Front if I tried,
This war ain't private:
I'm goin' inside.

"Fust, I found a
Hair-dresser's shop;
'Mister,' I say,
'Gimme a crop,
An' when that's cleared,
Don't make no gashes,
Scrape off my beard,
An' my moustaches.'

"Wal, from that place
When I depart,
I'd lost my face—
Kep' my old heart!
Out, slick an' smug,
New-like, I came
With a new mug—
And a new name.

"At the deepo
I slung it straight:
*Sam Dunn, Chill'goe,
Age, thirty-eight.*
Doc banged my ribs,
Like he would break 'em,
'Good,' says his nibs,
'Good as they make 'em!'

"That is how I
Served him up raw,
So's to git my
Share o' this War.
New heart, the chump!
M' old 'un, I'm in with it,
And—it's—a—trump:
You see me win with it!"

ST. JOHN ADCOCK
1914

Situation Normal

I'm a six foot t'ree from Brooklyn,
A hunnert eighty when I'm bare.
Me hand is big as hammers
And me chest's a mat o' hair.
I uster be a boxer,
In de Dead End I wuz tops.

I wuz raised on lemon extract,
T'hell wid whiskey slops.
De Moider, Inc., boys wuz me pals,
I scare guys wid me puss.
To your sixty-four buck question,
I'm a typist, pal, t'ank youse.

SGT. HANK CHERNICK

From *The Stars and Stripes*,
Italy, 1944.

The Fat-buttocked Bushmen

The Bushman's stature is not great,
    His jaw is quite prognathous;
Within his yellow, wool-starred pate
    His skull is not capacious.
His seamed membranous lips are thick,
    His malars are protrusive;
He sprays his words with dental click,
    His speech is most effusive.
He squints with epicanthous eye
    Across a nose prodigious;
He likes his ostrich-eggs quite high,
    His women steatopygous.

EARNEST A. HOOTON

Big Chief Wotapotami

Big Chief Wotapotami
Sat in the sun
And said, "Me hot am I."
Sat in the shade
And said, "Me cooler."
Such is the life
Of an Indian ruler.

Big Chief Wotapotami
Said to his tribe
(The Potawatami):
"White man come,
You get-um earful;
Want-um you boys
Be kind o' keerful."

DAVID McCORD

Reservation

Buffalo Moon and Sun-Go-Under
Lived with the loon by the Lake of Thunder,
Hunted the deer with a queer quartz arrow;
Now they've a cow and a plow and harrow.

Buffalo Moon and Sun-Go-Under
Lay by the spruce where the moose would blunder
Down to the stream and the gleam of water;
Sold for a dram and a lamb to slaughter.

Buffalo Moon and Sun-Go-Under
Rode with the proud in a cloud of wonder,
Rode all day till the rain came heavy;
Now it's the wheel of a real good Chevvy.

Buffalo Moon and Sun-Go-Under
Stood by the Canyon's grand asunder,
Looked on the stars, learned myth and fable;
The white man gave them West and Gable.

Buffalo Moon and Sun-Go-Under,
One rotund and the other rotunder,
One fecund and the other fecunder,
Live in a village (no pillage or plunder);
Live in peace (as the Soviét works)
Under the breeze of the national networks.

DAVID McCORD

I Wonder What Became of Rand, McNally. . . .

Mr. Rand and Mr. McNally,
Arbiters of hill and valley,
Portraitists of sea and land,
Mr. McNally and Mr. Rand,
Two sad cartographic chaps,
Sat in their office surrounded by maps.
Globes and maps around the room,
And on *their* maps a look of gloom.

"Time was when this business of ours was grand,"
Said Mr. McNally to Mr. Rand,
"When our toughest job was to sit and think
Shall France be purple and Britain pink?
Shall Spain be tinted a bright cerise,
And perhaps a dash of green for Greece?"

"But that," said Rand to Mr. McNally,
"Was before Benito got rough with Hallie,
When we didn't fret about changing borders,
And we just sat here receiving orders."

"Remember those days," McNally said,
"When we'd plan a map a month ahead,
And we'd know, if it came out at noon, let's say,
It was up to date the entire day?"

"Then the countries stayed as fixed by their founders,
And boundaries weren't made by bounders."
"Those days," said Rand, "are gone to*tally*."
"You said it, brother," said Mr. McNally.

NEWMAN LEVY

BIRDS & BEASTS & INSECTS SMALL

A simple bard of Nature I,
Whose vernal Muse delights to chant
The objects of the earth and sky,
The things that walk, the things that fly,
And those that can't.

DUM-DUM

"Notwithstanding which, O poet," spake the wood-
louse, very blandly,
"I am likewise the created,—I the equipoise of thee;
I the particle, the atom, I behold on either hand lie
The inane of measured ages that were embryos
of me."

ALGERNON CHARLES SWINBURNE

Hamlet. *Do you see yonder cloud that's almost in*
shape of a camel?
Polonius. *By th' mass, and 'tis like a camel indeed.*
Hamlet. *Methinks it is like a weasel.*
Polonius. *It is back'd like a weasel.*
Hamlet. *Or like a whale.*
Polonius. *Very like a whale.*

HAMLET; iii, 2

The Ass

The ass
  is decidedly middlecrass:
conventional, obtuse.
Reason, abuse,
are equally no use.
It is a platitude
that only a halter
can alter
the middlecrass assitude.

EDWIN ALLAN

A Considerable Speck
(Microscopic)

A speck that would have been beneath my sight
On any but a paper sheet so white
Set off across what I had written there.
And I had idly poised my pen in air
To stop it with a period of ink
When something strange about it made me think.
This was no dust speck by my breathing blown,
But unmistakably a living mite
With inclinations it could call its own.
It paused as with suspicion of my pen,
And then came racing wildly on again
To where my manuscript was not yet dry;
Then paused again and either drank or smelt—
With loathing, for again it turned to fly.
Plainly with an intelligence I dealt.
It semed too tiny to have room for feet,
Yet must have had a set of them complete
To express how much it didn't want to die.
It ran with terror and with cunning crept.
It faltered: I could see it hesitate;

Then in the middle of the open sheet
Cower down in desperation to accept
Whatever I accorded it of fate.

I have none of the tenderer-than-thou
Collectivistic regimenting love
With which the modern world is being swept.
But this poor miscroscopic item now!
Since it was nothing I knew evil of
I let it lie there till I hope it slept.

I have a mind myself and recognize
Mind when I meet with it in any guise.
No one can know how glad I am to find
On any sheet the least display of mind.

ROBERT FROST

The Hippopotamus

I shoot the Hippopotamus
With bullets made of platinum,
Because if I use leaden ones
His hide is sure to flatten 'em.

HILAIRE BELLOC

The Termite

Some primal termite knocked on wood
    And tasted it, and found it good,
And that is why your Cousin May
    Fell through the parlor floor today.

OGDEN NASH

The Elephant, or the Force of Habit

A tail behind, a trunk in front,
Complete the usual elephant.
The tail in front, the trunk behind,
Is what you very seldom find.

If you for specimens should hunt
With trunks behind and tails in front,
That hunt would occupy you long;
The force of habit is so strong.

A. E. HOUSMAN

The Flea

And here's the happy, bounding flea—
You cannot tell the he from she.
The sexes look alike, you see;
But she can tell and so can he.

ROLAND YOUNG

The Kangaroo

O Kangaroo, O Kangaroo,
Be grateful that you're in the zoo,
And not transmuted by a boomerang
To zestful, tangy Kangaroo meringue.

OGDEN NASH

The Turtle

The turtle lives 'twixt plated decks
Which practically conceal its sex.
I think it clever of the turtle
In such a fix to be so fertile.

OGDEN NASH

archygrams

the wood louse sits on a splinter
and sings to the rising sap
aint it awful how winter
lingers in springtimes lap

*   *   *

when the proud ibexes start from sleep
in the early alpine morns
at once from crag to crag they leap
alighting on their horns
and may a dozen times rebound
ere resting haughty on the ground
i do not like their trivial pride
nor think them truly dignified

DON MARQUIS

M

M was once a little mouse,
　　Mousy,
　　Bousy,
　　Sousy,
　　Mousy,
In the housy,
Little mouse!

EDWARD LEAR

Apex

The lion tamers wrestle with the lions in a cage.
With but a fragile whip they dare their charges' feral
　　rage.
They put their heads in tigers' mouths and do not
　　flinch a grain,
But . . . they never tried to take a cat five hundred
　　miles to Maine.

You hunters who bring back alive from Afric's roaring
　　shore
The nilghai and the elephant, the rhino and the boar;
Who load them on a steamer and evince no sign of
　　strain—
Let's see you drive a four-pound cat five hundred
　　miles to Maine!

Go cope with your rhinoceros bare-handed and alone,
Or kick a famished grizzly if for harmless fun you
    hone,
Or aggravate a timber wolf with pokings of a cane,
But do NOT try to drive a cat five hundred miles to
    Maine!

There is no word, there is no tongue, there is no ink
    to tell
One tenth of what one cat can raise of concentrated
    hell
When after two hours' driving to mistaken qualms
    you yield
And take poor puss to stretch her limbs in some adja-
    cent field.

And if you've done the things set forth in stanzas two
    and three,
You stand a chance, when Krazy from the leash has
    wriggled free
(Provided you are clad in steel with gloves and hat to
    match),
To get her back into the car without a bite or scratch.

Ye lion tamers, naturalists, and big-game hunters eke,
When *I'm* around be chary of your tendency to speak.
To hear you boast your petty deeds gives me a shoot-
    ing pain
For I have taken Krazy (phew!) five hundred miles to
    Maine.

                        BARON IRELAND

Moo!

Summer is over, the old cow said,
And they'll shut me up in a draughty shed
To milk me by lamplight in the cold,
But I won't give much for I am old.

It's long ago that I came here
Gay and slim as a woodland deer;
It's long ago that I heard the roar
Of Smith's white bull by the sycamore.
And now there are bones where my flesh should be;
My backbone sags like an old roof tree,
And an apple snatched in a moment's frolic
Is just so many days of colic.
I'm neither a Jersey nor Holstein now
But only a faded sort of cow.
My calves are veal and I had as lief
That I could lay me down as beef;
Somehow, they always kill by halves,—
Why not take me when they take my calves?
Birch turns yellow and sumac red,
I've seen this all before, she said,
I'm tired of the field and tired of the shed.
There's no more grass, there's no more clover;
Summer is over, summer is over.

ROBERT HILLYER

Great Fleas

Great fleas have little fleas upon their back to bite 'em,
And little fleas have lesser fleas, and so *ad infinitum*.
The great fleas themselves in turn have greater fleas to
     go on,
While these again have greater still, and greater still,
     and so on.

ANONYMOUS

Insect Wives

I'm told that certain insect wives, as soon
As they've enjoyed this buzzing honeymoon,
Not merely fire their hubbies from the hive
Or nest or hole, but eat them up alive.

He never has a chance to criticize her,
For she'll soon snack him as an appetizer;
He cannot bore for long his wedded kin—
She'll pack him, with the wedding cake, within.

Her widowhood advanced with every crunch,
She takes her bliss companionate with lunch;
While he, now freed from feminine abuses,
Devotes himself to draw her gastric juices.

No sexy problems fret this wifely bug;
She solves them all with her initial hug.
All wives will welcome such a dainty system
Of shaking mates as soon as they have kissed 'em!

RUDOLPH ALTROCCHI

The Duck

Behold the duck.
It does not cluck.
A cluck it lacks.
It quacks.
It is specially fond
Of a puddle or pond.
When it dines or sups,
It bottoms ups.

OGDEN NASH

The Ape

The sacred ape, now, children, see.
He's searching for the modest flea.
If he should turn around we'd find
He has no hair on his behind.

ROLAND YOUNG

Song for Thrift Week

As soon
As a squirrel
Has gathered
Its bin full,
A hunter
Stands ready
To pepper
Its skin full.

MILDRED WESTON

The Frog

What a wonderful bird the frog are—
When he stand he sit almost;
When he hop, he fly almost.
He ain't got no sense hardly;
He ain't got no tail hardly either.
When he sit, he sit on what he ain't got almost.

ANONYMOUS

The Kitten

The trouble with a kitten is
THAT
Eventually it becomes a
CAT.

OGDEN NASH

The Goat

The Billy goat's a handsome gent
But has a most far-reaching scent.
The Nanny goat is quite a belle.
Let's hope she has no sense of smell.

ROLAND YOUNG

Black and White Shuffle

Sev'n skunks lumbering in a row,
Taggin' mama, proud and slow,
Bushy tails all dipped in white,
Shoulder straps like cops at night,
Go on skunks and shuffle yo' shoes,
I'se sure got dem black-white blues.

Walking pert in broad daylight,
Blocking traffic shore ain't right,
You all am divine surprise,
Hold up Tiger, close dem eyes!
Go on skunks and shuffle yo' shoes,
I'se sure got dem black-white blues.

Seven li'l babies, watch 'em go!
One, three, seven form a row,
Hold you' temper, watch you' tail,
I ain't gwine to cross you' trail,
Go on skunks and shuffle yo' shoes,
I'se sure got dem black-white blues.

HARRY ELMORE HURD

the honey bee

the honey bee is sad and cross
and wicked as a weasel
and when she perches on you boss
she leaves a little measle

DON MARQUIS

The Answers

"When did the world begin and how?"
I asked a lamb, a goat, a cow:

"What's it all about and why?"
I asked a hog as he went by:

"Where will the whole thing end and when?"
I asked a duck, a goose, a hen:

And I copied all the answers too,
A quack, a honk, an oink, a moo.

ROBERT CLAIRMONT

The Dromedary

The Dromedary is a cheerful bird:
I cannot say the same about the Kurd.

HILAIRE BELLOC

The Firefly

The firefly's flame
Is something for which science has no name.
I can think of nothing eerier
Than flying around with an unidentified glow on a
person's posteerier.

OGDEN NASH

Gettin' Born

When once a chic busts through a egg
    He gives three little squeals,
Then works out backwards through a hole
    By kickin' with his heels.

Or maybe he'll keep peckin' 'round,
    With now and then some cursin',
Until his head pokes through and then
    Comes all his little person.

Or like as not he'll puff his chest,
    A grunt and then some kickin'—
He's standin' there out in the air,
    A promissory chicken.

ANTHONY EUWER

BOWLINES & SEASCAPES

*And Neddy he swore by butt and bend, and Billy by
     bend and bitt,*
*And nautical names that no man frames but your
     amateur nautical wit;*
*And Sam said, "Shiver my topping-lifts and scuttle my
     foc's'le yarn,*
*And may I be curst, if I'm not in first with a kipper-
     ling slued astarn!*

SIR OWEN SEAMAN

See, fore and aft, life's craft undone!
*   Crank plank, split spritsail—mark, sea's lark!*
That grey cold sea's old sprees, begun
*   When men lay dark i' the ark, no spark,*
All water—just God's fun!

ALGERNON CHARLES SWINBURNE

The Bowline

The bowline is the king of knots, or, if you like it,
      bends;
A bowline on a bollard is the best of journey's ends:
And, as long as men are mariners, I think it safe to say
This is a thing that never will be done another way.

In Life's unending upward urge how rare it is to find
A Terminus—an Ultimate—Perfection in its kind!
Time was when Michael Angelo was thought the Top
      in paint,
But many a pale young gentleman will tell you now he
      ain't:
The deed that dazzles us to-day, to-morrow will be
      drab:
The aeroplane is very *chic*—so was the hansom-cab.
A judgment of the House of Lords no mortal man may
      doubt,
Though Parliament, if it should please, may wipe that
      judgment out;
But if all the world's fine Parliaments were massed at
      Ponders End,
Here is a small particular that they could not amend;
Though the effete democracies, despairing, stooped to
      ask
The odious aid of tyrants and Herr Hitler tried the
      task;
Though the great Press itself engaged to find a better
      plan
And offered monstrous prizes to inspire the Little
      Man;
Though Jeans and Shaw and Nuffield were co-opted
      day by day,
This is a thing they could not do in any other way.

What ancient hairy tar, how many centuries ago,
Was author of the artifice we do not seem to know.

Maybe old Captain Noah, scarce aware what he was at,
Thus made a grass-rope ready when he sighted Ararat;
Maybe 'twas wise Ulysses when he made the sailors fast
Against the song of Sirens with a bowline to the mast;
Maybe by Captain Jason was the first example tied,
That some industrious Argonaut might paint the
     Argo's side.
Maybe the infant Raleigh, playing wistfully with
     string,
Took one more turn by accident and stumbled on the
     thing:
Or maybe after all 'twas no tough toiler of the sea,
But some Mamma who tethered thus some toddler to a
     tree;
Or at the earliest wife's remark, '*Again* you have for-
     got!'
The earliest husband's handkerchief received this
     noble knot.
Maybe primeval monkeys in the equinoctial gales
Preserved their equilibrium with bowlines in their
     tails.
At all events as long as men are mariners, I say,
Here is a thing that never will be done another way.

The sailor's knots have qualities he'd welcome in a
     bride—
Hold firm while they are wanted, yet are easily untied;
The more the strain you put on them, the tighter do
     they stick;
They are fastened in a flash but you can cast them off
     as quick.
The timber hitch, the reef knot, the sheet and fisher-
     man's bends,
The clove, the sweet, and simple hitch on which so
     much depends
Have each a special duty they do perfectly discharge

(Much more than you can say of men or matters, by
  and large).
All seamen in their memories preserve a secret niche
For the nameless benefactor who conceived the rolling
  hitch,
While manly tears my eyes invade with which I can't
  contend
When I discuss the Blackwall hitch or topsail halyard
  bend.
But the bowline is the king of knots, and it is grand to
  say—
Here is a thing that never will be done another way.

SIR A. P. HERBERT

A Grain of Salt

Of all the wimming doubly blest
The sailor's wife's the happiest,
For all she does is stay to home
And knit and darn—and let 'im roam.

Of all the husbands on the earth
The sailor has the finest berth,
For in 'is cabin he can sit
And sail and sail—and let 'er knit.

WALLACE IRWIN

In Prize

A ship was built in Glasgow, and oh, she looked a
  daisy—
(Just the way that some ships do!)
An' the only thing against 'er was she allus steered so
  crazy
(An' it's true, my Johnny Bowline, true!)

They sent 'er out in ballast to Oregon for lumber,
An' before she dropped her pilot she all but lost 'er
      number.

They sold 'er into Norway because she steered so
      funny,
An' she nearly went to glory before they drawed the
      money.

They sold 'er out o' Norway—they sold 'er into Chile,
An' Chile got a bargain because she steered so silly.

They chartered 'er to Germans with a bunch o'
      greasers forrard;
Old shellbacks wouldn't touch 'er because she steered
      so 'orrid.

But she'll fetch her price at auction, for, oh, she looks
      a daisy.
(Just the way that some ships do!)
An' the chap as tops the biddin' won't know she steers
      so crazy
(But it's true, my Johnny Bowline, true!)

                              CICELY FOX SMITH

The Pacific Engagement

or, A Poetical Dialogue between two
Courteous Admirals [1]

B.

At last we are met—but I hope with no other
Intent or design, but to spare one another.
Though we seem by our flags to be desperate foes,
Let us part, if you please, without banging or blows!

[1] Admirals John Byng and the Marquis de la Galissonière.

G.

But since fighting and wars are the arts which we
    trade in,
We must have a little, and short cannonading;
Our guns must be fired at a distance, but still
With no wicked intention to wound or to kill.

B.

As nigh to each other, good friends, as we ride,
A tar now and then must drop down on each side;
Our cannons must bounce, while our mock fight does
    last,
While I tear your rigging, you shatter my mast.

G.

Though the roar of my guns may your Britons alarm,
Yet assure 'em from me, they shall do 'em no harm;
They may hear my shot whizz, through the air without
    dread;
Directed by me, to fly over their head.

B.

To finish the farce, as we both have agreed,
Not five in your ship by my bullets shall bleed:
We'll fight a whole day amid volumes of smoke,
Nor an arm nor a leg of ten sailors be broke.

G.

Like victors we each will our colours display
And each boast a triumph—for running away!
While your King, and my King, shall vote a thanks-
    giving,
That their ships are all safe, and their troops are all
    living.

B.

Suppose our two monarchs should murmur and fret;
We can swear and protest that our powder was wet;
Or if that does not serve, we can drop a few hints,
That our pistols and muskets all wanted their flints:

G.

That our bullets by dozens dropt down in the main,
Which else would their hundreds and thousands have
    slain;
In the heat of the fight, and the smoke and the
    smother,
Forbid us to view, and to grapple each other.

B.

Ah, how had it vext us, when fighting, to see
A ball tear my ruffles, or singe your toupee;
A death to all spruce and gay finical blades,
A wound to receive in their martial cockades,

G.

That we battled in earnest to make folks believe,
Let us each shew a gash in our hat and our sleeve;
And to point out the dreadful effects of the war,
My thumb, and your finger, shall each have a scar. . . .

B.

How dreadful the scene, when the battle was o'er,
To have viewed our two decks all covered with gore;
But the statute pacific, we chose to fulfil,
Which forbid all good christians to murder and kill.

G.

To our cabins for safety then let us retreat;
Nor victors, nor vanquished, nor beating, nor beat;
While Richelieu with Blakeney for victory strains,
Each claiming a laurel, for dashing out brains,

B.

In triumph when back we return, to display
The harmless encounter and farce of the day;
Though envy may blast our renown, yet we hope
Each to merit a garland, instead of a rope. . . .

FROM *Bungiana,* 1756

Stephano's Song

The master, the swabber, the boatswain, and I,
  The gunner, and his mate,
Lov'd Mall, Meg, and Marian, and Margery,
  But none of us car'd for Kate.
  For she had a tongue with a tang,
  Would cry to a sailor, 'Go hang!'
She lov'd not the savour of tar nor of pitch;
Yet a tailor might scratch her where'er she did itch.
  Then to sea, boys, and let her go hang!

                                WILLIAM SHAKESPEARE

BRIDLEWISE

From the music of hooves and the snorting,
  From the cry of the hounds in their bliss,
Did he turn to the wholly unsporting
  Decision to fool us with this?

DUM-DUM

  Or if we rode, perhaps she did
    Pull sharply at the curb;
  But then the way in which she slid
    From horseback was superb!

C. S. CALVERLEY

Must we drag on this stupid existence forever,
  So idle and weary, so full of remorse,
While every one else takes his pleasure, and never
  Seems happy unless he is riding a horse?

EDWARD LEAR

The Famous Ballad of the Jubilee Cup

You may lift me up in your arms, lad, and turn my
    face to the sun,
For a last look back at the dear old track where the
    Jubilee Cup was won;
And draw your chair to my side, lad—no, thank ye, I
    feel no pain—
For I'm going out with the tide, lad, but I'll tell you
    the tale again.

I'm seventy-nine, or nearly, and my head it has long
    turned grey,
But it all comes back as clearly as though it was yes-
    terday—
The dust, and the bookies shouting around the clerk
    of the scales,
And the clerk of the course, and the nobs in force, and
    His Highness, the Pr*nce of W*les.

'Twas a nine-hole thresh to wind'ard, but none of us
    cared for that,
With a straight run home to the service tee, and a fin-
    ish along the flat.
'Stiff?' Ah, well you may say it! Spot-barred, and at
    five-stone-ten!
But at two and a bisque I'd ha' run the risk; for I was
    a greenhorn then.

So we stripped to the B. Race signal, the old red
    swallow-tail—
There was young Ben Bolt, and the Portland colt, and
    Aston Villa, and Yale;
And W. G., and Steinitz, Leander, and The Saint,
And the German Emperor's Meteor, a-looking as fresh
    as paint;

John Roberts (scratch), and Safety Match, The Lascar,
    and Lorna Doone,

43

Oom Paul (a bye), and Romany Rye, and me upon
    Wooden Spoon;
And some of us cut for partners, and some of us strung
    to baulk,
And some of us tossed for stations—But there, what
    use to talk?

Three-quarter-back on the Kingsclere crack was sta-
    tion enough for me,
With a fresh jackyarder blowing and the Vicarage goal
    a-lee!
And I leaned and patted her centre-bit, and eased the
    quid in her cheek,
With a 'Soh, my lass!' and a 'Woa, you brute!'—for she
    could do all but speak.

She was geared a thought too high, perhaps; she was
    trained a trifle fine;
But she had the grand reach forward! *I* never saw such
    a line!
Smooth-bored, clean-run, from her fiddle head with its
    dainty ear half-cock,
Hard-bit, *pur sang,* from her overhang to the heel of
    her off hind sock.

Sir Robert he walked beside me as I worked her down
    to the mark;
'There's money on this, my lad,' said he, 'and most
    of 'em's running dark;
But ease the sheet if you're bunkered, and pack the
    scrimmages tight,
And use your slide at the distance, and we'll drink to
    your health to-night!'

But I bent and tightened my stretcher. Said I to my-
    self, said I,—
'John Jones, this here is the Jubilee Cup, and you
    have to do or die.'

And the words weren't hardly spoken when the um-
   pire shouted 'Play!'
And we all kicked off from the Gasworks end with a
   'Yoicks!' and a 'Gone away!'

And at first I thought of nothing, as the clay flew by
   in lumps,
But stuck to the old Ruy Lopez, and wondered who'd
   call for trumps,
And luffed her close to the cushion, and watched each
   one as it broke,
And in triple file up the Rowley mile we went like a
   trail of smoke.

The Lascar made the running: but he didn't amount
   to much,
For old Oom Paul was quick on the ball, and headed
   it back to touch;
And the whole first flight led off with the right, as The
   Saint took up the pace,
And drove it clean to the putting green and holed it
   there with an ace.

John Roberts had given a miss in baulk, but Villa
   cleared with a punt;
And keeping her service hard and low The Meteor
   forged to the front,
With Romany Rye to windward at dormy and two to
   play,
And Yale close up—but a Jubilee Cup isn't run for
   every day.

We laid our course for the Warner—I tell you the pace
   was hot!
And again off Tattenham Corner a blanket covered
   the lot.
Check side! Check side! Now steer her wide! and
   barely an inch of room,

With The Lascar's tail over our lee rail, and brushing
    Leander's boom!

We were running as strong as ever—eight knots—but
    it couldn't last;
For the spray and the bails were flying, the whole field
    tailing fast;
And the Portland colt had shot his bolt, and Yale was
    bumped at the Doves,
And The Lascar resigned to Steinitz, stale-mated in
    fifteen moves.

It was bellows to mend with Roberts—starred three
    for a penalty kick:
But he chalked his cue and gave 'em the butt, and
    Oom Paul scored the trick—
'Off-side—no-ball—and at fourteen all! Mark cock!
    and two for his nob!'—
When W. G. ran clean through his lee, and beat him
    twice with a lob.

He yorked him twice on a crumbling pitch, and wiped
    his eye with a brace,
But his guy-rope split with the strain of it, and he
    dropped back out of the race;
And I drew a bead on The Meteor's lead, and chal-
    lenging none too soon,
Bent over and patted her garboard strake, and called
    upon Wooden Spoon.

She was all of a shiver forward, the spoondrift thick on
    her flanks,
But I'd brought her an easy gambit, and nursed her
    over the banks;
She answered her helm—the darling!—and woke up
    now with a rush,
While The Meteor's jock he sat like a rock—he knew
    we rode for his brush!

There was no one else left in it. The Saint was using
his whip,
And Safety Match, with a lofting catch, was pocketed
deep at slip;
And young Ben Bolt with his niblick took miss at
Leander's lunge,
But topped the net with the ricochet, and Steinitz
threw up the sponge.

But none of the lot could stop the rot—nay, don't ask
me to stop!—
The Villa had called for lemons, Oom Paul had taken
his drop,
And both were kicking the referee. Poor fellow! he
done his best;
But, being in doubt, he'd ruled them out—which he
always did when pressed.

So, inch by inch, I tightened the winch, and chucked
the sandbags out—
I heard the nursery cannons pop, I heard the bookies
shout:
'The Meteor wins!' 'No, Wooden Spoon!' 'Check!'
'Vantage!' 'Leg before!'
'Last lap!' 'Pass Nap!' At his saddle-flap I put up the
helm and wore.

You may overlap at the saddle-flap, and yet be loo'd
on the tape:
And it all depends upon changing ends, how a seven-
year-old will shape;
It was tack and tack to the Lepe and back—a fair ding-
dong to the Ridge,
And he led by his forward canvas yet as we shot 'neath
Hammersmith Bridge.

He led by his forward canvas—he led from his strongest suit—

But along we went on a roaring scent, and at Fawley
    I gained a foot.
He fisted off from the throttle, and gave me his wash
    —too late!
Deuce—vantage—check! By neck and neck, we rounded
    into the straight.

I could hear the 'Conquering 'Ero' a-crashing on
    Godfrey's band,
And my hopes fell sudden to zero, just there with the
    race in hand—
In sight of the Turf's Blue Ribbon, in sight of the
    umpire's tape,
As I felt the tack of her spinnaker crack, as I heard the
    steam escape!

Had I lost at that awful juncture my presence of
    mind? . . . but no!
I leaned and felt for the puncture, and plugged it
    there with my toe . . .
Hand over hand by the Members' Stand I lifted and
    eased her up,
Shot—clean and fair—to the crossbar there, and landed
    the Jubilee Cup!

'The odd by a head, and leg before,' so the Judge he
    gave the word:
And the Umpire shouted 'Over!' but I neither spoke
    nor stirred.
They crowded round: for there on the ground I lay in
    a dead-cold swoon,
Pitched neck and crop on the turf atop of my beauti-
    ful Wooden Spoon.

Her dewlap tire was punctured, her bearings all red-
    hot;
She'd a lolling tongue, and her bowsprit sprung. and
    her running gear in a knot;

And amid the sobs of her backers, Sir Robert loosened
   her girth
And led her away to the knacker's. She had raced her
   last on earth!

But I mind me well of the tear that fell from the eye
   of our noble Pr*nce,
And the things he said as he tucked me in bed—and
   I've lain there ever since;
Tho' it all gets mixed up queerly that happened be-
   fore my spill,—
But I draw my thousand yearly: it'll pay for the doc-
   tor's bill.

I'm going out with the tide, lad—You'll dig me a
   humble grave,
And whiles you will bring your bride, lad, and your
   sons (if sons you have),
And there, when the dews are weeping, and the echoes
   murmur 'Peace!'
And the salt, salt tide comes creeping and covers the
   popping-crease,

In the hour when the ducks deposit their eggs with a
   boasted force,
They'll look and whisper 'How was it?' and you'll take
   them over the course,
And your voice will break as you try to speak of the
   glorious first of June,
When the Jubilee Cup, with John Jones up, was won
   upon Wooden Spoon.

SIR ARTHUR QUILLER-COUCH

Horses

They head the list
   Of bad to bet on,
But I insist
   They're worse to get on.

RICHARD ARMOUR

The Racing-Man

My gentle child, behold this horse—
A noble animal, of *course*,
    But not to be relied on;
I wish he would not stand and snort;
Oh, frankly, he is *not* the sort
    Your father cares to ride on.

His head is tossing up and down,
And he has frightened half the town
    By blowing in their faces,
And making gestures with his feet,
While now and then he stops to eat
    In inconvenient places.

He nearly murdered me today
By trotting in the wildest way
    Through half a mile of forest;
And now he treads upon the kerb,
Consuming some attractive herb
    He borrowed from the florist.

I strike him roughly with my hand;
He does not seem to understand;
    He simply *won't* be bothered
To walk in peace, as I suggest,
A little way towards the West—
    He prances to the No'th'ard.

And yet, by popular repute,
He is a mild, well-mannered brute,
    And very well connected;
Alas! it is the painful fact
That horses hardly ever act
    As anyone expected.

Yet there are men prepared to place
A sum of money on a race
    In which a horse is running,
An animal as fierce as this,

As full of idle prejudice,
   And every bit as cunning;
And it is marvellous to me
That grown-up gentlemen can be
   So simple, so confiding;
I envy them, but, O my son,
I cannot think that they have done
   A great amount of riding.

SIR A. P. HERBERT

A Soldier of Weight

In the dim and distant ages, in the half-forgotten days,
Ere the East became the fashion and an Indian tour
   the craze,
Lived a certain Major-General, renowned throughout
   the State
As a soldier of distinction and considerable weight.

But though weightiness of mind is an invaluable
   trait,[1]
When applied to adiposity it's all the other way;
And our hero was confronted with an ever-growing
   lack
Of the necessary charger and the hygienic hack.

He had bought them by the dozen, he had tried them
   by the score,
But not one of them was equal to the burden that he
   bore;
They were conscious of the honour, they were sound
   in wind and limb,
They could carry a cathedral, but they drew the line
   at *him*.

[1] The English pronounce this *tray*. You had better do it too,
if you care for rhyme.

But he stuck to it, till finally his pressing needs were
    filled
By the mammoth of his species, a Leviathan in build,
A superb upstanding brown, of unexceptionable bone,
And phenomenally qualified to carry twenty stone.

And the General was happy; for the noble creature
    showed
An unruffled acquiescence with the nature of his load;
Till without the slightest warning, that superb up-
    standing brown
Thought it time to make a protest, which he did by
    lying down.

They appealed to him, reproached him, gave him
    sugar, cut his feed,
But in vain; for almost daily that inexorable steed,
When he heard his master coming, looked insultingly
    around,
And with cool deliberation laid him down upon the
    ground.

But they fought it out between them, till the unde-
    feated brute
Made a humorous obeisance at the General Salute!
Then his owner kicked him wildly in the stomach for
    his pranks,
Said he'd stand the beast no longer, and returned him
    to the ranks.

(An interval of about three years.)

Time has dulled our hero's anguish; time has raised
    our man of weight
To an even higher office in the service of the State;
And we find him at his yearly tour, inspecting at his
    ease
A distinguished corps of cavalry, the Someone's Own
    D. G.'s.

And our fat but famous man of war, accoutred to the
      nines,
Was engaged in making rude remarks, and going
      round the lines,
When he suddenly beheld across an intervening space
A Leviathan of horseflesh, the Behemoth of h's race.

'Colonel Robinson,' he shouted, with enthusiastic
      force,
'A remarkably fine horse, sir!' The remarkably fine
      horse
Gave a reminiscent shudder, looked insultingly
      around,
And with cold deliberation laid him down upon the
      ground!

DUM-DUM

Horse & Rider

> The rider
> Is fat
> As that ( )
> Or wider ( )
> In torso
> Of course
> The horse
> Is more so ( )

WEY ROBINSON

On a Clergyman's Horse Biting Him

The steed bit his master;
  How came this to pass?
He heard the good pastor
  Cry, 'All flesh is grass'.

ANONYMOUS

How I Brought the Good News from Aix to Ghent (or Vice Versa)

[It] runs (or rather gallops) roughly as follows: we quote from memory (having no boots of reference at hand):

I sprang to the rollocks and Jorrocks and me,
And I galloped, you galloped, he galloped, we gal-
    loped all three . . .
Not a word to each other; we kept changing place,
Neck to neck, back to front, ear to ear, face to face;
And we yelled once or twice, when we heard a clock
    chime,
"Would you kindly oblige us, *Is that the right time?*"
As I galloped, you galloped, he galloped, we gal-
    loped, ye galloped, they two shall have galloped;
    let us trot.

*　　　*　　　*　　　*

I unsaddled the saddle, unbuckled the bit,
Unshackled the bridle (the thing didn't fit)
And ungalloped, ungalloped, ungalloped, ungalloped
    a bit.
Then I cast off my bluff-coat, let my bowler hat fall,
Took off both my boots and my trousers and all—
Drank off my stirrup-cup, felt a bit tight,
And unbridled the saddle: it still wasn't right.

*　　　*　　　*　　　*

Then all I remember is, things reeling round
As I sat with my head 'twixt my ears on the ground—
For imagine my shame when they asked what I meant
And I had to confess that I'd been, gone and went
And *forgotten the news* I was bringing to Ghent,

Though I'd galloped and galloped and galloped and
    galloped and galloped
And galloped and galloped and galloped. (Had I not
    would have been galloped?)

Envoi

So I sprang to a taxi and shouted "To Aix!"
And he blew on his horn and he threw off his brakes,
And all the way back till my money was spent
We rattled and rattled and rattled and rattled and
    rattled
And rattled and rattled—
And eventually sent a telegram.

                        R. J. YEATMAN & W. C. SELLAR

CHILDREN & CHILDHOOD

Ah! cease thy tears and sobs, my little Life!
I did but snatch away the unclasped knife:
Some safer toy will soon arrest thine eye,
And to quick laughter change this peevish cry!
SAMUEL TAYLOR COLERIDGE

"Peek-a-boo!" say little Olaf.
"Yu can't find me. Ay ban hid."
Den ay used to look all over
For my little blue-eyed kid.
WILLIAM F. KIRK

Concerning Love

I wish she would not ask me if I love the Kitten more
    than her.
Of course I love her. But I love the Kitten too: and
    It has fur.

JOSEPHINE PRESTON PEABODY

A Father Does His Best

Said I to Lord & Taylor:
    "Hot are the summer skies,
    And my son Joe would like to go
    In a big straw hat in the year-old size.
    Have you got such a thing, for summer skies,
    A nice straw hat in the year-old size?"
Said Lord & Taylor: "No."

Said I to Saks Fifth Avenue:
    "The sunshine hurts Joe's eyes;
    He used to nap in a small white cap,
    But a big straw hat in the year-old size
    Would keep the sunshine out of his eyes.
    Have you got such a thing in the year-old size?"
Said Saks Fifth Avenue: "No."

Said I to Best & Company:
    "I think it might be wise
    When noons are red to cover Joe's head
    With a big straw hat in the year-old size.
    Can you sell me one, if you think it's wise,
    A big straw hat in the year-old size?"
Said Best & Company: "No."

Said I to the infant's mother:
    "It comes as a great surprise
    That our son Joe may never go
    In a big straw hat in the year-old size.

We had no trouble with his other supplies,
His Pyrex bottles, his spoon for eating,
His year-old pot and his year-old sheeting,
His feeding bib of heavy material
To catch the spray from the flying cereal,
 Rompers to match the color of his eyes
 In the year-old size;
These things were bought with the greatest ease,
The stores were willing and able to please,
His bands and his year-old shirts all fit,
His crew-neck sweater and his Arnold-Knit;
I bought him a bear and a rubber cat,
Yet now, when he needs a big straw hat,
 I don't know where to go.
Doesn't it come as a great surprise
That there's no straw hat in the year-old size
To keep the sun from the little lad's eyes?"
Said the infant's mother: "No."

E. B. WHITE

Amelia Mixed the Mustard

Amelia mixed the mustard,
 She mixed it good and thick;
She put it in the custard
 And made her Mother sick,
And showing satisfaction
 By many a loud huzza
"Observe" said she "the action
 Of mustard on Mamma."

A. E. HOUSMAN

Away with Bloodshed

Away with bloodshed, I love not such,
But Jane Eliza snores too much.

I bought a serpent that bites and stings
For three-and-sixpence or four shillings.

When Jane Eliza began to snore
I put it under her bedroom door.

The serpent had neither bit nor stung,
It had only just put out its tongue,

When Jane Eliza fell out of bed
And bumped upon it and killed it dead.

It showed off none of its pretty tricks
That cost four shillings or three-and-six;

It had no time to sting or bite
Nor even to utter the words "Good night."

So three-and-sixpence at least is gone,
And Jane Eliza, she still snores on.

A. E. HOUSMAN

Stans Puer ad Mensam

Attend my words, my gentle knave,
    And you shall learn from me
How boys at dinner may behave
    With due propriety.

Guard well your hands: two things have been
    Unfitly used by some;
The trencher for a tambourine,
    The table for a drum.

We could not lead a pleasant life,
    And 'twould be finished soon,
If peas were eaten with the knife,
    And gravy with the spoon.

Eat slowly: only men in rags
    And gluttons old in sin

Mistake themselves for carpet bags
    And tumble victuals in.

The privy pinch, the whispered tease,
    The wild, unseemly yell—
When children do such things as these,
    We say, "It is not well."

Endure your mother's timely stare,
    Your father's righteous ire,
And do not wriggle on your chair
    Like flannel in the fire.

Be silent: you may chatter loud
    When you are fully grown,
Surrounded by a silent crowd
    Of children of your own.

If you should suddenly feel bored
    And much inclined to yawning,
Your little hand will best afford
    A modest useful awning.

Think highly of the Cat: and yet
    You need not therefore think
That portly strangers like your pet
    To share their meat and drink.

The end of dinner comes ere long
    When, once more full and free,
You cheerfully may bide the gong
    That calls you to your tea.

SIR WALTER RALEIGH

A is an Apple

A is an apple, sour and green,
    Working in Tommy but cannot be seen.

ANONYMOUS

A Terrible Infant

I recollect a nurse call'd Ann,
    Who carried me about the grass,
And one fine day a fine young man
    Came up, and kiss'd the pretty lass.
She did not make the least objection!
        Thinks I, *"Aha!*
    When I can talk I'll tell Mamma"
—And that's my earliest recollection.

FREDERICK LOCKER-LAMPSON

Transportation Problem

Kiddy cars of little tikes,
Slightly older children's bikes,
Skis and sleds for winter needs,
Wagons, trucks, velocipedes,
Skooters, ice (and roller) skates—
How the stuff accumulates—
Piles of articles vehicular,
On the front porch in particular,
Things your children go like heck on,
And you fall and break your neck on.

RICHARD ARMOUR

Double Duty

Mothers who raise
    A child by the book
        Can, if sufficiently vexed,
Hasten results
    By applying the book
        As well as applying the text.

W. E. FARBSTEIN

A Memory

When I was as high as that
I saw a poet in his hat.
I think the poet must have smiled
At such a solemn gazing child.

Now wasn't it a funny thing
To get a sight of J. M. Synge,
And notice nothing but his hat?
Yet life is often queer like that.

L. A. G. STRONG

Infant Innocence

Reader, behold! this monster wild
Has gobbled up the infant child.
The infant child is not aware
It has been eaten by the bear.

A. E. HOUSMAN

Perambulator Poems

I

On my perambulator
I could cut notches
for every second-rater
who shows me watches.

II

For people
on trial
I don't smile,
but I keep one
on file.

And after
a while,
if they're
my style,
they can say
"Smile!"
and
I'll.

III

I affirm
that what makes
the germ,
the worm
squirm,
the whale
sperm,
the pachyderm,
and man live out
his term,
from here to Burma
on *terra firma,*
is the fundamental murmur
of the universe,
eh, Nurse?

IV

People—and a lot
I don't care for,
and wouldn't give a stewed fig
or the juice of a pear for—
will try to make friends
as like as not,
as if that's what
I take the air for.

V

When I was christened
they held me up
and poured some water
out of a cup.

The trouble was
it fell on me,
and I and water
don't agree.

A lot of christeners
stood and listened:
I let them know
that I was christened.

VI

As to naps:
They're all right
for saps,
perhaps,
to fill in
their gaps.
But real
chaps,
even in lace caps
and wraps,
don't collapse.

VII

Good days
I'm out,
bad days
I'm not;
and that's
about
how far
I've got.

DAVID McCORD

A Tonversation with Baby

"Was it a little baby
  With wide, unwinking eyes,
Propped in his baby carriage,
  Looking so wise?

"Oh, what a pwitty baby!
  Oh, what a sweety love!
What is oo thinkin', baby,
  And dweamin' of?

"Is oo wond'rin' 'bout de doggie
  A-fwiskin' here 'n dere?
Is oo watchin' de baby birdies
  Everywhere?

" 'N all de funny peoples
  'N a funny sings oo sees?
What is oo sinkin of, baby?
  Tell me, please.

" 'Z oo sinkin of tisses, tunnin,
  'N wannin 'n wannin for some?
O tweety goo swummy doodle,
  O yummy yum!"

Then spoke that solemn baby,
  Wise as a little gnome:
"You get in the baby carriage;
  I'll push you home."

MORRIS BISHOP

COLLEGE & CURRICULUM

Seventy-four and Twenty

Here goes a man of seventy-four,
Who sees not what life means for him,
And here another in years a score
Who reads its very figure and trim.

The one who shall walk to-day with me
Is not the youth who gazes far,
But the breezy wight who cannot see
What Earth's ingrained conditions are.

THOMAS HARDY

The Very Model of a Modern
College President

(Sir W. S. Gilbert)

I am the very model of a modern college president.
I'm always on the job, though nearly always a non-
  resident,
I tour about the country to assemblies gastronomical
And make all sorts of speeches from sublime to
  broadly comical,
I keep the trustees calm and the alumni all benevo-
  lent,
Restrain all signs of riot and publicity malevolent,
I know the market-value of each wage-slave profes-
  sorial,
And how much less he'll take for honorarium tutorial,
I'm on to all the low intrigues and rivalries divisional,
And on the budget how I wield my fountain-pen
  excisional!
So though I pile up mileage being generally non-
  resident
I am the very model of a modern college president!

I mix with all the business kings—the Lions and the
  Rotary,
Of heiresses and oil-tycoons I am a hopeful votary.
I'm fond of giving dinners in a lay-out that is squiffy-
  cal
And talking on the radio in accents quite pontifical,
I use the phrase "distinguished guest" at every oppor-
  tunity,
I welcome all alumni to my parlor every June at tea.
And though I like to see the neutrals' lonely hearts-
  that-burn at ease,
I always have a kindly word to say about fraternities,

67

I've shaken every human hand that's manicured and
   squeezable,
I pass the hat among the rich, the buck wherever
   feasible!
So though I pile up mileage being generally non-
   resident,
I am the very model of a modern college president!

HAROLD A. LARRABEE

Eleazar Wheelock

O, Eleazar Wheelock was a very pious man;
He went into the wilderness to teach the Indian,
With a Gradus ad Parnassum, a Bible, and a drum,
And five hundred gallons of New England rum.

> *Fill the bowl up! Fill the bowl up!*
> *Drink to Eleazar,*
> *And his primitive Alcazar,*
> *Where he mixed drinks for the heathen*
> *In the goodness of his soul.*

The big chief that met him was the Sachem of the
   Wah-hoo-wahs;
If he was not a big chief, there was never one you saw
   who was;
He had tobacco by the cord, ten squaws and more to
   come,
But he never yet had tasted of New England rum.

Eleazar and the big chief harangued and gesticulated;
They founded Dartmouth College and the big chief
   matriculated.
Eleazar was the faculty, and the whole curriculum
Was five hundred gallons of New England rum.

RICHARD HOVEY

Crossing Boston Common

One nears with Harvard-man expression
Who graces, doubtless, high profession;
He looks as smug, although near-sighted,
As if God had him copyrighted.

LOUISE DYER HARRIS

A Ballade of Any Father to Any Son

*(To be read in the Cockney, Lancashire, Scotch,
American or other marked accent)*

I 'ad no education, and my pile
  Began with pennies from the boots I blacked;
I said, "I'll raise my son in first-rate style,
  He shall start life with everything I lacked."
  You learnt some Greek and Latin, you were
     whacked,
While I coughed up at least 5,000 cool,
  Then you forgot it all, and then you slacked:
What was the use of sending you to school?

You cannot spell, your handwriting is vile,
  Your notions of geography are cracked,
You said the Danube flowed into the Nile,
  And then that Etna was a cataract,
  And the Sahara quite a fertile tract:
And now you say that you've been playing Boule
  And lost on every number that you backed:
What was the use of sending you to school?

Your car eats juice a gallon to the mile—
  If I'd been my old man I'd had you smacked!—
Don't stand there grinning like a crocodile!
  I'm damn well sick of you, and that's a fact:

My study with your bills is simply stacked,
And now yer Ma and me, it's something crool,
    We've had to have the under 'ousemaid sacked:
What was the use of sending you to school?

Envoy

Prince, it is not my way to fail in tact,
But you are such an utter bloody fool,
    Hey? You have never *heard* of Kellogg's Pact?
—What *was* the use of sending you to school?

SIR J. C. SQUIRE

The Old School Tie-Up

Eliot Cass was from Boston, Mass.
    Spike Jones from New Haven, Conn.
They headed the show at Boggs & Co.
    A business they carried on.
From Tues. to Fri. they saw eye to eye
    And peace would, in fact, prevail,
But beginning with Sat., things were not like that
For Cass was from Harvard—and getting fat—
    While slenderer Jones was Yale.

Through Oct. and Nov., Spike Jones would rove
    With the football team each week,
He was glad to confer on Wed. or Thur.,
    But on Sun. he refused to speak.
He explained on Mon. to everyone
    Each play—for an hour apiece—
And all the stenogs who worked for Boggs
Got terribly bored with the chorus of frogs
    Right up to the first of Dec.

From Jan. through Mar. Cass wandered far
    For hockey and basketball,

While Apr. and May found Jones away
　　Where the Eli batteries call.
A rift in the blue is the Eli Crew
　　But June brings Cass his dreams,—
And if Harvard led in the track, it's said
That all of the bookkeeping girls see red
　　As he talks of the Crimson Teams.

One day in Aug. it was like a morgue
　　In the office of Boggs & Co.
For the son of Jones, in solemn tones,
　　Said Harvard was where he'd go.
Jones hated to pass the relentless Cass
　　Whose cracks were becoming stale,
But 'twas Cass who wept on the first of Sept.
When he learned the secret his son had kept,
　　That *he* was going to Yale.

Now from Tues. to Fri. any passer-by
　　Finds Cass and Jones the same,
But look at them on that Sat. p.m.
　　When they go to the One Big Game.
For the Eli, Jones, utters awful groans
　　When the Harvard passes fail,
But we must confide he is satisfied
For Eliot sits on the Harvard side
　　And yells like hell for Yale.

LAURENCE McKINNEY

Epigram on an Academic Visit to the Continent

I went to Frankfort, and got drunk
With that most learn'd professor—Brunck:
I went to Worts, and got more drunken
With that more learn'd professor—Ruhncken.

RICHARD PORSON

Engineer's Yell

E to the X dy! dx!
E to the X dx!

Secant, cosine, tangent, sine,
Three-point-one-four-one-five-nine;

Square root, cube root, QED.
Slip stick! slide rule!
    'ray, U.C.!

       UNIVERSITY OF CALIFORNIA

On the Democracy of Yale

Here's to the town of New Haven,
  The Home of the Truth and the Light,
Where God talks to Jones in the very same tones
  That he uses with Hadley and Dwight.

       FREDERICK SCHEETZ JONES

Oxford & Cambridge

The King to Oxford sent a troop of horse,
For Tories own no argument but Force;
With equal skill to Cambridge books he sent,
For Whigs admit no force but Argument.

       SIR WILLIAM BROWNE

On Professor Drennan's Verse

Who forced the Muse to this alliance?
A Man of more degrees than parts—
The jilted Bachelor of Science
And Widower of Arts.

       ROY CAMPBELL

Baccalaureate

Summa is i-cumen in,
  Laude sing cuccu!
Laddes rede and classe lede,
Profesor bemeth tu—
  Sing cuccu!

Scholour striveth after Aye,
  Bleteth after shepskin ewe;
Writë theseth, honoure seazeth,
  Murie sing cuccu!

Cuccu, cuccu, wel singes A·B cuccu;
  Ne flunke thu naver nu;
  Sing cuccu, nu, sing cuccu,
  Sing cuccu, Phye Betta Cappe, nu!

                              DAVID McCORD

My Education

At school I sometimes read a book,
  And learned a lot of lessons;
Some small amount of pains I took,
  And showed much acquiescence
In what my masters said, good men!
  Yet after all I quite
Forgot the most of it: but then
              I learned to write.

At Lincoln's Inn I'd read a brief,
  Abstract a title, study
Great paper-piles, beyond belief
  Inelegant and muddy:
The whole of these as time went by
  I soon forgot: indeed
I tried to: yes: but by and by
              I learned to read.

By help of Latin, Greek and Law
I now can write and read too:
Then perish each forgotten saw,
Each fact I do not need too:
But still whichever way I turn
At one sad task I stick:
I fear that I shall never learn
               Arithmetic.

J. K. STEPHEN

DERRING-DO & DONE

"Go tell your tale, Lord Lovell," she said,
"To the maritime cavalree,
To your grandmother of the hoary head—
To any one but me . . ."

ANONYMOUS

The War Song of Dinas Vawr

The mountain sheep are sweeter,
But the valley sheep are fatter;
We therefore deemed it meeter
To carry off the latter.
We made an expedition;
We met a host and quelled it;
We forced a strong position,
And killed the men who held it.

On Dyfed's richest valley,
Where herds of kine were browsing,
We made a mighty sally,
To furnish our carousing.
Fierce warriors rushed to meet us;
We met them, and o'erthrew them:
They struggled hard to beat us;
But we conquered them, and slew them.

As we drove our prize at leisure,
The king marched forth to catch us:
His rage surpassed all measure,
But his people could not match us.
He fled to his hall-pillars;
And, ere our force we led off,
Some sacked his house and cellars,
While others cut his head off.

We there, in strife bewildering,
Spilt blood enough to swim in:
We orphaned many children,
And widowed many women.
The eagles and the ravens
We glutted with our foemen:
The heroes and the cravens,
The spearmen and the bowmen.

We brought away from battle,
And much their land bemoaned them,
Two thousand head of cattle,
And the head of him who owned them:
Edynfed, King of Dyfed,
His head was borne before us;
His wine and beasts supplied our feasts,
And his overthrow, our chorus.

THOMAS LOVE PEACOCK

Ludmilla

An Ode on the Occasion of Her Departure from These Shores

Ludmilla, the Soviet lassie,
    Has many a notch in her gun;
She thinks it a trifle to pick up a rifle
    And blow out the brains of a Hun.
If cartridges happen to fail her,
    She's equally expert with steel;
She uses a dagger to cut off the swagger
    Of ev'ry Hitlerian heel.

The Finns and Rumanians dread her;
    Their leader has only to cry:
"Ach, here comes Ludmilla, the demon guerrilla,"
    And back to their bases they fly.
Contrariwise, Russians adore her—
    The gal with the gat in her gown;
From Omsk to Tiflis the redoubtable miss
    Is toasted by country and town.

But where is the Muscovite hero
    Would venture Ludmilla to date?
Her great reputation for swift liquidation
    Would make her a perilous mate.

One man, and one only, is worthy;
  I move, Mr. Chief Commissar—
And the motion is carried—that she shall be married
  To Ivan Skavinsky Skavar.

ERNEST W. THIELE

Arac's Song

This helmet, I suppose,
Was meant to ward off blows,
  It's very hot,
  And weighs a lot,
As many a guardsman knows,
So off that helmet goes.

This tight-fitting cuirass
Is but a useless mass,
  It's made of steel,
  And weighs a deal,
A man is but an ass
Who fights in a cuirass,
So off goes that cuirass.

These brassets, truth to tell,
May look uncommon well,
  But in a fight
  They're much too tight,
They're like a lobster shell!

These things I treat the same
(I quite forget their name),
  They turn one's legs
  To cribbage pegs—
Their aid I thus disclaim,
Though I forget their name!

SIR W. S. GILBERT

Municipal

"Why is my District death-rate low?"
    Said Binks of Hezabad.
"Well, drains, and sewage-outfalls are
    "My own peculiar fad.
"I learnt a lesson once. It ran
    "Thus," quoth that most veracious man:—

It was an August evening and, in snowy garments
    clad,
I paid a round of visits in the lines of Hezabad;
When, presently, my Waler saw, and did not like at
    all,
A Commissariat elephant careering down the Mall.

I couldn't see the driver, and across my mind it
    rushed
That that Commissariat elephant had suddenly gone
    musth.[1]
I didn't care to meet him, and I couldn't well get
    down,
So I let the Waler have it, and we headed for the
    town.

The buggy was a new one and, praise Dykes, it stood
    the strain,
Till the Waler jumped a bullock just above the City
    Drain;
And the next that I remember was a hurricane of
    squeals,
And the creature making toothpicks of my five-foot
    patent wheels.

He seemed to want the owner, so I fled, distraught
    with fear,
To the Main Drain sewage-outfall while he snorted in
    my ear—

Reached the four-foot drain-head safely and, in darkness and despair,
Felt the brute's proboscis fingering my terror-stiffened hair.

Heard it trumpet on my shoulder—tried to crawl a little higher—
Found the Main Drain sewage-outfall blocked, some eight feet up, with mire;
And, for twenty reeking minutes, Sir, my very marrow froze,
While the trunk was feeling blindly for a purchase on my toes!

It missed me by a fraction, but my hair was turning grey
Before they called the drivers up and dragged the brute away.
Then I sought the City Elders, and my words were very plain.
They flushed that four-foot drain-head and—it never choked again!

You may hold with surface-drainage, and the sun-for-garbage cure,
Till you've been a periwinkle shrinking coyly up a sewer.
I believe in well-flushed culverts. . . .
                    This is why the death-rate's small;
And, if you don't believe me, get *shikarred* [2] yourself.
    That's all.

RUDYARD KIPLING

[1] Mad.   [2] Hunted.

DIALECT: IN & ON

The wit or the point o' what I spakes
  Ye got to find if ye can,
A wunnerful difference spellin' makes
  In the 'ands of a competent man!
I mayn't knaw much o' corliflower plants,
  I mayn't knaw 'oes from trowels,
But I does ma wark, if ma consonants
  Be properly mixed with ma vowels!
                    ANTHONY C. DEANE

Warm Babies

Shadrach, Meshach, Abednego,
Walked in the furnace to an' fro,
Hay foot, straw foot, fro an' to,
An' the flame an' the smoke flared up the flue.
Nebuchadnezzar he listen some,
An' he hear 'em talk, an' he say "How come?"
An' he hear 'em walk, an' he say "How so?
Dem babies was hawg tied an hour ago!"

Then Shadrach call, in an uppity way,
"A little more heat or we ain gwine stay!"
An' Shadrach bawl, so dat furnace shake:
"Lanlawd, heat! fo' de good Lawd's sake!"
Abednego yell, wid a loud "Kerchoo!"
"Is you out to freeze us, y' great big Jew!"
Nebuchadnezzar, he rare an' ramp,
An' call to his janitor, "You big black scamp!
Shake dem clinkers an' spend dat coal!
I'll bake dem birds, ef I goes in de hole!"
So he puts on the draf an' he shuts de door
So de furnace glow an' de chimbly roar.
Ol' Nebuchadnezzar, he smole a smile.
"Guess dat'll hold 'em," says he, "one while."
Then Shadrach, Meshach, Abednego
Walk on de hot coals to an' fro,
Gulp dem cinders like chicken meat
An' holler out fo' a mite mo' heat.
Ol' Nebuchadnezzar gives up de fight;
He open dat door an' he bow perlite.
He shade his eyes from the glare infernal
An' say to Abednego, "Step out, Colonel."
An' he add, "Massa Shadrach, I hopes you all
Won' be huffy at me at all."

Then Shadrach, Meshach, Abednego,
Hay foot, straw foot, three in a row,

Stepped right smart from dat oven door
Jes' as good as they wuz before,
An' far as Nebuchadnezzar could find,
Jes' as good as they wuz behind.

KEITH PRESTON

The Intro

'Er name's Doreen . . . Well, spare me bloomin' days!
    You could 'a' knocked me down wiv 'arf a brick!
Yes, me, that kids meself I know their ways,
    An' 'as a name fer smoogin' [1] in our click!
I jist lines up an' tips the saucy wink.
But strike! The way she piled on dawg! Yeh'd think
    A bloke wus givin' back-chat to the Queen. . . .
        'Er name's Doreen.

I seen 'er in the markit first uv all,
Inspectin' brums at Steeny Isaacs' stall.
    I backs me barrer in—the same ole way—
    An' sez, "Wot O! It's been a bonzer day.
'Ow is it fer a walk?" . . . Oh, 'oly wars!
The sort o' *look* she gimme! Jest becors
    I tried to chat 'er, like yeh'd make a start
        Wiv *any* tart.

An' I kin take me oaf I wus perlite,
An' never said no word that wasn't right,
    An' never tried to maul 'er, or to do
I didn't seem to 'ave the nerve—wiv 'er.
I felt as if I couldn't go that fur,
    An' start to sling off chiack like I used . . .
        Not intrajuiced!

[1] It would spoil the looks of this (and "Pilot Cove" which follows) to pepper it with footnotes for *smoogin'*, *click*, and the like. See page reference in *After All* for the glossary. Or you can take it in through the pores, as James Stephens says of the French language.

Nex' time I sighted 'er in Little Bourke,
Where she wus in a job. I found 'er lurk
   Wus pastin' labels in a pickle joint,
    A game that—any'ow, that ain't the point.
Once more I tried to chat 'er in the street,
But, bli'me! Did she turn me down a treat!
   The way she tossed 'er 'ead an' swished her skirt!
    Oh, it wus dirt!

A squarer tom, I swear, I never seen,
In all me natchril, than this 'ere Doreen.
   It wer'n't no guyver neither; fer I knoo
    That any other bloke 'ad Buckley's 'oo
Tried fer to pick 'er up. Yes, she wus square.
She jist sailed by an' lef' me standin' there
   Like any mug. Thinks I, "I'm out o' luck,"
    An' done a duck.

Well, I dunno. It's that way wiv a bloke.
If she'd a' breasted up to me an' spoke,
   I'd thort 'er jist a common bit o' fluff,
    An' then fergot about 'er, like enough.
It's jist like this. The tarts that's 'ard ter get
Makes you all 'ot to chase 'em, an' to let
   The cove called Cupid git an 'ammer-lock;
    An' lose yer block.

I know a bloke 'oo knows a bloke 'oo toils
In that same pickle found-ery. ('E boils
   The cabbitch storks or somethink.) Anyway,
    I gives me pal the orfis fer to say
'E 'as a sister in the trade 'oo's been
Out uv a job, an' wants to meet Doreen;
   Then we kin get an intro, if we've luck.
    'E sez, "Ribuck."

O' course we worked the oricle; you bet!
But, 'Struth, I ain't recovered frum it yet!

'Twas on a Saturd'y night, in Colluns Street,
  An'—quite be accident, o' course—we meet.
Me pal 'e trots 'er up an' does the toff—
'E allus wus a bloke fer showin' off.
  "This 'ere's Doreen," 'e sez. "This 'ere's the Kid."
    I dips me lid.

"This 'ere's Doreen," 'e sez. I sez "Good day."
An' bli'me, I 'ad nothin' more ter say!
  I couldn't speak a word, or meet 'er eye.
  Clean done me block! I never bin so shy,
Not since I wus a tiny little cub,
An' run the rabbit to the corner pub—
  Wot time the Summer days wus dry an' 'ot—
    Fer my ole pot.

Me! that 'as barracked tarts, an' torked an' larft,
An' chucked orf at 'em like a phonergraft!
  Gawstruth! I seemed to lose me pow'r o' speech.
  But, 'er! Oh, strike me pink! She is a peach!
The sweetest in the barrer! Spare me days,
I carn't describe that cliner's winnin' ways.
  The way she torks! 'Er lips! 'Er eyes! 'Er hair! . . .
    Oh, gimme air!

I dunno 'ow I done it in the end.
I rekerlect I arst to be 'er friend;
  An' tried to play at 'andies in the park,
  A thing she wouldn't sight. Aw, it's a nark!
I gotter swear when I think wot a mug
I must 'a' seemed to 'er. But still I 'ug
  That promise that she give me fer the beach.
    The bonzer peach!

Now, as the poit sez, the days drag by
On ledding feet. I wish't they'd do a guy.
  I dunno 'ow I 'ad the nerve ter speak,
  An' make that meet wiv 'er fer Sund'y week!

But strike! It's funny wot a bloke 'll do
When 'e's all out . . . She's gorn, when I come-to.
　　I'm yappin' to me cobber uv me mash. . . .
　　　　I've done me dash!

'Er name's Doreen . . . An' me—that thort I knoo
　　The ways uv tarts, an' all that smoogin' game!
An' so I ort; fer ain't I known a few?
　　Yet some'ow . . . I dunno. It ain't the same.
I carn't tell *wot* it is, but all I know,
I've dropped me bundle—an' I'm glad it's so.
　　Fer when I come ter think uv wot I been . . .
　　　　'Er name's Doreen.

C. J. DENNIS

Pilot Cove

"Young friend," 'e sez . . . Young friend! Well, spare
　　me days!
　　Yeh'd think I wus 'is own white-'eaded boy—
The queer ole finger, wiv 'is gentle ways.
　　"Young friend," 'e sez, "I wish't yeh bofe great joy."
The langwidge that them parson blokes imploy
　　Fair tickles me. The way 'e bleats an' brays!
　　　　"Young friend," 'e sez.

"Young friend," 'e sez . . . Yes, my Doreen an' me
　　We're gettin' hitched, all straight an' on the square,
Fer when I torks about the registry—
　　O 'oly wars! yeh should 'a' seen 'er stare;
　　"The registry?" she sez, "I wouldn't dare!
I know a clergyman we'll go an' see" . . .
　　　　"Young friend," 'e sez.

"Young friend," 'e sez. An' then 'e chats me straight;
　　An' spouts uv death, an' 'ell, 'an mortal sins.
"You reckernize this step you contemplate
　　Is grave?" 'e sez. An' I jist stan's an' grins;

Fer when I chips, Doreen she kicks me shins.
"Yes, very 'oly is the married state,
  Young friend," 'e sez.

"Young friend," 'e sez. An' then 'e mags a lot
 Of jooty an' the spiritchuil life,
To which I didn't tumble worth a jot.
 "I'm sure," 'e sez, "as you will 'ave a wife
 'Oo'll 'ave a noble infl'ince on yer life.
'Oo is 'er gardjin?" I sez, " 'Er ole pot"—
  "Young friend!" 'e sez.

"Young friend," 'e sez, "Oh fix yer thorts on 'igh!
 Orl marridges is registered up there!
An' you must cleave unto 'er till yeh die,
 An' cherish 'er wiv love an' tender care.
 E'en in the days when she's no longer fair
She's still yer wife," 'e sez. "Ribuck," sez I.
  "Young friend!" 'e sez.

"Young friend," 'e sez—I sez, "Now listen 'ere:
 This isn't one o' them impetchus leaps.
There ain't no tart a 'undredth part so dear
 As 'er. She 'as me 'eart an' soul fer keeps!"
 An' then Doreen, she turns away an' weeps;
But 'e jist smiles. "Yer deep in love, 'tis clear,
  Young friend," 'e sez.

"Young friend," 'e sez—an' tears wus in 'is eyes—
 "Strive 'ard. For many, many years I've lived.
An' I kin but recall wiv tears an' sighs
 The lives of some I've seen in marridge gived,"
 "My Gawd!" I sez. "I'll strive as no bloke strivved!
Fer don't I know I've copped a bonzer prize?"
  "Young friend," 'e sez.

"Young friend," 'e sez. An' in 'is gentle way
 'E pats the shoulder uv my dear Doreen,
"I've solim'ized grand weddin's in me day,

But 'ere's the sweetest little maid I've seen.
   She's fit fer any man, to be 'is queen;
An' you're more forchinit than you kin say,
      Young friend!" 'e sez.

"Young friend," 'e sez . . . A queer old pilot bloke
   Wiv silver 'air. The gentle way 'e dealt
Wiv 'er, the soft an' kindly way 'e spoke
   To my Doreen, 'ud make a statcher melt.
   I tell yeh, square an' all. I sort o' felt
A kiddish kind o' feelin' like I'd choke . . .
      "Young friend," 'e sez.

"Young friend," 'e sez, "you two on Choosday week,
   Is to be joined in very 'oly bonds.
To break them vows I 'opes yeh'll never seek;
   Fer I could curse them 'usbands 'oo absconds!"
   "I'll love 'er till I snuff it," I responds.
"Ah, that's the way I likes to 'ear yeh speak,
      Young friend," 'e sez.

"Young friend," 'e sez—an' then me 'and 'e grips—
   "I wish't yeh luck, you an' yer lady fair.
Sweet maid." An' sof'ly wiv 'is finger-tips,
   'E takes an' strokes me cliner's shinin' 'air.
   An' when I seen 'er standin' blushin' there,
I turns an' kisses 'er, fair on the lips.
      "Young friend!" 'e sez.

C. J. DENNIS

Mia Carlotta

Giuseppe, da barber, ees greata for "mash,"
He gotta da bigga, da blacka moustache,
Good clo'es an' good styla an' playnta good cash.

W'enevra Giuseppe ees walk on da street,
Da peopla dey talka, "how nobby! how neat!
How softa da handa, how smalla da feet."

He leefta hees hat an' he shaka hees curls,
An' smila weeth teetha so shiny like pearls;
Oh, manny da heart of da seelly young girls
                    He gotta.
          Yes, playnta he gotta—
                    But notta
                    Carlotta!

Giuseppe, da barber, he maka da eye,
An' lika da steam engine puffa an' sigh,
For catcha Carlotta w'en she ees go by.

Carlotta she walka weeth nose in da air,
An' look through Giuseppe weeth far-away stare,
As eef she no see dere ees som'body dere.

Giuseppe, da barber, he gotta da cash,
He gotta da clo'es an' da bigga moustache,
He gotta da seelly young girls for da "mash,"
                    But notta—
          You bat my life, notta—
                    Carlotta.
                    I gotta!
                                        T. A. DALY

Brooklynese Champion

I thought the winner had been found
    The day I heard a woman make
The butcher cut her off a pound
    Of fine and juicy soylern steak.

Imagine then the dizzy whirl
    That through my head did swiftly surge
The day I heard the gifted girl
    Who wished departing friends "Bon Verge."
                                        MARGARET FISHBACK

One Piecee Thing

One piecee thing that my have got,
Maskee [1] that thing my no can do.
You talkee you no sabey what?
    Bamboo.
        Quoted by LEWIS CARROLL

Teemothy Hatch

On the itching back
   Of Teemothy Hatch
There was one place
   That he couldna scratch.

At nicht poor Teem
   Would rise and screech
For that itching place
   That he couldna reach.

For years the prayers
   Of Teemothy Hatch
Were that he might itch
   Where he could scratch.

Then he told a Scot,
   By the name of Breese,
"Buried in ma back
   Is a sheeling piece."

That was lang ago;
   Noo his roof's unthatched:
But for forty years
   Was his back weel scratched.
        WILSON MACDONALD

[1] Without.

Sonnet on Stewed Prunes

Ay ant lak pie-plant pie so wery vell;
Ven ay skol eat ice-cream, my yaws du ache;
Ay ant much stuck on dis har yohnnie-cake
Or crackers yust so dry sum peanut shell.
And ven ay eat dried apples, ay skol svell
Until ay tenk my belt skol nearly break;
And dis har breakfast food, ay tenk, ban fake:
Yim Dumps ban boosting it, so it skol sell.
But ay tal yu, ef yu vant someteng fine,
Someteng so sveet lak wery sveetest honey,
Vith yuice dat taste about lak nice port vine,
Only it ant cost hardly any money,—
Ef yu vant someteng yust lak anyel fude,
Yu try stewed prunes. By yiminy! dey ban gude.

WILLIAM F. KIRK

EPICURES & FEEDERS

My stars, but I finished my oysters before I was sure
I'd begun.
The soup came in two-handled teacups, though a baby
could lift 'em with one.
There was fish à la somethin', a forkful, a potato that
looked like a pill;
Then a round little thing called a patty; sweetbread it
said on the bill.
Ice in a cup made of paper—takes longer to tell it than
eat;
Then turkey—a dab of red jelly, and one tiny sliver of
meat.
Mince pie 'bout the size of the arrows the Indians
chipped out of rock,
And coffee they poured in a thimble. That meal was
just shock after shock.
. . . . I golly, when I think of it!

ARTHUR H. FOLWELL

Now to the banquet we press;
Now for the eggs, the ham;
Now for the mustard and cress,
Now for the strawberry jam!

SIR W. S. GILBERT

Find me such a man
As Lippo yonder, built upon the plan
Of heavy storage, double-navelled, fat
From his own giblet's oils . . .

BAYARD TAYLOR

A Ternarie of Littles, upon a Pipkin of Jellie Sent to a Lady

A little Saint best fits a little Shrine,
A little Prop best fits a little Vine,
As my small Cruse best fits my little Wine.

A little Seed best fits a little Soyle,
A little Trade best fits a little Toyle:
As my small Jarre best fits my little Oyle.

A little Bin best fits a little Bread,
A little Garland fits a little Head:
As my small stuffe best fits my little Shed.

A little Hearth best fits a little Fire,
A little Chappell fits a little Quire,
As my small Bell best fits my little Spire.

A little Streame best fits a little Boat;
A little lead best fits a little Float;
As my small Pipe best fits my little Note.

A little meat best fits a little bellie,
As sweetly, Lady, give me leave to tell ye,
This little pipkin fits this little Jellie.

ROBERT HERRICK

The Pilgrims' Thanksgiving Feast

The Pilgrims landed, worthy men,
  And, saved from wreck on raging seas,
They fell upon their knees, and then
  Upon the Aborigines.

In thankfulness they planned a feast
  On what the land could then afford.
The grace consumed an hour at least,
  Whence rose the phrase, "the festive bored."

What meat to choose they did not know,
  Until upon a maple limb
A turkey-gobbler gobbled, so
  They took the hint and gobbled him.

ARTHUR GUITERMAN

Marble-Top

At counters where I eat my lunch
  In dim arcades of industry,
I cock my elbows up and munch
  Whatever food occurs to me.

By many mirrors multiplied,
  My silly face is not exalted;
And when I leave I have inside
  An egg-and-lettuce and a malted.

And just to hear the pretty peal
  Of merry maids at their pimento
Is more to me than any meal
  Or banquet that I ever went to.

E. B. WHITE

Bacon and Eggs

Now blest be the Briton, his beef and his beer,
And all the strong waters that keep him in cheer,
But blest beyond cattle and blest beyond kegs
Is the brave British breakfast of bacon and eggs—

  Bacon and eggs,
  Bacon and eggs;
    Sing bacon,
    Red bacon,
  Red bacon and eggs!

Thus armed and thus engined, well-shaven and gay,
We leap to our labours and conquer the day,
While paltry pale foreigners, meagre as moles,
Must crawl through the morning on coffee and rolls—

> *Coffee and rolls,*
> *Barbarous rolls;*
> *Sing coffee,*
> *Black coffee,*
> *Vile coffee and rolls!*

What wonder the Frenchman, blown out with new
   bread,
Gesticulates oft and is light in the head!
Our perfect control of our arms and our legs
We owe to our ballast of bacon and eggs—

> *Bacon and eggs,*
> *Unemotional eggs;*
> *Sing bacon,*
> *Fat bacon,*
> *Brave bacon and eggs!*

What wonder that Fortune is careful to place
Her loveliest laurels on men of our race,
While sorrow is heaped upon Prussians and Poles
Who shame the glad morning with coffee and rolls—

> *Coffee and rolls,*
> *Ladylike rolls;*
> *Sing coffee,*
> *Pooh! coffee,*
> *Black coffee and rolls!*

What wonder the Russian looks redly because
Our England, old England, is much what it was!
We fight to the finish, we drink to the dregs
And dare to be Daniels on bacon and eggs—

> *Bacon and eggs,*
> *Masculine eggs;*
> *Sing bacon,*
> *Bring bacon,*
> *And fry me two eggs!*

But gross Europeans who constantly munch
Too little at breakfast, too freely at lunch,
Sit sated in *cafés*, incapable souls,
And go to the devil on coffee and rolls—

> *Coffee and rolls,*
> *Windy wet rolls;*
> *At coffee*
> *I'm scoffy,*
> *I execrate rolls!*

O breakfast! O breakfast! The meal of my heart!
Bring porridge, bring sausage, bring fish for a start,
Bring kidneys and mushrooms and partridges' legs,
But let the foundation be bacon and eggs—

> *Bacon and eggs,*
> *Bacon and eggs;*
> *Bring bacon,*
> *Crisp bacon,*
> *And let there be eggs!*

SIR A. P. HERBERT

Table For One

I know a tavern in the town,
By which I mean a place to eat,
And there I go to sit me down
Alone and in a sheltered seat.
I order coffee, with a roll,
And think the place exactly right
To loaf and to invite my soul
While reading something fairly bright.

What happens then? A carpenter
Erects new doors, or walls, or shelves.
Above his din the manager
And waiters shout among themselves.
The porters come with pails and mops.
The bus boy fills the sugar bowls.
A waiter wipes the table tops.
The cooks are flinging casseroles.
The cashier types the luncheon list.
The counterman makes orange-juice.

O waiters, go away! Desist!
O orange-grinder, call a truce!
O tavern-keeper, hire a hall
And there have all your housework done.
I do not wish to know at all
The way your private life is run.

JOHN HOLMES

The Cheese-Mites Asked

The cheese-mites asked how the cheese got there,
    And warmly debated the matter;
The orthodox said it came from the air,
    And the heretics said from the platter.

ANONYMOUS

Eating Song

*(Being a Rendering of the Fervours of our best
Drinking Songs into the equivalent terms of a
kindred Art)*

If you want to drive wrinkles from belly and brow,
You must tighten the skin, as I tighten it now;
For at gobbets of bacon I sit at my ease,
And I button my mouth over dollops of cheese,

And I laugh at the Devil, who plays on his pipes
With the wind from a famishing traveller's tripes.
The French call it dining to peddle and peck,
But an Englishman's watchword is "Full to the neck!"
Does the parson deny it?—he's lean as a cat,
And the men that I like are all puffy and fat:
Perhaps you'll find music in heaven, but by George!
You won't get a thundering suetty gorge.
So down with your victuals, and stuff till you burst,
And let him who refuses a morsel be curst!

SIR WALTER RALEIGH

On China Blue

On china blue my lobster red
   Precedes my cutlet brown,
With which my salad green is sped
   By yellow Chablis down.

Lord, if good living be no sin,
   But innocent delight,
O polarize these hues within
   To one eupeptic white.

SIR STEPHEN GASELEE

You Hire a Cook

You hire a cook, but she can't cook yet;
You teach her by candle, bell, and book yet;
You show her, as if she were in her cradle,
Today, the soup, tomorrow, a ladle.
Well, she doesn't learn, so although you need her,
You decide that somebody else should feed her:—
But you're kind by birth; you hate to fire her;
To tell a woman you don't require her—
So you wait and wait, and before you do it,
What thanks do you get? She beats you to it!

SAMUEL HOFFENSTEIN

Assorted Relishes

Celery

When forced to wait and wait for luncheon,
A stalk or two will serve to munch on,
A use which would, indeed, be laudable,
If only it weren't quite so audible.

Olives

Unless its innards are pimento,
Each olive leaves its own memento,
And therefore, should you nibble any,
The seeds will testify how many.

Radishes

Though pretty things, they like as not
Are either pithy or too hot,
Nor do you know, till you have bitten,
If you've a tiger or a kitten.

Pickles

Since people are of many minds
About the sundry sorts and kinds,
Some way is needed to empower one
To tell a sweet one from a sour one.

Onions

The onion eater and his brother,
Though inoffensive to each other,
Are by their diet alienated
From those who've not participated.

RICHARD ARMOUR

FAR FROM SOMEWHERE

Everywhere is far from somewhere else:
The rain doth freeze for me—for you snow melts:
Sun on the tundra, moon cool on the veldts.

PRIMUS

Pan in Vermont

(About the 15th of this month you may expect our
    Mr.——, with the usual Spring Seed, etc.,
    Catalogues.—*Florists' Announcement*)

It's forty in the shade to-day the spouting eaves de-
    clare;
The boulders nose above the drift, the southern slopes
    are bare;
Hub-deep in slush Apollo's car swings north along the
    Zod-
iac. Good lack, the Spring is back, and Pan is on the
    road!

His house is Gee & Tellus' Sons,—so goes his jest with
    men—
He sold us Zeus knows what last year; he'll take us in
    again.
Disguised behind a livery-team, fur-coated, rubber-
    shod—
Yet Apis from the bull-pen lows—he knows his brother
    God!

Now down the lines of tasselled pines the yearning
    whispers wake—
Pitys of old thy love behold. Come in for Hermes'
    sake!
How long since that so-Boston boot with reeling Mae-
    nads ran?
Numen adest! Let be the rest. Pipe and we pay, O Pan.

(What though his phlox and hollyhocks ere half a
    month demised?
What though his ampelopsis clambered not as adver-
    tised?
Though every seed was guaranteed and every standard
    true—

Forget, forgive they did not live! Believe, and buy
    anew!)

Now o'er a careless knee he flings the painted page
    abroad—
Such bloom hath never eye beheld this side the Eden
    Sword;
Such fruit Pomona marks her own, yea, Liber oversees
That we may reach (one dollar each) the Lost Hes-
    perides!.

Serene, assenting, unabashed, he writes our orders
    down:—
Blue Asphodel on all our paths—a few true bays for
    crown—
Uncankered bud, immortal flower, and leaves that
    never fall—
Apples of Gold, of Youth, of Health—and—thank you,
    Pan, that's all.

He's off along the drifted pent to catch the Windsor
    train,
And swindle every citizen from Keene to Lake Cham-
    plain;
But where his goat's-hoof cut the crust—beloved, look
    below—
He's left us (I'll forgive him all) the may-flower 'neath
    her snow!

RUDYARD KIPLING

On the Aristocracy of Harvard

And this is good old Boston,
    The home of the bean and the cod,
Where the Lowells talk only to Cabots
    And the Cabots talk only to God.

JOHN COLLINS BOSSIDY

A Correction

When we told you minus twenty
Here this morning, that seemed plenty.
We were trying to be modest
(Said he spitting in the sawdust),
And moreover did our guessing
By the kitchen stove while dressing.
Come to dress and make a sortie,
What we found was minus forty.

Franconia, N. H.   ROBERT FROST

The American Traveller

To Lake Aghmoogenegamook,
    All in the State of Maine,
A man from Witteguergaugaum came
    One evening in the rain.

"I am a traveller," said he,
    "Just started on a tour,
And go to Nomjamskillicock
    To-morrow morn at four."

He took a tavern bed that night;
    And, with the morrow's sun,
By way of Sekledobskus went,
    With carpet-bag and gun.

A week passed on; and next we find
    Our native tourist come
To that sequestered village called
    Genasagarnagum.

From thence he went to Absequoit,
    And there, quite tired of Maine—
He sought the mountains of Vermont,
    Upon a railroad train.

Dog Hollow, in the Green Mount State,
    Was his first stopping place;
And then Skunk's Misery displayed
    Its sweetness and its grace.

By easy stages then he went
    To visit Devil's Den;
And Scramble Hollow, by the way,
    Did come within his ken.

Then via Nine Holes and Goose Green
    He travelled through the State;
And to Virginia, finally,
    Was guided by his fate.

Within the old Dominion's bounds
    He wandered up and down;
To-day, at Buzzard Roost ensconced,
    To-morrow at Hell Town.

At Pole Cat, too, he spent a week,
    Till friends from Bull Ring came,
And made him spend a day with them
    In hunting forest-game.

Then, with his carpet-bag in hand,
    To Dog Town next he went,
Though stopping at Free Negro Town,
    Where half a day he spent.

From thence, to Negationburg
    His route of travel lay;
Which having gained, he left the State
    And took a southward way.

North Carolina's friendly soil
    He trod at fall of night,
And, on a bed of softest down,
    He slept at Hell's Delight.

Morn found him on the road again,
    To Lousy Level bound;
At Bull's Tail, and Lick Lizard, too,
    Good provender he found.

The country all about Pinch Gut
    So beautiful did seem
That the beholder thought it like
    A picture in a dream.

But the plantations near Burnt Coat
    Were even finer still,
And made the wondering tourist feel
    A soft delicious thrill.

At Tear Shirt, too, the scenery
    Most charming did appear,
And Snatch It in the distance far,
    And Purgatory near.

But, spite of all these pleasant scenes,
    The tourist stoutly swore
That home is brightest, after all,
    And travel is a bore.

So back he went to Maine straightway:
    A little wife he took;
And now is making nutmegs at
    Moosehicmagunticook.

                              ROBERT H. NEWELL

Hotel Lobby

Here's tropic flora
That astounds
The simple traveller.
Here abounds

The Mazda blossom,
By whose glare
Exotic fauna
Takes the air.

Amazing palms
Rear stalk on stalk
Where parrot pages
Strut and squawk

Unmindful
Of the eyes that burn
Behind the undergrowth
Of fern.

Off in the brush
A saxophone
Reiterates
The tribal moan.

A tom-tom throbs
An urgent plea.
The natives move
Uneasily.

With sullen grace
A leopard slinks
After a dashing pelt
Of lynx.

The jungle's stirring!
We will wait
For bigger game
To congregate.

Sequestered
On the mezzanine
We can observe
And be unseen.

> Oh, strange
> And awe-inspiring sight—
> A jungle water-hole
> By night!
>
> MILDRED WESTON

New England

Here where the wind is always north-north-east
And children learn to walk on frozen toes,
Wonder begets an envy of all those
Who boil elsewhere with such a lyric yeast
Of love that you will hear them at a feast
Where demons would appeal for some repose,
Still clamoring where the chalice overflows
And crying wildest who have drunk the least.

Passion is here a soilure of the wits,
We're told, and Love a cross for them to bear;
Joy shivers in the corner where she knits
And Conscience always has the rocking-chair,
Cheerful as when she tortured into fits
The first cat that was ever killed by Care.

> EDWIN ARLINGTON ROBINSON

Come to Britain

A Humble Contribution to the Movement

Oh, why does New York go to France for its fun
When they might be as jolly in South Kensington?
Why flock to the Continent? Surely they know
We've got a whole Continent parked in Soho.

> Come to Britain! for Britain's the best.
> It's eleven o'clock, and the nation's at rest.
> The curfew is pealing, all's quiet at Ealing,

And no one can say we're offensively gay;
An income-tax form is the only thing cheap,
But come to Britain and have a good sleep.

Why go to Paris, you travelling swells,
When you've never had fun in our country hotels?
There isn't a bath, and the bell doesn't ring,
But you don't come to Britain for that sort of thing.

Come to Britain! The rooms are so old
And so picturesque that you won't mind the cold.
The bed's over there and the light's over here;
Don't put out your boots if you want them this
*   year;*
The maid has a beard, the cold mutton perspires,
But come to Britain and visit the Shires!

Some of you find that Mentone is dull—
Come over and try a wet Sunday in Hull.
Take luncheon in bed, and get up when you dine,
But order your hot-water-bottle for nine.

Come to Britain and lead the gay life!
As a rule it's illegal to bathe with your wife;
We censor all dramas that mention pyjamas,
But still there's a thrill in our girl-guides at drill;
And we've swings in the parks, and municipal boats,
So come to Britain and sow your wild oats!

Come to Britain! We've done what we could
To make the place healthy and wholesome and
*   good.*
Your whiskey will cost you much less in the States,
And here, between drinks, we have tedious waits,
But the Albert Memorial's always on show,
So come to Britain, and let yourselves go!

SIR A. P. HERBERT

Edinburgh

A bonny burgh is Edinbro', the city brave and bright
That spreads in green and gray below the castle on the
    height;
And there on lovely Princes Street the people group in
    knots
To talk about the latest news of Mary Queen of Scots.

The castle is a gallant keep and one you're bound to
    view;
A military pensioner will kindly take you through,
Rehearsing inexhaustibly the plots and counterplots
That made it insalubrious for Mary Queen of Scots.

You'll see the ancient Canongate, you'll see the house
    of Knox,
With churches here and churches there, all strictly
    orthodox;
You'll see the work of colorists who lavished paint in
    pots
On old and recent likenesses of Mary Queen of Scots.

And when amid the gorse and sheep you've climbed to
    Arthur's Seat,
Where Arthur, says the legend, watched his chivalry
    retreat,
Your eye shall rest on Holyrood and other sacred spots
Connected with the tragedy of Mary Queen of Scots.

You'll see the marble statue of the Wizard of the
    North;
You'll see the cantilever bridge that spans the Firth of
    Forth,
A noble bridge, yet when 'twas done the builders
    cursed their lots
Because it wasn't patronized by Mary Queen of Scots.

A blessing on the bonny burgh and all it holds en-
shrined,
On every house of native rock, on every close and
wynd,
And send it good historians to clear whatever blots
May rest upon the memory of Mary Queen of Scots!

ARTHUR GUITERMAN

"Il est Cocu—le Chef de Gare!"

The Teuton sang the "Wacht am Rhein"
   And "Lieber Augustin," while we
Had "Long Long Trail" and "Clementine"
   And "Old Kit Bag" (to give but three);
   Good songs, and yet, you must agree,
The "poilu's" theme was richer, vaster,
   —Double-distilled felicity!—
"He has been duped—the station-master!"

A joyous thought, an anodyne
   For gelignite and T.N.T.
A song to cure those saturnine
   Red singing-men of Battersea;
   And, whosoever wrote it, he
Deserves a tomb of alabaster
   Graven on which these words should be:
"He has been duped—the station-master!"

When I am tired of Gertrude Stein
   ("She said she said that she said she . . . !")
When the expressionistic line
   Has palled, and Sitwells weary me,
   When bored with psycho-prosody,
Obscurist and grammaticaster
   Give me that song of Picardy:
"He has been duped—the station-master!"

Envoy

Prince, did you hear the soldiery
Singing of that obscure disaster—
(Zenith of Gallic pleasantry!)
"He has been duped—the station-master!"

H. S. MACKINTOSH

The Immoral Arctic

The Eskimo, explorers state,
    Little regards the marriage vow.
Lightly the bride deceives her mate.
    It makes you sort of wonder how.

Come forth, my love; the Northern Light
    Wavers in glory o'er the snow;
We'll dedicate to love this night.
    It's only forty-five below.

Your husband in the igloo snores,
    Heedless of love's adventurers.
Come forth to God's great out-of-doors!
    You'd better put on all your furs.

And it will be sufficient bliss
    To sit and drink your beauty in.
I dare not kiss you, for a kiss
    Is likely to remove the skin.

The Eskimo's incontinence
    Is what explorers make report of.
I don't contest the evidence;
    But still, it makes you wonder, sort of.

MORRIS BISHOP

Cologne

In Köhln, a town of monks and bones,
And pavements fang'd with murderous stones,

And rags, and hags, and hideous wenches;
I counted two and seventy stenches,
All well defined, and several stinks!
Ye Nymphs that reign o'er sewers and sinks,
The river Rhine, it is well known,
Doth wash your city of Cologne;
But tell me, Nymphs! what power divine
Shall henceforth wash the river Rhine?

SAMUEL TAYLOR COLERIDGE

On My Joyful Departure from the Same

As I am a rhymer,
And now at least a merry one,
Mr. Mum's Rudesheimer
And the church of St. Geryon
Are the two things alone
That deserve to be known
In the body and soul-stinking town of Cologne.

SAMUEL TAYLOR COLERIDGE

The Spectre

The moment I glanced at the mirk-windowed mansion
    that lifts from the woodlands of Dankacre, Lincs.,
To myself I said softly: "Confide in me, pilgrim, why
    is it the heart in your bosom thus sinks?
What's amiss with this region? It's certainly England;
    the moon, there, is rising, and there Vega blinks."

A drear wind sighed bleakly; it soughed in the silence;
    it sobbed as if homesick for Knucklebone, Notts.;
The moon with her mountains showed spectral and
    sullen; the corn-crake and nightjar craked, jarred,
    from their grots;

And aloft from its mistletoe nest in an oak-tree, a
    scritch-owlet's scritch froze my blood into clots.

I called on my loved one asleep 'neath the myrtles
    whose buds turn to berries in Willowlea, Herts.;
I mused on sweet innocent scenes where in summer
    the deer browse, the doves croon, the butterfly
    darts;
But, alas! these devices proved vain, horror loured,
    my terror was such as no metre imparts.

For afar o'er the marshes the booming of bitterns, like
    the bitterns that boomed once from Bootle in
    Lancs.,
Came mingled with wailings from Dowsing and
    Dudgeon of sea-gulls lamenting o'er Bluddi-
    thumbe Banks—
My bowels turned to water; my knees shook; my skin
    crept; and the hairs on my cranium rose up in
    hanks.

And lo! from an attic, there peered out a visage, with
    eyes like brass bed-knobs and beak like a hawk's;
And it opened the casement, and climbed down the
    ivy, with claws like a trollop's, on legs like a
    stork's;
And I screamed and fled inland, from mansion and
    moonshine, till I saw the sun rising on Pep-y-gent,
    Yorks.

                        WALTER DE LA MARE

Tourist Time

    This fat woman in canvas knickers
    Gapes seriously at everything.
    We might be a city of the dead
    Or cave men
    Instead of simple town folk.

We have nothing to show
That can't be seen better somewhere else,
Yet for this woman the wonder ceases not.

Madam, the most extraordinary thing in this town
Is the shape of your legs.

O communication!
O rapid transit!

F. R. SCOTT

Étude Géographique

Out West, they say, a man's a man; the legend still
    persists
That he is handy with a gun, and careless with his
    fists.
The fact is, though, you may not hear a stronger word
    than "Gosh!"
From Saskatoon, Saskatchewan, to Walla Walla, Wash.

In western towns 'tis many years since it was last the
    rage
For men to earn their daily bread by holding up the
    stage,
Yet story writers still ascribe such wild and woolly
    bosh
To Saskatoon, Saskatchewan, and Walla Walla, Wash.

The gents who roam the West today are manicured
    and meek,
They shave their features daily and they bathe three
    times a week.
They tote the tame umbrella and they wear the mild
    galosh
From Saskatoon, Saskatchewan, to Walla Walla, Wash.

But though the West has frowned upon its old
    nefarious games,
It still embellishes the map with sweet, melodious
    names,
Which grow in lush profusion like the apple and the
    squash
From Saskatoon, Saskatchewan, to Walla Walla, Wash.

STODDARD KING

Says I to Myself

Says I to myself,
glad I shall be,
when I am free,
O Rome from thee,
& over the sea,
high diddledydee.

EDWARD LEAR

GRAPE JUICE & MR. COLLINS

If on my theme I rightly think,
There are five reasons why men drink,
Good wine, a friend, or being dry,
Or lest we should be, by and by,
Or any other reason why.

HENRY ALDRICH

None so knowing as he
At brewing a jorum of tea,
Ha! ha!
A pretty stiff jorum of tea.

SIR W. S. GILBERT

The Laird o' Phelps spent Hogmanay declaring he
was sober,
Counted his feet to prove the fact and found he had
one foot over.

LOUIS MacNEICE

I think that some have died of drought,
And some have died of drinking;
I think that naught is worth a thought—
And I'm a fool for thinking!

WINTHROP MACKWORTH PRAED

Bathtub Gin

Oh, ancient sin, Oh, bathtub gin,
  How rare and how robust,
Bouquet of tin and porcelain
  And little grains of rust.
Our cares dissolved as you evolved,
  Your beauty was benumbing,
You rose full-armored from the bath
  Like Venus from the plumbing.

When hardened hearts in foreign parts
  Deride your name with scorn,
And whisper calumnies and say
  That you were basely born,
I plait a wreath of juniper,
  My thirsty tonsils ache
To fill my skin with bathtub gin
  Like Father used to make.

PHILIP H. RHINELANDER

prohibition

prohibition makes you
want to cry
into your beer and
denies you the beer
to cry into

DON MARQUIS

A Glass of Beer

The lanky hank of a she in the inn over there
Nearly killed me for asking the loan of a glass of beer;
May the devil grip the whey-faced slut by the hair,
And beat bad manners out of her skin for a year.

That parboiled ape, with the toughest jaw you will see
On virtue's path, and a voice that would rasp the dead,
Came roaring and raging the minute she looked at me,
And threw me out of the house on the back of my
    head!

If I asked her master he'd give me a cask a day;
But she, with the beer at hand, not a gill would ar-
    range!
May she marry a ghost and bear him a kitten, and may
The High King of Glory permit her to get the mange.

JAMES STEPHENS

Said Aristotle unto Plato

Said Aristotle unto Plato,
   "Have another sweet potato?"
Said Plato unto Aristotle,
   "Thank you, I prefer the bottle."

OWEN WISTER

Forbidden Drink

"No one will milk a cow within
The area!" So reads the sign.
Since drinking milk is such a sin,
Cheer up, we'll get along on wine.

ROBERT LOVETT

Italy: May, 1944

Drinking

The thirsty earth soaks up the rain,
And drinks, and gapes for drink again.
The plants suck in the earth, and are
With constant drinking fresh and fair;

The sea itself—which one would think
Should have but little need of drink—
Drinks ten thousand rivers up,
So filled that they o'erflow the cup.
The busy sun—and one would guess
By's drunken fiery face no less—
Drinks up the sea, and when he's done,
The moon and stars drink up the sun:
They drink and dance by their own light;
They drink and revel all the night.
Nothing in nature's sober found,
But an eternal health goes round.
Fill up the bowl then, fill it high,
Fill up the glasses there; for why
Should every creature drink but I;
Why, man of morals, tell me why?

ABRAHAM COWLEY

Down in a Wine Vault

Down in a wine vault underneath the city
    Two old men were sitting; they were drinking
        booze.
Torn were their garments, hair and beards were gritty;
    One had an overcoat but hardly any shoes.

Overhead the street cars through the streets were run-
        ning
    Filled with happy people going home to Christmas;
In the Adirondacks the hunters all were gunning,
    Big ships were sailing down by the Isthmus.

In came a Little Tot for to kiss her granny,
    Such a little totty she could scarcely tottle,
Saying, "Kiss me, Grandpa! Kiss your little Nanny!"
    But the old man beaned her with a whiskey bottle!

Outside the snowflakes began for to flutter,
   Far at sea the ships were sailing with the seamen,
Not another word did Angel Nanny utter.
   Her grandsire chuckled and pledged the Whiskey
      Demon! . . .

DON MARQUIS

Then as to Feasting

Then as to feasting, it doesn't agree with me—
Each single Goblet is equal to three with me,
Wine is my foe tho' I still am a friend of it,
Hock becomes hic—with a cup at the end of it.

OLIVER WENDELL HOLMES

Moan in the Form of a Ballade

I went to someone's dinner and a play,
   And supper, with a man whose name was Duff,
Or Herbert Spencer, or the poet Gray.
   I felt inclined to chatter like a chough.
   The Cardinal, whose health I drank, was Puff,
When all at once the wine went to my head,
   I felt as if at sea about to luff.
I can't remember how I went to bed.

The chairs and tables glimmered far away;
   I thought I heard Sir William Wellenough
Remark upon the road to Mandalay,
   How much he liked a little bit of fluff.
   Then everybody played at Blind Man's Buff;
It must have been, I think, my nose that bled.
   I heard a player shout "I'll call the bluff."
I can't remember how I went to bed.

I'm feeling very far from well to-day;
  I cannot bear the taste of smoke or snuff,
Nor anything that's brought upon a tray,
  My brow is fevered and my voice is gruff.
  I've taken what is called a *Quantum Suff,*
Or *Nisi prius* as the lawyer said.
  The doctor came and left me in a huff.
I can't remember how I went to bed.

Envoy

  Prince, have you heard of that tremendous stuff
That startles into life the quiet dead?
  I drank it till I felt I'd had enough.
I can't remember how I went to bed.

MAURICE BARING

Liquor & Longevity

The horse and mule live 30 years
And nothing know of wines and beers.
The goat and sheep at 20 die
And never taste of Scotch or Rye.
The cow drinks water by the ton
And at 18 is mostly done.
The dog at 15 cashes in
Without the aid of rum and gin.
The cat in milk and water soaks
And then in 12 short years it croaks.
The modest, sober, bone-dry hen
Lays eggs for nogs, then dies at ten.
All animals are strictly dry:
They sinless live and swiftly die;
But sinful, ginful rum-soaked men
Survive for three score years and ten.
And some of them, a very few,
Stay pickled till they're 92.

ANONYMOUS

The Grapes of Wrath

Speaking of wine
There is a little-known story of Marshal Foch.
When the German envoys arrived
To ask for armistice
They were given their lunch
Apart, by themselves.
And by the Marshal's express command
They were served a very rare vintage.
And you might take care, said Foch,
That they observe the label.

It was of the year 1870.

CHRISTOPHER MORLEY

A Ballade of Diminishing Control
(Dialogue of Passenger and Driver)

Yes, I admit that Proust is rather good,
   But don't you think old Johnson was a lout?
—Just here the bowmen of King Harold stood—
   Of course I'll stop—it ended in a rout—
   My poor old father passed me on the gout,
I seldom touch a drink or a cigar—
   An admirable inn, beyond a doubt—
What *was* that thing we thought of in the car?

What? One more hostelry? D'you think I could?
   All right! The Spring is here, and one should sprout,
Besides, I see the wines are from the wood—
   If only I were equal to a bout!—
   A small one—no, a large one—the mahout
Of whom I spoke, alas, was drowned in tar—
   It's always thus, the best go up the spout—
What was that thing we thought of in the car?

Now, don' you shink you might put up that hood?
  I don' shee why you should ashume that pout—
I only shaid you *might,* not that you *should*—
  Don' be an ash, I shay I didn't shout!—
  Here, mish, my frien' an' me, we want shome
      shtout—
Shorry, I shought zhis wash zhe private bar—
  Well now, zhe breeding habitsh of zhe trout—
What wash zhat shing we *shought* of in zhe car?

Envoy

  Hi! Here'sh a pub! Put on zhat brake, you tout!
I dunno where zhe bloody hell we are—
  —Yesh! Jush one more before zhey turn ush out—
Wa' wash zhat shing we shought of in zhe car?

SIR J. C. SQUIRE

Hangover

My head is like lead, and my temples they bulge,
And my tongue feels like something I wouldn't di-
    vulge,
But it's always the way when I overindulge,
                    Overindulge . . .

The wages of sin they tell me is death,
Like the grim retribution that fell on Macbeth,
And the wages of gin is a terrible breath,
                    Terrible breath . . .

My eyes are on fire, my forehead I clutch,
And it's hard to stand up, my condition is such,
But it's always this way when I've taken too much,
                    Taken too much . . .

I feel like a fish that has recently died,
Like the rind of a melon that's left at low tide,
And I can't eat my breakfast, I know 'cause I've tried,
                    My, how I tried . . .

I'm feeling unhappy, I needn't relate.
I wish I could blame it on something I ate,
But it's always this way when I stay up too late,
Stay up too late . . .

My feet are unsteady, the carpet revolves
With a sinister eddy. My courage dissolves,
And I wish I had followed my better resolves,
My better resolves . . .

PHILIP H. RHINELANDER

Recipe

(From *Two Gentlemen of Soho*)

Pluck me ten berries from the juniper,
And in a beaker of strong barley-spirit
The kindly juices of the fruit compress.
This is our Alpha. Next clap on your wings,
Fly south for Italy, nor come you back
Till in the cup you have made prisoner
Two little thimblefuls of that sweet syrup
The Romans call Martini. Pause o'er Paris
And fill two eggshells with the French Vermouth.
Then home incontinent, and in one vessel
Cage your three captives, but in nice proportions,
So that no one is master, and the whole
Sweeter than France, but not so sweet as Italy.
Wring from an orange two bright tears, and shake,
Shake a long time the harmonious trinity,
Then in two cups like angels' ears present them,
And see there swims an olive in the bowl,
Which when the draught is finished shall remain
Like some sad emblem of a perished love.
This is our Omega.

SIR A. P. HERBERT

Tomato Juice

(A Song of the Sea)

Life is a most extraordinary thing.
  I sit and see the coast of Spain go by,
And watch the circling sea-birds on the wing;
  The sun is o'er the yard-arm and I cry,
  'Steward, it is the moment for a can—
    But not of beer. Bring something soft and cheap;
For England's far, and I'm a better man;
  Bring me the best tomato-juice you keep.'
And here is news to make the Devil grin—
Tomato-juice is twopence more than gin!

Ozone is in my lungs; and in my soul
  Ozone is present. I would drink a toast
In some demure and unfermented bowl
  To Nancy Astor and the healthy host;
For they are right: and always I will be
  Unalcoholic as a heather-bell.
I will take naught but vitamins and tea,
  Preserve my liver and my wealth as well.
But, oh! sobriety's as dear as sin—
Tomato-juice is twopence more than gin!

If there is anything that I desire
  It is a beaker of tomato-juice—
With Worcester sauce, a dash of it, for fire—
  Anti-scorbutic, purifying, puce.
And if these ladies—as I think they do—
  Expect refreshment of a liquid kind,
I would delight them with tomatoes too
  And put the Demon Alcohol behind;
But I have duties to my kith and kin—
Tomato-juice is twopence more than gin!

So, Steward, bring them Sweet Martinis all!
　　Life is a most extraordinary thing:
False values eyerywhere the saints appal,
　　The good men suffer and the wicked sing.
Whenever I determine to be good
　　I know that some misfortune will befall.
I am a martyr, much misunderstood;
　　So, Steward, mix a cocktail for us all.
But what a ship! How can the angels win?
Tomato-juice is twopence more than gin!

SIR A. P. HERBERT

A Toast

Here's to ye absent Lords, may they
Long in a foreign country stay,
Drinking at other ladies' boards
The health of other absent Lords.

ANONYMOUS

Wine Jelly

Lips that touch wine jelly
Will never touch mine, Nellie.

ANONYMOUS

HABITANT

Venez ici, mon cher ami, an' sit down by me—so
An' I will tole you story of old tam long ago—
W'en ev'ryt'ing is happy—w'en all de bird is sing
An' me!—I'm young an' strong lak moose an' not
  afraid no t'ing.

WILLIAM HENRY DRUMMOND

Pierre of Timagami in New York

Oui, oui, Monsieur, Timagami,
  I leeve dere half ma life;
De hodder half she's up dere now;
  Babette, dat ees ma wife.

I doan' lak much dese New York girls;
  Dey ees too pale and thin;
Where dey leave off, by gar, ma friend,
  Babette she just begin.

Timagami has million lakes;
  Two million lakes, maybe.
Our grocers geev wan lake away
  Wit' hevery pound of tea.

De fir trees in Timagami
  Dey grow so beeg and high
We have to take dem down at night
  To let de stars go by.

De we have storms? Sapré, dose winds
  Are swifter dan reindeer;
Dey sometimes blow a town away;
  Dat's how I came down here.

I doan' lak travel in a crowd,
  I lak to go alone.
By gar, eet's cheaper dan de bus
  To travel by cyclone.

Our cheeldren een Timagami
  Doan' play no Blindman's Buff;
De grizzly bear won't play wit' dem
  Because dey get too tough.

De Yankee girl, wen chile is born,
  To hospital dey go,
And stay two week; and sometime tree,
  For why I'd lak to know.

Wen our last leetle keed she come,
 (Dat's nombre twenty-four)
Babette she took ten minute rest,
 Den feenish scrub de floor.

De we leeve long up in dat north?
 Come up dere and you'll see
Lots men one hundred years of age
 Seet on dere grandad's knee.

We've plentie moose up dere, and wen
 You see one running loose
Wit' thirty leetle moose behind
 Dat's French-Canadian moose.

Gude-bye, ma fren', come up some day
 And mak Canadian whoop.
We geev you wheesky blanc all night;
 For breakfas' nice pea-soup.

WILSON MACDONALD

Armand Dussault

Armand Dussault ees easy-mark
 Mos' heverybody know.
He naiver lose hees temper once:
 He ees too beeg an' slow.

De leetle boys dey com' at night
 An' steal hees eggs an' hen;
An' den com' back, wen he doan' look,
 An' steal som' more again.

Dey know dat he can't run because
 He ees so slow an' beeg.
An' so one fellow steal hees cow,
 Anodder steal hees peeg.

Armand had very pretty wife;
    Her tongue eet run her wild.
She naiver stop her talking once
    Since she was leetle child.

One day a handsome neighbor-man
    He stole dat wife away,
An' took her to United State
    An' kep' her dere to stay.

But Armand he doan' get heem mad;
    He smile and say to me:
"Las' Sonday, at de church, de pries'
    Preach, 'Love your enemy.'

"An' so I love de man dat stole
    Ma rake an' hoe an' plow.
I even love a leetle bit
    De man dat stole ma cow.

"I love de man dat stole ma pipe:
    My love for heem ees small.
But dat good man, who stole my wife,
    I love heem bes' of all."

WILSON MACDONALD

De Baby Show

Joe Beauchamp ees conceited man.
    He trow heem out hees ches'.
He teenk heemself an' all he own
    Ees better dan de res'.

He mak' beeg money in de mine,
    And buy great house an' lot:
An' den dose friends he used to know
    He very queek forgot.

Hees car eet ees a Roysey-Rolls,
  An' heverywhere he go
Dat car do seexty mile an hour
  For jus' to mak' heem show.

One day he stop my wife an' say:
  "Ees dat your leetle lad?"
She answer, "Oui," an' den he laugh:
  "He's homely, dat's too bad.

"He look lak' hees ole man," he say.
  "He's got no shape, an' fat."
An' den he look at me and smile:
  "Doan' blame de keed for dat."

I was so mad I couldn't speak:
  I swallow me my tongue.
I wish Joe Beauchamp he was dead:
  I'd lak' to see heem hung.

Now once a year een Ville Marie
  Dey hole a Baby Show.
Dey have a band an' heveryting,
  An' heverybody go.

Joe Beauchamp sent hees baby dere,
  All scented up lak' rose;
An' nurse maid by heem all de time
  To keep heem clean hees nose.

Ma baby he was enter too:
  He have such preety eyes.
But judges doan' see dat, and geev'
  Joe's baby de first prize.

But jus' as judges go to geev'
  Dat baby boy de cup,
He yell heem "Whoop," and keek hees toes.
  An' trow hees breakfas' up.

I say to Joe: "Ma baby's looks
    May not be bes' in town;
But when he go to Baby Show
    He keep hees breakfas' down."
                    WILSON MACDONALD

The Wreck of the "Julie Plante"

A Legend of Lac St. Pierre

On wan dark night on Lac St. Pierre,
    De win' she blow, blow, blow,
An' de crew of de wood scow *Julie Plante*
    Got scar't an' run below—
For de win' she blow lak hurricane
    Bimeby she blow some more,
An' de scow bus' up on Lac St. Pierre
    Wan arpent from de shore.

De captinne walk on de fronte deck,
    An' walk de hin' deck too—
He call de crew from up de hole
    He call de cook also.
De cook she's name was Rosie,
    She come from Montreal,
Was chambre maid on lumber barge,
    On de Grande Lachine Canal.

De win' she blow from nor'-eas'-wes',—
    De sout' win' she blow too,
W'en Rosie cry "Mon cher captinne,
    Mon cher, w'at I shall do?"
Den de captinne t'row de big ankerre,
    But still the scow she dreef,
De crew he can't pass on de shore,
    Becos' he los' hees skeef.

De night was dark lak' wan black cat,
  De wave run high an' fas',
W'en de captinne tak de Rosie girl
  An' tie her to de mas'.
Den he also tak' de life preserve,
  An' jomp off on de lak',
An' say, "Good-bye, ma Rosie dear,
  I go drown for your sak'."

Nex' morning very early
  'Bout ha'f-pas' two—t'ree—four—
De captinne—scow—an' de poor Rosie
  Was corpses on de shore,
For de win' she blow lak' hurricane
  Bimeby she blow some more,
An' de scow bus' up on Lac St. Pierre,
  Wan arpent from de shore.

MORAL

Now all good wood scow sailor man
  Tak' warning by dat storm
An' go an' marry some nice French girl
  An' leev on wan beeg farm.
De win' can blow lak' hurricane
  An' s'pose she blow some more,
You can't get drown on Lac St. Pierre
  So long you stay on shore.

                    WILLIAM HENRY DRUMMOND

HISTORY, SCIENCE & HIGH THOUGHT

In short, while scientists unborn
Prepare to search the stars and roses,
The snail is on his ancient thorn
And God in conference with Moses.

SAMUEL HOFFENSTEIN

On the Vanity of Earthly Greatness

The tusks that clashed in mighty brawls
Of mastodons, are billiard balls.

The sword of Charlemagne the Just
Is ferric oxide, known as rust.

The grizzly bear whose potent hug
Was feared by all, is now a rug.

Great Caesar's bust is on the shelf,
And I don't feel so well myself!

ARTHUR GUITERMAN

Eschatology

I have no care for Systematic Theology,
But oh, the recurrent hour of bile that brings
Fainness for specialization in Eschatology
(Greek, you recall, for the study of all Last Things)!

Come, day when the wealth of the world is less than
      tuppence,
The seas unfretted, and the monuments down,
When the proud have got their ultimate come-up-
      pance,
And on the seventh New York the sand lies brown:

And all my sloth and failure, all my passion
One with the sorrow of the Gaul and Goth,
And all our fireproof homes are burnt and ashen,
And in the moth-proof closets dwells the moth;

And every most unspeakable thing is spoken,
Rust in the rust-resisting pipes of brass,
And all unbreakable things at last are broken;
Shatter'd the non-shatterable glass.

MORRIS BISHOP

On a Great Election

The accursed power which stands on Privilege
(And goes with Women, and Champagne and Bridge)
Broke—and Democracy resumed her reign:
(Which goes with Bridge, and Women and Champagne).

HILAIRE BELLOC

Merry Old Souls

Old Ben Franklin was a merry old soul, ·
He walked up Market Street munching a roll,
And a girl laughed loud, and her laughter was so
    ranklin'
That old Ben Franklin made her Mrs. Ben Franklin.

Old Julius Caesar was a merry old soul,
To be a Roman emperor was all his goal;
But he put away the crown; he was such an old teaser
That the mob put the finger on Gaius Julius Caesar.

Old Isaac Newton was a merry old soul,
He invented gravitation when out for a stroll,
And no one up to now has succeeded in refutin'
The good old hypothesis of old Isaac Newton.

Old Savonarola was a merry old soul,
He held all of Florence under rigid control;
The people didn't like it, and doped his Coca-Cola,
And then they heated Florence with old Savonarola.

Rabelais also was a merry old soul;
Many of his writings are very, very droll;
Censors in the customhouse treat him rather shabbily
By cutting out the better bits of Master Francis
    Rabelais.

MORRIS BISHOP

The Problem of the Poles

My suffering Public, take it not amiss
If, rising from the narrow bonds of Rhyme,
I seek the nobler Blankness of the bards,
Where one may stretch oneself, and go ahead,
Not pausing, save for breath, or fat, round words
To build his thought withal. I cannot help it.
I am constrained thereto by such a theme,
So deep a mystery and so obscure,
That I can tackle it no other way.
Permit me, then. And, with apologies,
I now pronounce the purpose of my song.

There is a class of man that seems to be
(Thanks, kindly Muse, that wrought so fair a line!)
Afflicted with a mad desire to scale
Our high terrestrial poles—or North or South—
Say North. Indeed, I understand that two
Claim to have done it. I propose to show
They haven't, and, what's more, they never will.

(There are two North Poles really—I know that;
But for simplicity we'll call them one.)

Take first the compass. This, as you're aware,
Inevitably, with unerring nose,
Points to the North. I'm sure I don't know why;
Such is its mad, mad humour. Now, suppose
You stick it *on* the Pole; how does it act?

First you would say that, as it seeks the North,
And, as that lies directly underneath,
It points straight downward. So it would appear,
But, mark you, what about the other end?

This (which, with deference, we'll call the Tail)
Has an affinity toward the South,

Equal and opposite in all respects.
One end looks North, the other end looks South.

If, then, your nose points downward to the earth,
From the position of your unshamed Tail
The South Pole must be clean above your head.
But, as you're standing on the northern end
Of the terrestrial axis, for a fact,
The South Pole, being at the other end,
Must stick out right away beneath your feet.
So that your Tail, which points toward the skies,
Must at the same time look the other way.
Dash it, it can't do both. So that won't do.

Now for another. This is harder still.
Science, for travail of geographers,
Draws a straight line through Greenwich, pole to pole,
Which she calls nought or zero, which you will.
Now any place that isn't on that line,
Considered in connection with the poles,
Has bearings East or West. Contrariwise,
All of this world that isn't East or West
Must be in line with Greenwich. Mustn't it?

Now then, suppose a person climbs the Pole,
In what direction must that person .gaze?
South. For up there there *is* no East or West;
And, though he screw his head off, he can still
Only look Southward. Thus his line of sight,
As it sees nothing lying East or West,
No matter where he looks, must pass through Green-
    wich.
And, as he slowly circles round his Pole,
And yet can never look away from Greenwich,
It follows that that quaint old-fashioned spot
Moves, with his eye, clean round the world and back.
But Greenwich can't go doing things like that,
And so where are you? Here we are again.

But wait a minute. No. I'll tell you what.
Man, in the limits of his finite mind,
Of finite things alone has cognisance.
All that is real, everything that *is,*
Must have three thingamies (Dimensions. Thanks),
Or else it's non-existent. Now a line,
Being, as Euclid crushingly observed,
Length without breadth, which is ridiculous,
Has one di-thingamy, which doesn't count.

We see, then, that meridian through Greenwich,
Saving in Science's disordered brain,
Doesn't exist—and every spot where man
Can rest his foot is something East or West;
There is no atom on this mundane orb
But has its little bearings. Very well.
Now put that person up his Pole again.

Recalling what we said of him before,
It becomes clear to an unbiassed mind
That the position which he occupies
Has bearings neither East nor West. And so,
If we apply the paragraph above,
Wherever else his doubtful post may be,
It forms no part of this terrestrial globe.
That is to say, there is no Pole at all.
Which being satisfactorily proved,
I fail to see why people want to go there.

DUM-DUM

Canopus

When quacks with pills political would dope us,
     When politics absorbs the livelong day,
I like to think about the star Canopus,
     So far, so far away.

Greatest of visioned suns, they say who list 'em;
　　To weigh it science always must despair.
Its shell would hold our whole dinged solar system,
　　Nor ever know 'twas there.

When temporary chairmen utter speeches,
　　And frenzied henchmen howl their battle hymns,
My thoughts float out across the cosmic reaches
　　To where Canopus swims.

When men are calling names and making faces,
　　And all the world's ajangle and ajar,
I meditate on interstellar spaces
　　And smoke a mild seegar.

For after one has had about a week of
　　The arguments of friends as well as foes,
A star that has no parallax to speak of
　　Conduces to repose.

BERT LESTON TAYLOR

A Narrative

Bill dug a well
And knelt down to it;
Frank bought a telescope
And stared up through it;
Both looking for truth
Since nobody knew it.
Bill sought dark,
No light reflected;
Frank sought light,
With dark neglected.
One looked up,
One looked down;
And a long-drawn fight

Began in our town.
Was Bill in the right
Looking down his well?
Was Frank our hope,
With his telescope?
We could not tell.

But when Frank said
"I find that dark
Is what makes light,"
Bill raised his head:
"I can't find night
Without a spark,"
Was what Bill said.
"Let's look at your well,"
Said Frank to Bill;
And Bill looked up
Through the telescope.
"What do you see?"
Said Bill to Frank.
"Stars and an echo of dark," said Frank.
"What do you see?"
Said Frank to Bill.
"Dark and the echo of stars," said Bill.

One looked up,
One looked down;
And the fight goes on
All over our town.
Was Bill our hope
At the telescope?
Did Frank do right
To take Bill's well?
No one can tell.
They're at it still.

THEODORE SPENCER

Stairs

Here's to the man who invented stairs
And taught our feet to soar!
He was the first who ever burst
Into a second floor.

The world would be downstairs today
Had he not found the key;
So let his name go down to fame,
Whatever it may be.

OLIVER HERFORD

"The Art of Our Necessities is Strange"
(Chant Royal)

The subject today, my friends, is Stinted Praise
   For Certain Useful but Mysterious Things.
Let's start with electricity. When one pays
   (As pay one must) the bill for what it brings,
Is he whom I have designated "one"
Aware of how the current's job is done?
   No, sir. Can he explain the Frigidaire?
   Can he address this meeting and lay bare
How we get "Darn That Dream" or "Ave Maria"
   By radio? Neither can I. The radio's there,
But how it works I haven't the least idea.

What greets each day my uninstructed gaze?
   Machines! One washes clothes, one sews, one flings
Itself about and dusts. Another obeys
   A thermostat, and in the basement sings
About the price of oil. The breakfast bun,
The luncheon roll, the tea-time sally lunn—
   These punctuate a life of rumble and glare
   And whirring and buzz and drone and chugging
     and blare.

(That was a dash of onomatopoeia.)
    The Machine's ubiquitous—I mean it's everywhere—
But how it works I haven't the least idea.

Heavy the hand that A. G. Bell still lays
    Upon us all. Bosses or underlings,
We spend a goodly part of all our days
    Answering or causing telephonic rings.
And there are men who find professional fun
In figuring out eclipses of the sun.
    The telephone! The spectrograph! A pair
    Of swell incomprehensibles! I declare
Each one to be a honey; each is to me a
    Friend, a pal; for each I deeply care;
But how it works I haven't the least idea.

Just listen to the late J. Milton's phrase:
    "How sweetly did they float upon the wings."
Sweetly, my eye! For flying spells malaise.
    If there be one who to the good earth clings,
It's me. O monstrous man-made birds! Well, none
Shall ferry me to rudely achieved oblivion!
    (I once knew a lady who had wings. I'll share
    That dame with you, that gal from memory's lair:
"Psyche at the Pool." Remember? Wasn't she a
    Pip?) A plane's all right for those who dare—
But how it works I haven't the least idea.

A saw; a hammer; paper and pen; the ways
    Of these I know. And when DiMaggio swings,
When Katie Hepburn acts, when Heifetz plays,
    I know just how these babies pull the strings.
But now silk stockings are from brick dust spun;
Big, shiny, smokeless locomotives run
    On liquid vaseline; the movies tear
    Three-colored leaves from nature's book, and wear
A polychromatic dress. There seems to be a
    Trend. To each device, my muse, be fair!
But how it works I haven't the least idea.

Envoy

O Conant, Hutchins, not for me a chair
  Of Phys or Chem! But couldn't Edsel spare
A driver's seat (with car)? In some degree a-
  llergic to such, I'd manage the thing, I swear!
But how it works I haven't the least idea.

FORREST IZARD

Kind of an Ode to Duty

O Duty,
Why hast thou not the visage of a sweetie or a cutie?
Why glitter thy spectacles so ominously?
Why art thou clad so abominously?
Why art thou so different from Venus
And why do thou and I have so few interests mutually
      in common between us?
Why art thou fifty per cent martyr
And fifty-one per cent Tartar?

Why is it thy unfortunate wont
To try to attract people by calling on them either to
      leave undone the deeds they like, or to do the
      deeds they don't?
Why art thou so like an April post-mortem
On something that died in the ortumn?
Above all, why dost thou continue to hound me?
Why art thou always albatrossly hanging around me?

Thou so ubiquitous,
And I so iniquitous.
I seem to be the one person in the world thou art
      perpetually preaching at who or to who;
Whatever looks like fun, there art thou standing be-
      tween me and it, calling yoo-hoo.
O Duty, Duty!

How noble a man should I be hadst thou the visage
    of a sweetie or a cutie!
But as it is thou art so much forbiddinger than a
    Wodehouse hero's forbiddingest aunt
That in the words of the poet, When Duty whispers
    low, Thou must, this erstwhile youth replies, I
    just can't.

OGDEN NASH

On the Antiquity of Microbes

Adam
Had 'em.
STRICKLAND GILLILAN

I Marvel at the Ways of God

I marvel at the ways of God,
    For time and time again
I see Him paint such lovely clouds
    Above such awkward men.

E. B. WHITE

A Hot-Weather Song

I feel so exceedingly lazy,
I neglect what I oughtn't to should!
My notion of work is so hazy
That I couldn't to toil if I would.

I feel so exceedingly silly
That I say all I shouldn't to ought!
And my mind is as frail as a lily;
It would break with the weight of a thought!

DON MARQUIS

P Is for Paleontology

Consider the sages who pulverize boulders,
And burrow for elbows and shinbones and shoulders,
And shovel the loot from a hill or a dale of it,
And lovingly carry off pail after pail of it.

Anon a remarkable Tyrannosaurus
As tall as a steeple is standing before us,
Rebuilt from a bit of the skin or a scale of it
Or maybe as much as a single toe-nail of it.

Curators are handy to speak of its habits,
To say that it fed on the forebears of rabbits,
To mimic the whine or the whistle or wail of it
And tell (in a whisper) the female or male of it.

But though in the quest for some primitive lemur,
They fish out a fragment of petrified femur,
I wish they'd not fashion a four-footed whale of it
Without ever knowing the head or the tail of it.*

MILTON BRACKER

* And I don't give a darn for the Harvard or Yale of it.

Senex to Matt. Prior

Ah! Matt.: old age has brought to me
Thy wisdom, less thy certainty:
The world's a jest, and joy's a trinket:
I knew that once: but now—I think it.

J. K. STEPHEN

On Troy

I give more praise to Troy's redoubt
For Love kept in, than War kept out.

OLIVER ST. JOHN GOGARTY

THE HUMAN RACE

I wish I loved the Human Race;
I wish I loved its silly face;
I wish I liked the way it walks;
I wish I liked the way it talks;
And when I'm introduced to one
I wish I thought What Jolly Fun!

SIR WALTER RALEIGH

The Anatomy of Humor

"What is funny?" you ask, my child,
  Crinkling your bright-blue eye.
"Ah, that is a curious question indeed,"
  Musing, I make reply.

"Contusions are funny, not open wounds,
  And automobiles that go
Crash into trees by the highwayside;
  Industrial accidents, no.

"The habit of drink is a hundred per cent,
  But drug addiction is nil.
A nervous breakdown will get no laughs;
  Insanity surely will.

"Humor, aloof from the cigarette,
  Inhabits the droll cigar;
The middle-aged are not very funny;
  The young and the old, they are.

"So the funniest thing in the world should be
  A grandsire, drunk, insane,
Maimed in a motor accident,
  And enduring moderate pain.

"But why do you scream and yell, my child?
  Here comes your mother, my honey,
To comfort you and to lecture me
  For trying, she'll say, to be funny."

MORRIS BISHOP

Sunday Morning

There's one joins sweetly in the quavering hymn,
Hears prayer and reading, never lets a sigh,
Christian in docile breath and breast and limb,
But Pagan in the corner of her eye.

L. A. G. STRONG

When a Man's Busy

When a man's busy, why, leisure
Strikes him as wonderful pleasure:
'Faith, and at leisure once is he?
Straightway he wants to be busy.

ROBERT BROWNING

The Archaeologist of the Future

Five thousand years have fled, let us suppose,
And lo, an archaeologist appears,
Searching for records of our joys and fears.
And haply out of all our verse and prose
One book alone remains. How it will pose
His plodding brain, after that flight of years,
To come on Alice swimming in her tears,
Or Father William, an eel upon his nose!

He'll stare and gasp at Tweedle-dee and -dum
And gape at incandescent words that mock
Invention, Bandersnatch and Jabberwock,
And, fancying angry eggs and talking flowers,
No doubt will think his fifth millennium
A far less entertaining time than ours.

LEONARD BACON

A Hero in the Land of Dough

Another nickel in the slot
And you will hit the Lucky Dot—
Down will pour the Great Jack Pot.

Up the avenue you'll go
A hero in the land of dough—
Ticker tape will fall like snow.

You will be the lucky one
Lolling in the summer sun
Watching lucky horses run,

Watching lucky numbers spin,
You will be the next to win—
Put another nickel in.

ROBERT CLAIRMONT

We Have Been Here Before

I think I remember this moorland,
　The tower on the tip of the tor;
I feel in the distance another existence;
　I think I have been here before.

And I think you were sitting beside me
　In a fold in the face of the fell;
For Time at its work'll go round in a circle,
　And what is befalling, befell.

"I have been here before!" I asserted,
　In a nook on a neck of the Nile.
I once in a crisis was punished by Isis,
　And you smiled. I remember your smile.

I had the same sense of persistence
　On the site of the seat of the Sioux;
I heard in the teepee the sound of a sleepy
　Pleistocene grunt. It was you.

The past made a promise, before it
　Began to begin to begone.
This limited gamut brings you again. Damn it,
　How long has this got to go on?

MORRIS BISHOP

Third Row, Centre

The stage is lighted, the first act half over.
These, the too ample ones, subside and fret,
Fussing with furs, with program and lorgnette,
And finally the dialogue, discover
Where the bright leading-lady with her lover
Moves in the scenic brilliance of the set.
Expressionless they stare at the duet
And gradually their sighing breath recover.

Their escorts, redolent of excellent wine,
Liqueurs, and quite superior cigars,
Slump in their seats and estimate the star's
Height, weight, and substance, and relax the spine
Musing upon the question of her charms
Were she transferred to their own broadcloth arms.

Fish-eyed, they drowse for two hours and a half
Save for the intermissions when they push
Into the aisle and join the lobby's crush
And stare about, and vacuously laugh,
Innerly woeful with no more to quaff,
Putting the barnyard waddlers to the blush
For solid flesh, and sure in any hush
To give the play a brazen epitaph.

So the plot thickens, and the second act,
That even pricks the critics with its pace,
Brings something near to pathos on each face,
As the eyes goggle and the brows contract
And yearningly those vasty bosoms heave,
And, like the mute stalled ox, those others grieve.

Uncomfortably they stir and cough and stir
And wonder dimly what it's all about,
Sniffing at truffles with a quivering snout
When any questionable lines occur,

But otherwise in trance, as they prefer.
And so, at last, their evening is worn out;
And the house-lights come on; and with the rout
They exit in their usual hauteur.

High above Broadway blaze the great sky-signs.
Blare, in the street, a thousand taxi klaxons.
All over town Semites and Anglo-Saxons
Strengthen their old commercial battle-lines . . .
And now in chariots of a newer Rome
The furs and opera-hats are bowling home.

WILLIAM ROSE BENÉT

To Sit in Solemn Silence

To sit in solemn silence in a dull, dark dock,
In a pestilential prison, with a life-long lock,
Awaiting the sensation of a short, sharp shock,
From a cheap and chippy chopper on a big black block!

SIR W. S. GILBERT

Cynicus to W. Shakspere

You wrote a line too much, my sage,
　　Of seers the first, and first of sayers;
For only half the world's a stage,
　　And only all the women players.

J. K. STEPHEN

A Christian Is a Man Who Feels

A Christian is a man who feels
Repentance on a Sunday
For what he did on Saturday
And is going to do on Monday.

T. R. YBARRA

To a Human Skeleton

(Encountered in the Museum of Natural History)

It's hard to think,
    Albeit true,
That without flesh
    I'd be like you,

And harder still
    To think, old pal,
That one of these
    Fine days I shall.

RICHARD ARMOUR

INCENSE & NONSENSE

And what mean all these mysteries to me
Whose life is full of indices and surds?

$$x^2 + 7x + 53$$
$$= \tfrac{11}{3}$$

LEWIS CARROLL

The Dormouse and the Doctor

There once was a Dormouse who lived in a bed
Of delphiniums (blue) and geraniums (red),
And all the day long he'd a wonderful view
Of geraniums (red) and delphiniums (blue).

A Doctor came hurrying round, and he said:
"Tut-tut, I am sorry to find you in bed.
Just say 'Ninety-nine,' while I look at your chest. . . .
Don't you find that chrysanthemums answer the best?"

The Dormouse looked round at the view and replied
(When he'd said "Ninety-nine") that he'd tried and
    he'd tried,
And much the most answering things that he knew
Were geraniums (red) and delphiniums (blue).

The Doctor stood frowning and shaking his head,
And he took up his shiny silk hat as he said:
"What the patient requires is a change," and he went
To see some chrysanthemum people in Kent.

The Dormouse lay there, and he gazed at the view
Of geraniums (red) and delphiniums (blue),
And he knew there was nothing he wanted instead
Of delphiniums (blue) and geraniums (red).

The Doctor came back and, to show what he meant,
He had brought some chrysanthemum cuttings from
    Kent.
"Now *these*," he remarked, "give a *much* better view
Than geraniums (red) and delphiniums (blue)."

They took out their spades and they dug up the bed
Of delphiniums (blue) and geraniums (red),
And they planted chrysanthemums (yellow and white).
"And *now*," said the Doctor, "we'll *soon* have you
    right."

The Dormouse looked out, and he said with a sigh:
"I suppose all these people know better than I.
It was silly, perhaps, but I *did* like the view
Of geraniums (red) and delphiniums (blue)."

The Doctor came round and examined his chest,
And ordered him Nourishment, Tonics, and Rest,
"How very effective," he said, as he shook
The thermometer, "all these chrysanthemums look!"

The Dormouse turned over to shut out the sight
Of the endless chrysanthemums (yellow and white).
"How lovely," he thought, "to be back in a bed
Of delphiniums (blue) and geraniums (red)."

The Doctor said, "Tut! It's another attack!"
And ordered him Milk and Massage-of-the-back,
And Freedom-from-worry and Drives-in-a-car,
And murmured, "How sweet your chrysanthemums
    are!"

The Dormouse lay there with his paws to his eyes,
And imagined himself such a pleasant surprise:
"I'll *pretend* the chrysanthemums turn to a bed
Of delphiniums (blue) and geraniums (red)!"

The Doctor next morning was rubbing his hands,
And saying, "There's nobody quite understands
These cases as I do! The cure has begun!
How fresh the chrysanthemums look in the sun!"

The Dormouse lay happy, his eyes were so tight
He could see no chrysanthemums, yellow or white,
And all that he felt at the back of his head
Were delphiniums (blue) and geraniums (red).

And that is the reason (Aunt Emily said)
If a Dormouse gets in a chrysanthemum bed,
You will find (so Aunt Emily says) that he lies
Fast asleep on his front with his paws to his eyes.

                                        A. A. MILNE

The Owl and the Pussy-Cat

The Owl and the Pussy-Cat went to sea
   In a beautiful pea-green boat,
They took some honey, and plenty of money
   Wrapped up in a five-pound note.
The Owl looked up to the stars above,
   And sang to a small guitar,
"O lovely Pussy! O Pussy, my love,
   "What a beautiful Pussy you are,
      "You are,
      "You are!
   "What a beautiful Pussy you are!"

Pussy said to the Owl, "You elegant fowl!
   "How charmingly sweet you sing!
"O let us be married! too long we have tarried:
   "But what shall we do for a ring?"
They sailed away for a year and a day,
   To the land where the Bong-tree grows,
And there in a wood a Piggy-wig stood,
   With a ring at the end of his nose,
      His nose,
      His nose,
   With a ring at the end of his nose.

"Dear Pig, are you willing to sell for one shilling
   "Your ring?" Said the Piggy, "I will."
So they took it away, and were married next day
   By the Turkey who lives on the hill.
They dined on mince, and slices of quince,
   Which they ate with a runcible spoon;
And hand in hand, on the edge of the sand,
   They danced by the light of the moon,
      The moon,
      The moon,
   They danced by the light of the moon.

EDWARD LEAR

Lullaby of the Catfish and the Crab

Strange was the wooing!
To his undoing
Clara the Catfish came
Down through the shimmering
Green sea glimmering,
Mewing with eyes of flame;
Casper would grasp her,
His claws would grab.
Oh, pity Casper,
Casper the Crab!

O waly, waly,
This happened daily.
Clara the Catfish swum
(Would "swam" be better?)
She left a letter.
It read, "Well! Well! Hum! Hum!"
Casper, exasper-
ated, was rab-
id with rage. Poor Casper,
Casper the Crab!

Clara was always
Through watery hallways
Wavily out of reach.
Scuttling and squirmish
Casper would skirmish
Dimly the deep-sea beach.
"Oh," he would gasp, "her
I ne'er shall nab!"
Desolate Casper,
Casper the Crab!

His last endeavor
Fixed him forever.
Clara swam down with a pout.

He leapt to reach her,
Impetuous creature,
And turned himself inside out.
And they heard him jabber
With his last gasp,
"Alas poor Cabber,
Cabber the Crasp!"

WILLIAM ROSE BENÉT

The Bees' Song

Thouzandz of thornz there be
On the Rozez where gozez
The Zebra of Zee:
Sleek, striped, and hairy,
The steed of the Fairy
Princess of Zee.

Heavy with blozzomz be
The Rozez that growzez
In the thickets of Zee,
Where grazez the Zebra,
Marked Abracadeeebra
Of the Princess of Zee.

And he nozez the poziez
Of the Rozez that growzez
So luvez'm and free,
With an eye, dark and wary,
In search of a Fairy,
Whose Rozez he knowzez
Were not honeyed for he,
But to breathe a sweet incense
To solace the Princess
Of far-away Zee.

WALTER DE LA MARE

Little Birds

Little Birds are dining
　　Warily and well,
　　Hid in mossy cell;
Hid, I say, by waiters,
Gorgeous in gaiters—
　　I've a tale to tell.

Little Birds are feeding
　　Justices with jam,
　　Rich in frizzled ham;
Rich, I say, in oysters
Haunting shady cloisters—
　　That is what I am.

Little Birds are teaching
　　Tigresses to smile,
　　Innocent of guile;
Smile, I say, not smirkle—
Mouth a semicircle,
　　That's the proper style.

Little Birds are sleeping
　　All among the pins,
　　Where the loser wins;
Where, I say, he sneezes
When and how he pleases—
　　So the tale begins.

Little Birds are writing
　　Interesting books,
　　To be read by cooks;
Read, I say, not roasted—
Letter-press, when toasted,
　　Loses its good looks.

Little Birds are playing
　　Bagpipes on the shore,
　　Where the tourists snore.

"Thanks!" they cry. " 'Tis thrilling!
Take, oh, take this shilling!
    Let us have no more!"

Little Birds are bathing
    Crocodiles in cream,
    Like a happy dream;
Like, but not so lasting—
Crocodiles when fasting,
    Are not all they seem!

Little Birds are choking
    Baronets with bun,
    Taught to fire a gun;
Taught, I say, to splinter
Salmon in the winter—
    Merely for the fun.

Little Birds are hiding
    Crimes in carpet-bags,
    Blessed by happy stags;
Blessed, I say, though beaten—
Since our friends are eaten
    When the memory flags.

Little Birds are tasting
    Gratitude and gold,
    Pale with sudden cold;
Pale, I say, and wrinkled—
When the bells have tinkled
    And the tale is told.

LEWIS CARROLL

archy experiences a seizure

the cockroach stood by the mickle
    wood in the flush of the astral dawn
and he sniffed the air from the hidden
    lair where the khyber swordfish spawn

and the bilge and belch of the glutton
   welsh as they smelted their warlock cheese
surged to and fro where the grinding
   floe wrenched at the headlands knees
half seas over under up again
and the barnacles white in the moon
the pole stars chasing its tail like a pup again
and the dish ran away with the spoon

DON MARQUIS

Incidents in the Life of My Uncle Arly

O my agèd Uncle Arly!
Sitting on a heap of Barley
   Thro' the silent hours of night,—
Close beside a leafy thicket:—
On his nose there was a Cricket,—
In his hat a Railway-Ticket;—
   (But his shoes were far too tight).

Long ago, in youth, he squander'd
All his goods away, and wander'd
   To the Tiniskoop-hills afar.
There on golden sunsets blazing,
Every evening found him gazing,—
Singing,—"Orb! you're quite amazing!
   "How I wonder what you are!"

Like the ancient Medes and Persians,
Always by his own exertions
   He subsisted on those hills;—
Whiles,—by teaching children spelling,—
Or at times by merely yelling,—
Or at intervals by selling
   "Propter's Nicodemus Pills."

Later, in his morning rambles
He perceived the moving brambles
   Something square and white disclose:—
'Twas a First-class Railway-Ticket;
But, on stooping down to pick it
Off the ground,—a pea-green Cricket
   Settled on my uncle's Nose.

Never—never more,—oh! never,
Did that Cricket leave him ever,—
   Dawn or evening, day or night;—
Clinging as a constant treasure,—
Chirping with a cheerious measure,—
Wholly to my uncle's pleasure,—
   (Though his shoes were far too tight).

So for three-and-forty winters,
Till his shoes were worn to splinters,
   All those hills he wander'd o'er,—
Sometimes silent;—sometimes yelling;—
Till he came to Borley-Melling,
Near his old ancestral dwelling;—
   (But his shoes were far too tight).

On a little heap of Barley
Died my agèd Uncle Arly,
   And they buried him one night;—
Close beside the leafy thicket;—
There,—his hat and Railway-Ticket;—
There,—his ever-faithful Cricket;—
   (But his shoes were far too tight).

                              EDWARD LEAR

The Pobble Who Has No Toes

The Pobble who has no toes
   Had once as many as we;
When they said, "Some day you may lose them all;"—
   He replied,—"Fish fiddle de-dee!"

And his Aunt Jobiska made him drink,
Lavender water tinged with pink,
For she said, "The World in general knows
"There's nothing so good for a Pobble's toes!"

The Pobble who has no toes,
    Swam across the Bristol Channel;
But before he set out he wrapped his nose
    In a piece of scarlet flannel.
For his Aunt Jobiska said, "No harm
"Can come to his toes if his nose is warm;
"And it's perfectly known that a Pobble's toes
"Are safe,—provided he minds his nose."

The Pobble swam fast and well,
    And when boats or ships came near him
He tinkledy-binkledy-winkled a bell,
    So that all the world could hear him.
And all the Sailors and Admirals cried,
When they saw him nearing the further side,—
"He has gone to fish, for his Aunt Jobiska's
"Runcible Cat with crimson whiskers!"

But before he touched the shore,
    The shore of the Bristol Channel,
A sea-green Porpoise carried away
    His wrapper of scarlet flannel.
And when he came to observe his feet,
Formerly garnished with toes so neat,
His face at once became forlorn
On perceiving that all his toes were gone!

And nobody ever knew
    From that dark day to the present,
Whoso had taken the Pobble's toes,
    In a manner so far from pleasant.
Whether the shrimps or crawfish gray,
Or crafty Mermaids stole them away—

Nobody knew; and nobody knows
How the Pobble was robbed of his twice five toes!

The Pobble who has no toes
   Was placed in a friendly Bark,
And they rowed him back, and carried him up,
   To his Aunt Jobiska's Park.
And she made him a feast at his earnest wish
Of eggs and buttercups fried with fish;—
And she said,—"It's a fact the whole world knows,
"That Pobbles are happier without their toes."

EDWARD LEAR

Antigonish

As I was going up the stair
   I met a man who wasn't there!
He wasn't there again today!
   I wish, I *wish* he'd stay away!

HUGHES MEARNS

Aunt Eliza

In the drinking-well
   Which the plumber built her,
Aunt Eliza fell . . . .
   . . . We must buy a filter.

HARRY GRAHAM

Grandpapa

Grandpapa fell down a drain;
Couldn't scramble out again.
Now he's floating down the sewer
There's one grandpapa the fewer.

HARRY GRAHAM

The Walloping Window-blind

A capital ship for an ocean trip
  Was *The Walloping Window-blind;*
No gale that blew dismayed her crew
  Or troubled the captain's mind.
The man at the wheel was taught to feel
  Contempt for the wildest blow,
And it often appeared, when the weather had cleared,
  That he'd been in his bunk below.

The boatswain's mate was very sedate,
  Yet fond of amusement, too;
And he played hop-scotch with the starboard watch
  While the captain tickled the crew.
And the gunner we had was apparently mad,
  For he sat on the after-rail,
And fired salutes with the captain's boots,
  In the teeth of the booming gale.

The captain sat in a commodore's hat,
  And dined, in a royal way,
On toasted pigs and pickles and figs
  And gummery bread, each day.
But the cook was Dutch, and behaved as such;
  For the food that he gave the crew
Was a number of tons of hot-cross buns,
  Chopped up with sugar and glue.

And we all felt ill as mariners will,
  On a diet that's cheap and rude;
And we shivered and shook as we dipped the cook
  In a tub of his gluesome food.
Then nautical pride we laid aside,
  And we cast the vessel ashore
On the Gulliby Isles, where the Poohpooh smiles,
  And the Anagazanders roar.

Composed of sand was that favored land,
  And trimmed with cinnamon straws;
And pink and blue was the pleasing hue
  Of the Tickletoeteaser's claws.
And we sat on the edge of a sandy ledge
  And shot at the whistling bee;
And the Binnacle-bats wore water-proof hats
  As they danced in the sounding sea.

On rubagub bark, from dawn to dark,
  We fed, till we all had grown
Uncommonly shrunk,—when a Chinese junk
  Came by from the torriby zone.
She was stubby and square, but we didn't much care,
  And we cheerily put to sea;
And we left the crew of the junk to chew
  The bark of the rubagub tree.

CHARLES E. CARRYL

Calico Pie

    Calico Pie,
    The little Birds fly
Down to the calico tree,
    Their wings were blue,
    And they sang "Tilly-loo!"
    Till away they flew,—
And they never came back to me!
    They never came back!
    They never came back!
They never came back to me!

    Calico Jam,
    The little Fish swam
Over the syllabub sea,
    He took off his hat,
    To the Sole and the Sprat,
    And the Willeby-wat,—

But he never came back to me!
　He never came back!
　He never came back!
He never came back to me!

　Calico Ban,
　The little Mice ran,
To be ready in time for tea,
　Flippity flup,
　They drank it all up,
　And danced in the cup,—
But they never came back to me!
　They never came back!
　They never came back!
They never came back to me!

　Calico Drum,
　The Grasshoppers come,
The Butterfly, Beetle, and Bee,
　Over the ground,
　Around and round,
　With a hop and a bound,—
But they never came back!
　They never came back!
　They never came back!
They never came back to me!

EDWARD LEAR

The Great Auk's Ghost

The Great Auk's ghost rose on one leg,
　Sighed thrice and three times winkt,
And turned and poached a phantom egg,
　And muttered, "I'm extinct."

RALPH HODGSON

Patience

When ski-ing in the Engadine
My hat blew off down a ravine.
My son, who went to fetch it back,
Slipped through an icy glacier's crack
And then got permanently stuck.
It really was infernal luck:
My hat was practically new—
I loved my little Henry too—
And I may have to wait for years
Till either of them reappears.

HARRY GRAHAM

Jabberwocky

'Twas brillig, and the slithy toves
    Did gyre and gimble in the wabe:
All mimsy were the borogoves,
    And the mome raths outgrabe.

"Beware the Jabberwock, my son!
    The jaws that bite, the claws that catch!
Beware the Jubjub bird, and shun
    The frumious Bandersnatch!"

He took his vorpal sword in hand:
    Long time the manxome foe he sought—
So rested he by the Tumtum tree,
    And stood awhile in thought.

And, as in uffish thought he stood,
    The Jabberwock, with eyes of flame,
Came whiffling through the tulgey wood,
    And burbled as it came!

One, two! One, two! And through and through
    The vorpal blade went snicker-snack!
He left it dead, and with its head
    He went galumphing back.

"And hast thou slain the Jabberwock?
    Come to my arms, my beamish boy!
O frabjous day! Callooh! Callay!"
    He chortled in his joy.

'Twas brillig, and the slithy toves
    Did gyre and gimble in the wabe:
All mimsy were the borogoves,
    And the mome raths outgrabe.

                              LEWIS CARROLL

At Dingle Bank

He lived at Dingle Bank—he did;—
He lived at Dingle Bank;
And in his garden was one Quail,
Four tulips, and a Tank;
And from his windows he could see
The otion and the River Dee.

His house stood on a Cliff,—it did,
In aspic it was cool:
And many thousand little boys
Resorted to his school,
Where if of progress they could boast
He gave them heaps of buttered toast.

But he grew rabid-wroth, he did,
If they neglected books,
And dragged them to adjacent cliffs
With beastly Button Hooks,
And there with fatuous glee he threw
Them down into the otion blue.

And in the sea they swam, they did,—
All playfully about,
And some eventually became
Sponges, or speckled trout:—
But Liverpool doth all bewail
Their Fate;—likewise his Garden Quail.

                    EDWARD LEAR

The Suicide's Grave

On a tree by a river a little tom-tit
          Sang "Willow, titwillow, titwillow!"
And I said to him, "Dicky-bird, why do you sit
          Singing 'Willow, titwillow, titwillow'?
Is it a weakness of intellect, birdie?" I cried,
"Or a rather tough worm in your little inside?"
With a shake of his poor little head he replied,
          "Oh, willow, titwillow, titwillow!"

He slapped at his chest, as he sat on that bough,
          Singing "Willow, titwillow, titwillow!"
And a cold perspiration bespangled his brow,
          Oh, willow, titwillow, titwillow!
He sobbed and he sighed, and a gurgle he gave,
Then he threw himself into the billowy wave,
And an echo arose from the suicide's grave—
          "Oh, willow, titwillow, titwillow!"

Now, I feel just as sure as I'm sure that my name
          Isn't Willow, titwillow, titwillow,
That 'twas blighted affection that made him exclaim,
          "Oh, willow, titwillow, titwillow!"
And if you remain callous and obdurate, I
Shall perish as he did, and you will know why,
Though I probably shall not exclaim as I die,
          "Oh, willow, titwillow, titwillow!"

                    SIR W. S. GILBERT

The Hunting of the Snark
Fit the First
The Landing

"Just the place for a Snark!" the Bellman cried,
  As he landed his crew with care;
Supporting each man on the top of the tide
  By a finger entwined in his hair.

"Just the place for a Snark! I have said it twice:
  That alone should encourage the crew.
Just the place for a Snark! I have said it thrice:
  What I tell you three times is true."

The crew was complete: it included a Boots—
  A maker of Bonnets and Hoods—
A Barrister, brought to arrange their disputes—
  And a Broker, to value their goods.

A Billiard-marker, whose skill was immense,
  Might perhaps have won more than his share—
But a Banker, engaged at enormous expense,
  Had the whole of their cash in his care.

There was also a Beaver, that paced on the deck,
  Or would sit making lace in the bow:
And had often (the Bellman said) saved them from
      wreck,
  Though none of the sailors knew how.

There was one who was famed for the number of
      things
  He forgot when he entered the ship:
His umbrella, his watch, all his jewels and rings,
  And the clothes he had bought for the trip.

He had forty-two boxes, all carefully packed,
  With his name painted clearly on each:

But, since he omitted to mention the fact,
   They were all left behind on the beach.

The loss of his clothes hardly mattered, because
   He had seven coats on when he came,
With three pairs of boots—but the worst of it was,
   He had wholly forgotten his name.

He would answer to "Hi!" or to any loud cry,
   Such as "Fry me!" or "Fritter my wig!"
To "What-you-may-call-um!" or "What-was-his-name!"
   But especially "Thing-um-a-jig!"

While, for those who preferred a more forcible word,
   He had different names from these:
His intimate friends called him "Candle-ends,"
   And his enemies "Toasted-cheese."

"His form is ungainly—his intellect small—"
   (So the Bellman would often remark)
"But his courage is perfect! And that, after all,
   Is the thing that one needs with a Snark."

He would joke with hyænas, returning their stare
   With an impudent wag of the head:
And he once went a walk, paw-in-paw, with a bear,
   "Just to keep up its spirits," he said.

He came as a Baker: but owned, when too late—
   And it drove the poor Bellman half-mad—
He could only bake Bride-cake—for which, I may state,
   No materials were to be had.

The last of the crew needs especial remark,
   Though he looked an incredible dunce:
He had just one idea—but, that one being "Snark,"
   The good Bellman engaged him at once.

He came as a Butcher: but gravely declared,
   When the ship had been sailing a week,

He could only kill Beavers. The Bellman looked
 scared,
 And was almost too frightened to speak:

But at length he explained, in a tremulous tone,
 There was only one Beaver on board;
And that was a tame one he had of his own,
 Whose death would be deeply deplored.

The Beaver, who happened to hear the remark,
 Protested, with tears in its eyes,
That not even the rapture of hunting the Snark
 Could atone for that dismal surprise!

It strongly advised that the Butcher should be
 Conveyed in a separate ship:
But the Bellman declared that would never agree
 With the plans he had made for the trip:

Navigation was always a difficult art,
 Though with only one ship and one bell:
And he feared he must really decline, for his part,
 Undertaking another as well.

The Beaver's best course was, no doubt, to procure
 A second-hand dagger-proof coat—
So the Baker advised it—and next, to insure
 Its life in some Office of note:

This the Banker suggested, and offered for hire
 (On moderate terms), or for sale,
Two excellent Policies, one Against Fire,
 And one Against Damage From Hail.

Yet still, ever after that sorrowful day,
 Whenever the Butcher was by,
The Beaver kept looking the opposite way,
 And appeared unaccountably shy.

LEWIS CARROLL

The Great Panjandrum Himself

So she went into the garden
to cut a cabbage-leaf
to make an apple-pie;
and at the same time
a great she-bear, coming down the street,
pops its head into the shop.
What! no soap?
So he died,
and she very imprudently married the Barber.
And there were present
the Picninnies,
and the Joblillies,
and the Garyulies,
and the great Panjandrum himself,
with the little round button at top;
and they all fell to playing the game
of catch-as-catch-can,
till the gunpowder ran out at the heels of their boots.

ANONYMOUS

Words without Music

The man sat in the gallery,
His feet were in the orchestry.—Longfellow

ANONYMOUS

Presence of Mind

When, with my little daughter Blanche,
    I climbed the Alps, last summer,
I saw a dreadful avalanche
    About to overcome her;

And, as it swept her down the slope,
  I vaguely wondered whether
I should be wise to cut the rope
  That held us twain together.

    *   *   *   *

I must confess I'm glad I did,
But still I miss the child—poor kid!

HARRY GRAHAM

INVECTIVE & EPIGRAM

I have an arrow that will find its mark,
A mastiff that will bite without a bark.

RALPH WALDO EMERSON

The Japanese

How courteous is the Japanese;
He always says, "Excuse it, please."
He climbs into his neighbor's garden,
And smiles, and says, "I beg your pardon";
He bows and grins a friendly grin,
And calls his hungry family in;
He grins, and bows a friendly bow;
"So sorry, this my garden now."

OGDEN NASH

On a Politician

Here, richly, with ridiculous display,
The Politician's corpse was laid away.
While all of his acquaintance sneered and slanged,
I wept: for I had longed to see him hanged.

HILAIRE BELLOC

Thoughts for St. Stephen

Instead of the Puritans landing on Plymouth Rock
(Said Jo Davidson, the delightful sculptor)
How much pleasanter this country would have been
If Plymouth Rock
Had landed on the Puritans.

CHRISTOPHER MORLEY

At the Grave of a Land-Shark

There was no land, they used to tell,
Old Miller couldn't trade or sell;
A clever man! I wonder how
He'll turn the lot he's stuck with now!

ERNEST G. MOLL

The Artist

The Artist and his Luckless Wife
They lead a horrid haunted life,
Surrounded by the things he's made
That are not wanted by the trade.

The world is very fair to see;
The Artist will not let it be;
He fiddles with the works of God,
And makes them look uncommon odd.

The Artist is an awful man,
He does not do the things he can;
He does the things he cannot do,
And we attend the private view.

The Artist uses honest paint
To represent things as they ain't,
He then asks money for the time
It took to perpetrate the crime.

SIR WALTER RALEIGH

On Some South African Novelists

You praise the firm restraint with which they write—
I'm with you there, of course:
They use the snaffle and the curb all right,
But where's the bloody horse?

ROY CAMPBELL

Quatrain

Jack eating rotten cheese, did say,
Like Samson I my thousands slay:
I vow, quoth Roger, so you do.
And with the self-same weapon too.

BENJAMIN FRANKLIN

Epigram

Bring hemlock, black as Cretan cheese,
And mix a sacramental brew;
A worthy drink for Socrates,
Why not for you?

ROBERT HILLYER

Tower of Ivory

This was decreed by superior powers
In a moment of wisdom sidereal,
That those who dwell upon ivory towers
Shall have heads of the same material.

LEONARD BACON

On Scott's
"The Field of Waterloo"

On Waterloo's ensanguined plain
Lie tens of thousands of the slain;
But none, by sabre or by shot,
Fell half so flat as Walter Scott.

THOMAS, LORD ERSKINE

The Humorist

He must not laugh at his own wheeze:
A snuff box has no right to sneeze.

KEITH PRESTON

Engraved on the Collar
of His Highness' Dog

I am his Highness' dog at Kew.
Pray tell me, sir, whose dog are you?

ALEXANDER POPE

To R. K.

> As long I dwell on some stupendous
> And tremendous (Heaven defend us!)
> Monstr'-inform'-ingens-horrendous
> Demoniaco-seraphic
> Penman's latest piece of graphic.
>
> BROWNING

Will there never come a season
Which shall rid us from the curse
Of a prose which knows no reason
And an unmelodious verse:
When the world shall cease to wonder
At the genius of an Ass,
And a boy's eccentric blunder
Shall not bring success to pass:

When mankind shall be delivered
From the clash of magazines,
And the inkstand shall be shivered
Into countless smithereens:
When there stands a muzzled stripling,
Mute, beside a muzzled bore:
When the Rudyards cease from kipling
And the Haggards Ride no more.

J. K. STEPHEN

Pillow Cases

The Army recently let a contract for 1,000,000 duck-feather pillows and the Navy one for 650,000 pillows filled with chicken feathers.—*The New York Times*.

Sleep sound, O soldier, through the night
In fair or stormy weather,
Sleep sound from dusk to dawn, sleep tight
Upon the duckling's feather.

Sleep well, O sailor, as your ship
　　Plows through the bounding billows,
Sleep well, despite the roll and dip,
　　On chicken-feather pillows.

Sleep fitfully, you brass-hat cluck,
　　Or in your sleep be stricken
Who for the soldier chose the duck
　　And for the gob the chicken.

RICHARD ARMOUR

If The Man Who Turnips Cries

If the man who turnips cries,
Cry not when his father dies,
'Tis a proof that he had rather
Have a turnip than his father.

SAMUEL JOHNSON

My Bishop's Eyes

My Bishop's eyes I've never seen
Though the light in them may shine;
For when he prays, he closes his,
And when he preaches, mine.

ANONYMOUS

Lord Clive

What I like about Clive
Is that he is no longer alive.
There is a great deal to be said
For being dead.

EDMUND CLERIHEW BENTLEY

This House Where Once a Lawyer Dwelt

This house where once a lawyer dwelt
   Is now a smith's. Alas!
How rapidly the iron age
   Succeeds the age of brass!

WILLIAM ERSKINE

Warning

This road isn't passable
Not even jackassable.

JESSE DOUGLAS

LIFE & LETTERS

This is all we ever say:
Ego, mei, mihi, me.
CHRISTOPHER MORLEY

Inscription in a Library

Goode friend for Iesus sake forbeare
To lifte the bookes enstalled here
Blest be the man who reades a tome
But curst be he that takes one home.

W. G. WENDELL

I Like to Quote

I like to quote the fragrant lines of Keats,
    And often I am caught by Shelley's tone,
And yet for clever thoughts and quaint conceits
    Give me some little lyric of my own.

MITCHELL D. FOLLANSBEE

Epitaph in Anticipation

G. B. S.

Where the ramparts tower in flame or shadow
    He came and saw and wagged his jaw.
Thrice fortunate, the Colorado
    Has had its glimpse of Bernard Shaw.

LEONARD BACON

The Canadian Authors Meet

Expansive puppets percolate self-unction
Beneath a portrait of the Prince of Wales.
Miss Crotchet's muse has somehow failed to function,
Yet she's a poetess. Beaming, she sails

From group to chattering group, with such a dear
Victorian saintliness, as is her fashion,
Greeting the other unknowns with a cheer—
Virgins of sixty who still write of passion.

The air is heavy with "Canadian" topics,
And Carman, Lampman, Roberts, Campbell, Scott
Are measured for their faith and philanthropics,
Their zeal for God and King, their earnest thought.

The cakes are sweet, but sweeter is the feeling
That one is mixing with the *literati;*
It warms the old and melts the most congealing.
Really, it is a most delightful party.

Shall we go round the mulberry bush, or shall
We gather at the river, or shall we
Appoint a poet laureate this Fall,
Or shall we have another cup of tea?

O Canada, O Canada, Oh can
A day go by without new authors springing
To paint the native maple, and to plan
More ways to set the selfsame welkin ringing?

F. R. SCOTT

On his Books

When I am dead, I hope it may be said:
'His sins were scarlet, but his books were read.'

HILAIRE BELLOC

The Bards We Quote

Whene'er I quote I seldom take
From bards whom angel hosts environ;
But usually some damned rake
    Like Byron.

Of Whittier I think a lot,
My fancy to him often turns;
But when I quote 'tis some such sot
    As Burns.

I'm very fond of Bryant, too,
He brings to me the woodland smelly;
Why should I quote that "village roo,"
    P. Shelley?

I think Felicia Hemans great,
I dote upon Jean Ingelow;
Yet quote from such a reprobate
    As Poe.

To quote from drunkard or from rake
Is not a proper thing to do.
I find the habit hard to break,
    Don't you?

                        BERT LESTON TAYLOR

A Salute to the Modern Language Association, Convening in the Hotel Pennsylvania, December 28th-30th

The Modern Language Association
    Meets in the Hotel Pennsylvania,
And the suave Greeters in consternation
    Hark to the guests indulging their mania

For papers on "Adalbert Stifter as the Spokesman of
        Middle-Class Conservatism,"
    And "The American Revolution in the *Gazette de
        Leyde* and the *Affaires de l'Angleterre et de
        l'Amérique,*"
    And "Emerson and the Conflict Between Platonic and
        Kantian Idealism,"
    And "Dialektgeographie und Textkritik,"

And "Vestris and Macready: Nineteenth-Century
        Management at the Parting of the Ways,"
    And "Pharyngeal Changes in Vowel and Consonant
        Articulation,"

And "More Light on Molière's Theater in 1672-73,
    from *Le Registre* d'Hubert, Archives of the
    Comédie Française,"
And "Diderot's Theory of Imitation."

May culture's glossolalia, clinging
    In Exhibit Rooms and Parlor A,
Sober a while the tempestuous singing
    Of fraternal conventions, untimely gay;

May your influence quell, like a panacea,
    A business assembly's financial fevers,
With the faint, sweet memory of "Observaciones sobre
    la aspiración de H en Andalucía,"
And "The Stimmsprung (Voice Leap) of Sievers."

                       MORRIS BISHOP

A Little Bow to Books on How To

For years I've read the books on how to
    Do this and that, awake and live,
Make friends, influence people, bow to
    The blows or blessings Fate may give,

How to invest, or raise a crocus,
    How to relax, or how to take it,
Read other people's hocus-pocus
    Or, if one likes one's own, to make it.

How to breathe, or browse, or think,
    Or get a job, or be polite,
Grow hair, or run a skating rink,
    Make good by day, make love by night,

How to rejoice, alone or married,
    How to distinguish saints from sinners,
How not to end it all when harried,
    How to eat corn at formal dinners,

How to, how to, how, how, how, how,
   Do this, do that, and these and those, too;
I yawn, but not before I bow
   To those great minds the money flows to.
IRWIN EDMAN

Book & Bookplate

This bookplate, that thou here seest put,
It was for Mr. Henderson cut:—
He ends it with a Latin phrase
(From Horace); this is what it says:—
"O thou sweet soother of my cares,
Be helpful to my proper pray'rs."
I hoped that it was me he meant;
But oh, that was not his intent.
He neither read the book nor cut it,
But pasted in his plate and shut it,
And sold it when the price had risen.
I'm glad the book's no longer his'n.
JOHN MASEFIELD

The Reader Writes

What poets mean by what they mean
Is tougher than it's ever been.

Some swear that Ezra Pound's the ticket;
I get lost in Ezra's thicket.

I'm stumped by what the lilacs bring
To T. S. Eliot in the spring.

I sit up late at night deciding
What goes on in Laura Riding.

Ah, never will the masses know
What Auden means, who loves them so.

Rare is the nugget I can fish out
From subtleties the poets dish out;

In fact, I think it's time we had some
Poets who are plain and gladsome,

Who shun the effort it must cost
To seem more deep that Robert Frost.

CARL CRANE

On a Certain Scholar

He never completed his History of Ephesus,
But his name got mentioned in numerous prefaces.

W. CRADDLE

A Parable for Poetasters

I gathered marble Venus in my arms
Just as the rabble shouted on the stair.
I said, "From her the sea withdrew its storms,
And gently on her body breathed the air."
The floor went down: she crashed to many pieces.
Discovered later by a Commissar,
He roared, "New forms! New forms!"
And wrote a thesis.

OLIVER ST. JOHN GOGARTY

Review of a Cook Book

Vague in plot but clear in style,
    Its characters escape me.
Flavor marks it all the while,
    And how it's helped to shape me!

LOUISE DYER HARRIS

The Purist to Her Love

Whatever its function,
Like's not a conjunction.

And if you continue
Committing that sin, you

Will drive me to Reno's
Consoling casinos.

MARGARET FISHBACK

Fate and the Younger Generation

It is strange to think of the Annas, the Vronskys, the
    Pierres, all the Tolstoyan lot
wiped out.

And the Alyoshas and Dmitris and Myshkins and
    Stavrogins, the Dostoevsky lot
all wiped out.

And the Tchekov wimbly-wambly wet-legs all wiped
    out.

Gone! Dead, or wandering in exile with their feathers
    plucked,
anyhow, gone from what they were, entirely.

Will the Proustian lot go next?
And then our English imitation intelligentsia?
Is it the *Quos vult perdere Deus* business?

Anyhow the Tolstoyan lot simply asked for extinction:
Eat me up, dear peasant!—So the peasant ate him.
And the Dostoevsky lot wallowed in the thought:
Let me sin my way to Jesus!—So they sinned them-
    selves off the face of the earth.

And the Tchekov lot: I'm too weak and lovable to
　　　live!—So they went.
Now the Proustian lot: Dear darling death, let me
　　　wriggle my way towards you
like the worm I am!—So he wriggled and got there.
Finally our little lot: I don't want to die, but by Jingo
　　　if I do!—
—Well, it won't matter so very much, either.

D. H. LAWRENCE

Thoughts on Editors

Editur et edit

No, editors don't care a button
　　　What false and faithless things they do;
They'll let you come and cut their mutton,
　　　And then they'll have a cut at you.

With Barnes I oft my dinner took,
　　　Nay, met ev'n Horace Twiss to please him;
Yet Mister Barnes traduced my book,
　　　For which may his own devils seize him!

With Doctor Bowring I drank tea,
　　　Nor of his cakes consumed a particle;
And yet th' ungrateful LL.D.
　　　Let fly at me next week an article.

John Wilson gave me suppers hot,
　　　With bards of fame like Hogg and Packwood,
A dose of black strap then I got,
　　　And after a still worse of *Blackwood*.

Alas, and must I close the list
　　　With thee, my Lockhart, of the *Quarterly*,
So kind, with bumper in they fist,—
　　　With pen, so *very* gruff and tartarly.

Now in thy parlour feasting me,
   Now scribbling at me from thy garrett,—
Till 'twixt the two in doubt I be
   Which sourest is, thy wit or claret.

THOMAS MOORE

To Henry David Thoreau
(After reading a tribute to him in Fortune)

Thoreau, you've come into your own
   Along with all the streamlined sages,
Your sentences acquire tone
   On Fortune's heavy coated pages,

Henry, you've won your accolade,
   Fortune agrees your thoughts are useful;
You rate even now, shrewd Yankee sage,
   With thinkers practical and Luce-ful.

Henry, you fled to Walden Pond;
   Your flight became a textbook fable;
Your influence now soars beyond
   The schoolroom to the tycoon's table.

"The mass of men," I think you wrote,
   "Lead lives of quiet desperation";
They die. Their words live on to quote
   With costly colored illustration.

You fled, I know, the market-place,
   Your townsmen's lives, cheap and external,
But you've come back at last to grace
   The great world in its suavest journal.

Now Walden Pond is far away,
   And you long dead, shrewd Yankee mentor;
But every seer must have his day,
   And right in Rockefeller Center.

IRWIN EDMAN

To Minerva

(From the Greek)

My temples throb, my pulses boil,
  I'm sick of Song, and Ode, and Ballad—
So, Thyrsis, take the Midnight Oil,
  And pour it on a lobster salad.

My brain is dull, my sight is foul,
  I cannot write a verse, or read,—
Then, Pallas, take away thine Owl,
  And let us have a lark instead.

THOMAS HOOD

There is No Opera Like "Lohengrin"

But one Apocalyptic Lion's whelp (in flesh
called William Lyon Phelps) purrs: After all,
there is no opera like "Lohengrin"!
My father, a Baptist preacher, a good man,
is now with God—and every day is Christmas.
Apart from questions of creative genius,
there are no gooder men than our good writers.
Lyman Abbott and I, who never can read Dante,
still find cathedrals beautifully friendly.
Hell is O.K.; Purgatory bores me; Heaven's dull.
There is no opera like "Lohengrin"!
Miss Lulu Bett's outline is a Greek statue.
Augustus Thomas' "Witching Hour" 's a masterpiece;
Housman's Second Volume is a masterpiece;
Anglo-Americans well know Ollivant's
masterpiece, "Bob, Son of Battle," that masterpiece!
There is no opera like "Lohengrin"!
In verse, these masterpieces are worth reading:
"The Jar of Dreams," by Lilla Cabot Perry;
"Waves of Unrest," by Bernice Lesbia Kenyon.

(O Charlotte Endymion Porter! Percy Bysshe Shelley?
Helen Archibald Clark! O women with three names!)
Anna Hempstead Branch read all the Bible
through in a few days. Speaking of Milton,
bad manners among critics are too common,
but gentlemen should not grow obsolete.
Often we fall asleep—not when we're bored,
but when we think we are most interesting.
There is no opera like "Lohengrin"!
I sometimes think there are no persons who
can do more good than good librarians can.
American books grow easier to hold;
dull paper and light weight is the ideal.

                                        JOHN WHEELWRIGHT

archy a low brow

boss i saw a picture
of myself in a paper
the other day
writing on a typewriter
with some of my feet
i wish it was as easy
as that what i have to do
is dive at each key
on the machine
and bump it with my head
and sometimes it telescopes
my occiput into my
vertebrae and i have a
permanent callous
on my forehead
i am in fact becoming
a low brow think of it
me with all my learning
to become a low brow

hoping that you
will remain the same
i am as ever your
faithful little bug
                    archy
                DON MARQUIS

The Height of the Ridiculous

I wrote some lines once on a time
    In wondrous merry mood,
And thought, as usual, men would say
    They were exceeding good.

They were so queer, so very queer,
    I laughed as I would die;
Albeit, in the general way,
    A sober man am I.

I called my servant, and he came;
    How kind it was of him
To mind a slender man like me,
    He of the mighty limb!

"These to the printer," I exclaimed,
    And, in my humorous way,
I added (as a trifling jest),
    "There'll be the devil to pay."

He took the paper, and I watched,
    And saw him peep within;
At the first line he read, his face
    Was all upon the grin.

He read the next; the grin grew broad,
    And shot from ear to ear;
He read the third; a chuckling noise
    I now began to hear.

The fourth; he broke into a roar;
  The fifth; his waistband split;
The sixth; he burst five buttons off,
  And tumbled in a fit.

Ten days and nights, with sleepless eye,
  I watched that wretched man,
And since, I never dare to write
  As funny as I can.

                    OLIVER WENDELL HOLMES

Ballade of the Goth

In days of old when Spenser sang,
  And Art and Letters were akin,
The halls of Verse re-echoing rang
  With voice of bard and paladin;
Now are those singers gathered in,
  Their garments given to the moth,
And o'er their bones there gleams the grin
  Of Saxon, Icelander, and Goth.

Shakespeare and Milton may go hang,
  For what knew they of sage Alcuin?
St. Patrick's Dean wrote modern slang,
  And Wordsworth is not worth a pin;
Poor ghosts of poets, worn and thin,
  Brayed all to pieces by the wrath
Symphonious, from the lion's skin
  Of Saxon, Icelander, and Goth.

And now does that barbaric gang
  Invade all learning, and begin,
From San Francisco to Penang,
  To stroke the beard, and wag the chin,

And drown all music in their din,
    And cut all letters to their cloth,
And brain all poets with the shin
    Of Saxon, Icelander, and Goth.

Envoy

Prince of Examiners! They sin
    Who brush our Art aside like froth.
Be of good cheer; 'tis ours to spin
    The Saxon, Icelander, and Goth.

        SIR WALTER RALEIGH

Deep Stuff

Sampling the books the moderns bring,
    In honesty I must confess
I liked the old Pierian spring
    More than the "stream of consciousness."

'Twas just a shallow, surface seep,
    That crystal, classic spring, I know,
And yet, why should we bore so deep
    To get this muddy modern flow?

        KEITH PRESTON

Thoughts
(after looking through an annotated classic)

I saw a bus marked X A N A D U
And climbed aboard to ride right through
To see great Kubla's pleasure-dome
And all his world of polychrome.
With eager eyes, I once or twice
Glimpsed golden towers of strange device
And caught, or thought I caught, the sound
Of Alph's vast river underground.

Despite of all the driver said
That moved me much to strike him dead,
He told us why, as on we flew,
The Khan had rationed honey-dew
And even clapped a ceiling price
On malted milk of Paradise.
With Kubla's frosty caves in sight,
He lectured on the troglodyte
And made such talk I couldn't hear
The horns of Elfland blowing clear.

Weave a circle round him thrice,
And close your eyes with holy dread.

Awearied much, the bell I pressed,
Leaped to a bank of thyme to rest,
Then laughed to see my dream come true,
For, lo, I was in Xanadu;
And with the multitude gave cry
As Kubla Khan came riding by
With press of urchins all about
His golden court and goblin route.
But when the Abyssinian maid
Her dulcimeric music played,
I raised a daemon-lover shout—
The driver stopped and threw me out.
This much I learned in Xanadu:
"$C_2 H_5 O H$, eschew."

ROY DAVIS

As I Was Laying on the Green

As I was laying on the green,
A small English book I seen.
Carlyle's *Essay on Burns* was the edition,
So I left it laying in the same position.

ANONYMOUS

Us Potes

Swift was sweet on Stella;
  Poe had his Lenore;
Burns's fancy turned to Nancy
  And a dozen more.

Pope was quite a trifler;
  Goldsmith was a case;
Byron'd flirt with any skirt
  From Liverpool to Thrace.

Sheridan philandered;
  Shelley, Keats, and Moore
All were there with some affair
  Far from lit'rachoor.

Fickle is the heart of
  Each immortal bard.
Mine alone is made of stone—
  Gotta work too hard.

              FRANKLIN P. ADAMS

A Classic Waits for Me

*(With Apologies to Walt Whitman, Plus a Trial
Membership in the Classics Club)*

A classic waits for me, it contains all, nothing is lack-
    ing,
Yet all were lacking if taste were lacking, or if the
    endorsement of the right man were lacking.
O clublife, and the pleasures of membership,
O volumes for sheer fascination unrivalled.
Into an armchair endlessly rocking,
Walter J. Black my president,
I, freely invited, cordially welcomed to membership,

My arm around John Kieran, Hendrik Willem van
      Loon, Pearl S. Buck,
My taste in books guarded by the spirit of William
      Lyon Phelps
(From your memories, sad brothers, from the fitful
      risings and callings I heard),
I to the classics devoted, brother of rough mechanics,
      beauty-parlor technicians, spot welders, radio-
      program directors
(It is not necessary to have a higher education to ap-
      preciate these books),
I, connoisseur of good reading, friend of connoisseurs
      of good reading everywhere,
I, not obligated to take any specific number of books,
      free to reject any volume, perfectly free to reject
      Montaigne, Erasmus, Milton,
I, in perfect health except for a slight cold, pressed for
      time, having only a few more years to live,
Now celebrate this opportunity.
Come, I will make the club indissoluble,
I will read the most splendid books the sun ever shone
      upon,
I will start divine magnetic groups,
   With the love of comrades,
     With the life-long love of distinguished commit-
      tees.

I strike up for an Old Book.
Long the best-read figure in America, my dues paid,
      sitter in armchairs everywhere, wanderer in
      populous cities, weeping with Hecuba and with
      the late William Lyon Phelps,
Free to cancel my membership whenever I wish.
Turbulent, fleshy, sensible,
Never tiring of clublife,
Always ready to read another masterpiece provided it

has the approval of my president, Walter J. Black,

Me imperturbe, standing at ease among writers,

Rais'd by a perfect mother and now belonging to a perfect book club,

Bearded, sunburnt, gray-neck'd, astigmatic,

Loving the masters and the masters only

(I am mad for them to be in contact with me),

My arm around Pearl S. Buck, only American woman to receive the Nobel Prize for Literature,

I celebrate this opportunity.

And I will not read a book nor the least part of a book but has the approval of the Committee,

For all is useless without that which you may guess at many times and not hit, that which they hinted at,

All is useless without readability.

By God! I will accept nothing which all cannot have their counterpart of on the same terms (89¢ for the Regular Edition or $1.39 for the De Luxe Edition, plus a few cents postage).

I will make inseparable readers with their arms around each other's necks,

By the love of classics,

By the manly love of classics.

E. B. WHITE

To John Taylor

With Pegasus upon a day,
    Apollo weary, flying,
Through frosty hills the journey lay,
    On foot the way was plying.

Poor slipshod giddy Pegasus
    Was but a sorry walker;

To Vulcan then Apollo goes,
  To get a frosty calker.

Obliging Vulcan fell to work,
  Threw by his coat and bonnet,
And did Sol's business in a crack;
  Sol paid him with a sonnet.

Ye Vulcan's sons of Wanlockhead,
  Pity my sad disaster;
My Pegasus is poorly shod—
  I'll pay you like my master.
                    ROBERT BURNS

"Forever"

Forever! 'Tis a single word!
  Our rude forefathers deemed it two:
Can you imagine so absurd
          A view?

Forever! What abysms of woe
  The word reveals, what frenzy, what
Despair! For ever (printed so)
          Did not.

It looks, ah me! how trite and tame!
  It fails to sadden or appal
Or solace—it is not the same
          At all.

O thou to whom it first occurred
  To solder the disjoined, and dower
Thy native language with a word
          Of power:

We bless thee! Whether far or near
  Thy dwelling, whether dark or fair
Thy kingly brow, is neither here
          Nor there.

But in men's hearts shall be thy throne,
   While the great pulse of England beats:
Thou coiner of a word unknown
      To Keats!

And nevermore must printer do
   As men did longago; but run
"For" into "ever," bidding two
      Be one.

Forever! passion-fraught, it throws
   O'er the dim page a gloom, a glamour:
It's sweet, it's strange; and I suppose
      It's grammar.

Forever! 'Tis a single word!
   And yet our fathers deemed it two:
Nor am I confident they erred;
      Are you?

                      C. S. CALVERLEY

After Reading the Reviews of "Finnegans Wake"

Nothing has been quite the same
Since I heard your liquid name,
Since it cast a magic spell,
Anna Livia Plurabelle.

Maid or river, bird or beast,
Doesn't matter in the least;
Quite enough that tongue may tell
Anna Livia Plurabelle.

What you've done, you'll never guess,
To my stream of consciousness!
Hang the meaning! What the hell!
Anna Livia Plurabelle.

                      MELVILLE CANE

Commercial Candour

*(On the outside of a sensational novel is printed
the statement: "The back of the cover will tell you
the plot.")*

Our fathers to creed and tradition were tied,
They opened a book to see what was inside,
And of various methods they deemed not the worst
Was to find the first chapter and look at it first.
And so from the first to the second they passed,
Till in servile routine they arrived at the last.
But a literate age, unbenighted by creed,
Can find on two boards all it wishes to read;
For the front of the cover shows somebody shot
And the back of the cover will tell you the plot.

Between, that the book may be handily padded,
Some pages of mere printed matter are added,
Expanding the theme, which in case of great need
The curious reader might very well read
With the zest that is lent to a game worth the winning,
By knowing the end when you start the beginning;
While our barbarous sires, who would read every word
With a morbid desire to find out what occurred
Went dearily drudging through Dickens and Scott.
But the back of the cover will tell you the plot.

The wild village folk in earth's earliest prime
Could often sit still for an hour at a time
And hear a blind beggar, nor did the tale pall
Because Hector must fight before Hector could fall:
Nor was Scheherazade required, at the worst,
To tell her tales backwards and finish them first;
And the minstrels who sang about battle and banners
Found the rude camp-fire crowd had some notion of
          manners.
Till Forster (who pelted the people like crooks,

The Irish with buckshot, the English with books),
Established the great educational scheme
Of compulsory schooling, that glorious theme.
Some learnt how to read, and the others forgot,
And the back of the cover will tell you the plot.

O Genius of Business! O marvellous brain,
Come in place of the priests and the warriors to reign!
O Will to Get On that makes everything go—
O Hustle! O Pep! O Publicity! O!
Shall I spend three-and-sixpence to purchase the book,
Which we all can pick up on the bookstall and look?
Well, it may appear strange, but I think I shall not,
For the back of the cover will tell you the plot.

G. K. CHESTERTON

Lines

*Written on receiving from the Librarian of a
College which educates "the mountain youth of
Tennessee," a request for "a book" to assist in the
re-formation of the Library, which was recently
destroyed by fire.*

Mine ears have heard your distant moan,
  O mountain youth of Tennessee;
Even the bowels of a stone
  Would melt at your librarian's plea.
Although we're parted by the ocean,
  I'm most distressed about your fire:
Only I haven't any notion
  What sort of volume you require.

I have a Greene, a Browne, a Gray,
  A Gilbert White, a William Black,
Trollope and Lovelace, Swift and Gay
  And Hunt and Synge: nor do I lack

More sober folk for whom out there
    There may be rather better scope,
Three worthy men of reverend air,
    A Donne, a Prior, and a Pope.

Peacock or Lamb, discreetly taken,
    Might fill the hungry mountain belly,
Or Hogg or Suckling, Crabbe or Bacon
    (Bacon's not Shakespeare, Crabbe *is* Shelley).
And if—for this is on the cards—
    You do not like this mental food,
I might remit less inward bards:
    My well-worn Spenser or my Hood.

Longfellows may be in your line
    (Littles we know are second-raters),
Or one might speed across the brine
    A Mayflower full of Pilgrim Paters.
Or, then, again, you may devote
    Yourselves to less æsthetic lore,
Yet if I send you out a Grote
For all I know you'll ask for More.

O thus proceeds my vacillation:
    For now the obvious thought returns
That after such a conflagration
    A fitting sequel might be Burns.
And now again I change my mind
    And, almost confidently, feel
That since to Beg you are inclined
    You might like Borrow, say, or Steele. . . .

Envoy

Yes, Prince, this song *shall* have an end.
    A sudden thought has come to me—
The thing is settled: I shall send
    A Tennyson to Tennessee!

SIR J. C. SQUIRE

A Sonnet

Two voices are there: one is of the deep;
It learns the storm-cloud's thunderous melody,
Now roars, now murmurs with the changing sea,
Now bird-like pipes, now closes soft in sleep:
And one is of an old half-witted sheep
Which bleats articulate monotony,
And indicates that two and one are three,
That grass is green, lakes damp, and mountains steep:
And, Wordsworth, both are thine: at certain times
Forth from the heart of thy melodious rhymes,
The form and pressure of high thoughts will burst:
At other times—good Lord! I'd rather be
Quite unaquainted with the A.B.C.
Than write such hopeless rubbish as thy worst.

J. K. STEPHEN

Ballade of the Poetic Life

The fat men go about the streets,
  The politicians play their game,
The prudent bishops sound retreats
  And think the martyrs much to blame;
  Honour and Love are halt and lame
And Greed and Power are deified,
  The wild are harnessed by the tame;
For this the poets lived and died.

Shelley's a trademark used on sheets:
  Aloft the sky in words of flame
We read "What porridge had John Keats?
  Why, Brown's! A hundred years the same!"
  Arcadia's an umbrella frame,
Milton's a toothpaste: from the tide
  Sappho's been dredged to rouge my Dame—
For this the poets lived and died.

And yet, to launch ideal fleets,
 Lost regions in the stars to claim,
To face all ruins and defeats,
 To sing a beaten world to shame,
 To hold each bright impossible aim
Deep in the heart: to starve in pride
 For fame, and never know their fame—
For this the poets lived and died.

Envoy

Princess, inscribe beneath my name
"He never begged, he never sighed,
 He took his medicine as it came"—
For this the poets lived—and died.

SIR J. C. SQUIRE

The Philosopher

Lao-tzŭ

"Those who speak know nothing;
Those who know are silent."
These words, as I am told,
Were spoken by Lao-tzŭ.
If we are to believe that Lao-tzŭ
 Was himself *one who knew,*
How comes it that he wrote a book
Of five thousand words?
 Translated by ARTHUR WALEY

Obit on Parnassus

Death before forty's no bar. Lo!
 These had accomplished their feats:
Chatterton, Burns, and Kit Marlowe,
 Byron and Shelley and Keats.

Death, the eventual censor,
    Lays for the forties, and so
Took off Jane Austen and Spenser,
    Stevenson, Hood, and poor Poe.

You'll leave a better-lined wallet
    By reaching the end of your rope
After fifty, like Shakespeare and Smollett,
    Thackeray, Dickens, and Pope.

Try for the sixties—but say, boy,
    That's when the tombstones were built on
Butler and Sheridan, the play boy,
    Arnold and Coleridge and Milton.

Three score and ten—the tides rippling
    Over the bar; slip the hawser.
Godspeed to Clemens and Kipling,
    Swinburne and Browning and Chaucer.

Some staved the debt off but paid it
    At eighty—that's after the law.
Wordsworth and Tennyson made it,
    And Meredith, Hardy, and Shaw.

But Death, while you make up your quota,
    Please note this confession of candor—
That I wouldn't give an iota
    To linger till ninety, like Landor.

                                    F. SCOTT FITZGERALD

About the Shelleys

'Twas not my wish
To be Sir Bysshe,
But 'twas the whim
Of my son Tim.
    Quoted by WORDSWORTH

Britannia Rules of Orthography

From British novels a thrill I get
That I sadly miss in the American tale—
The thrill of a heroine suffragette
In gaol.

They touch on Life in the Quivering Raw,
With the frankest noun and the straightest verb,
And all of them—Hewlett, Bennett, and Shaw—
Say kerb.

Domestic voices are flabby and weak
In the Search for Truth that the age requires.
Would Ade or Tarkington dare to speak
Of tyres?

Hail to Conrad, Galsworthy, Wells,
To the crunching might of their books and dramas,
And the Lure of the East when Kipling spells
Pyjamas.

                                        FIRTH

Anthologistics

Since one anthologist put in his book
Sweet things by Morse, Bone, Potter, Bliss and Brook,
All subsequent anthologists, of course
Have quoted Bliss, Brook, Potter, Bone and Morse.
For, should some rash anthologist make free
To print selections, say, from you and me,
Omitting with a judgment all his own
The classic Brook, Morse, Potter, Bliss and Bone,
Contemptuous reviewers, passing by
Our verses, would unanimously cry,
"What manner of anthology is this
That leaves out Bone, Brook, Potter, Morse and Bliss!"

                                        ARTHUR GUITERMAN

LIMERICKS

Well, it's partly the shape of the thing
That gives the old limerick wing:
  These accordion pleats
  Full of airy conceits
Take it up like a kite on a string.

ANONYMOUS

A clergyman out in Dumont
Keeps tropical fish in the font;
    Though it always surprises
    The babes he baptizes,
It seems to be just what they want.

MORRIS BISHOP

A certain young gourmet of Crediton
Took some pâté de foie gras and spread it on
    A chocolate biscuit,
    Then murmured, "I'll risk it."
His tomb bears the date that he said it on.

REV. CHARLES INGE

There was a young person named Tate
Who went out to dine at 8.8,
    But I will not relate
    What that person named Tate
And his tête-à-tête ate at 8.8.

CAROLYN WELLS

A flea and a fly in a flue
Were imprisoned, so what could they do?
    Said the fly, "Let us flee,"
    Said the flea, "Let us fly,"
So they flew through a flaw in the flue.

ANONYMOUS

An epicure, dining at Crewe,
Found quite a large mouse in his stew.
    Said the waiter, "Don't shout,
    And wave it about,
Or the rest will be wanting one, too!"

ANONYMOUS

There was a young man of Devizes,
Whose ears were of different sizes;
   The one that was small
   Was of no use at all,
But the other won several prizes.

                ANONYMOUS

There was an old person of Tring
Who, when somebody asked her to sing,
   Replied, "Isn't it odd?
   I can never tell *God
Save the Weasel* from *Pop Goes the King!*"

                ANONYMOUS

I wish that my Room had a Floor;
I don't so much care for a Door,
   But this walking around
   Without touching the ground
Is getting to be quite a bore!

              GELETT BURGESS

A silly young fellow named Hyde
In a funeral procession was spied;
   When asked, "Who is dead?"
   He giggled and said,
"I don't know; I just came for the ride."

                ANONYMOUS

Said old Peeping Tom of Fort Lee:
"Peeping ain't what it's cracked up to be;
   I lose all my sleep,
   And I peep and I peep,
And I find 'em all peeping at me."

              MORRIS BISHOP

There was a young man of Madrid
Who imagined that he was the Cid:
   When they asked of him "Why?"
   He could only reply
That he didn't know why, but he did.
ANONYMOUS

When you go to a store in Ascutney,
There is no use to ask them for chutney.
   You may beg, you may tease,
   You may go to your knees:
It will do you no good, they ain't got any.
RICHARD H. FIELD

At the village emporium in Woodstock
Of chutney they keep quite a good stock;
   They're more given to gluttony
   Than the folk of Ascutney
Who neither of liquors nor foods talk.
FREDERICK WINSOR

A sleeper from the Amazon
Put nighties of his gra'mazon—
   The reason, that
   He was too fat
To get his own pajamazon.
ANONYMOUS

There was an old man of Tarentum,
Who gnashed his false teeth till he bent 'em.
   When they asked him the cost
   Of what he had lost,
He replied, "I can't say, for I rent 'em."
ANONYMOUS

There once was a man of Calcutta
Who spoke with a terrible stutter.
   At breakfast he said,
   "Give me b-b-b-bread,
And b-b-b-b-b-b-butter."

                ANONYMOUS

There was a young lady of Twickenham,
Whose shoes were too tight to walk quick in 'em;
   She came back from her walk,
   Looking white as a chalk,
And took 'em both off and was sick in 'em.

                OLIVER HERFORD

The bottle of perfume that Willie sent
Was highly displeasing to Millicent;
   Her thanks were so cold
   They quarrelled, I'm told,
Through that silly scent Willie sent Millicent.

                ANONYMOUS

There once was a bonnie Scotch laddie,
Who said as he put on his plaidie:
   "I've just had a dish
   O' unco' guid fish."
What *had* 'e had? had 'e had haddie?

                ANONYMOUS

A beautiful lady named Psyche
Is loved by a fellow named Yche.
   One thing about Ych
   The lady can't lych
Is his beard, which is dreadfully spyche.

                ANONYMOUS

My Face

As a beauty I am not a star,
There are others more handsome, by far,
  But my face—I don't mind it
  For I am behind it.
It's the people in front get the jar!
ANTHONY EUWER

There was a young woman named Bright,
Whose speed was much faster than light.
  She set out one day,
  In a relative way,
And returned on the previous night.
ANONYMOUS

A tutor who tooted a flute,
Tried to teach two young tooters to toot.
  Said the two to the tutor,
  "Is it harder to toot, or
To tutor two tooters to toot?"
CAROLYN WELLS

There was a young fellow of Perth,
Who was born on the day of his birth;
  He was married, they say,
  On his wife's wedding day,
And he died when he quitted the earth.
ANONYMOUS

There was a fat canon of Durham,
Who trod on a cloister-bred wurrum;
  Said he to the beadle,
  "Prepare the cathed'l,
And let us proceed to inter'm."
ANONYMOUS

The Death of Polybius Jubb

He died in attempting to swallow,
Which proves that, though fat, he was hollow—
For in gasping for space
He swallowed his face,
And hadn't the courage to follow.

ROY CAMPBELL

There was a young man of Sid. Sussex,
Who insisted that $w + x$
    Was the same as xw;
    So they said, "Sir, we'll trouble you
To confine that idea to Sid. Sussex."

ARTHUR C. HILTON

There was an old fellow of Trinity
Who solved the square root of Infinity,
    But it gave him such fidgets
    To count up the digits,
He chucked Math and took up Divinity.

ANONYMOUS

There's a vaporish maiden in Harrison
Who longed for the love of a Saracen.
    But she had to confine her
    Intent to a Shriner,
Who suffers, I fear, by comparison.

MORRIS BISHOP

Said a great Congregational preacher
To a hen, "You're a beautiful creature."
    And the hen, just for that,
    Laid an egg in his hat,
And thus did the Hen reward Beecher.

ANONYMOUS

There was a young fellow named Hall,
Who fell in the spring in the fall;
   'Twould have been a sad thing
   If he'd died in the spring,
But he didn't—he died in the fall.

                    ANONYMOUS

Miss Minnie McFinney, of Butte,
Fed always, and only, on frutte.
   Said she: "Let the coarse
   Eat of beef and of horse,
I'm a peach, and that's all there is tutte."

                    ANONYMOUS

No matter how grouchy you're feeling,
You'll find the smile more or less healing.
   It grows in a wreath
   All around the front teeth,
Thus preserving the face from congealing.

                ANTHONY EUWER

There was a young lady of Woosester
Who usest to crow like a roosester;
   She usest to climb
   Two trees at a time,
But her sisester usest to boosest her.

                    ANONYMOUS

   A clergyman, in want
   Of a second-hand movable font,
     Would dispose, for the same,
     Of a portrait (in frame)
   Of the Bishop, elect, of Vermont.

          RONALD ARBUTHNOTT KNOX

There was a faith-healer of Deal
Who said, "Although pain isn't real,
    If I sit on a pin
    And I puncture my skin
I dislike what I *fancy* I feel!"

                  ANONYMOUS

There was an old person of Leeds,
And simple indeed were his needs.
    Said he: "To save toil
    Growing things in the soil,
I'll just eat the packets of seeds!"

                  ANONYMOUS

MAD DOGS & ENGLISHMEN

For Allah created the English mad—the maddest of all mankind!

RUDYARD KIPLING

But in spite of all temptations
To belong to other nations,
He remains an Englishman!

SIR W. S. GILBERT

Elegy in a Country Churchyard

The men that worked for England
They have their graves at home:
And bees and birds of England
About the cross can roam.

But they that fought for England,
Following a falling star,
Alas, alas for England
They have their graves afar.

And they that rule in England,
In stately conclave met,
Alas, alas for England
They have no graves as yet.

G. K. CHESTERTON

I Was a Bustle-Maker Once, Girls

When I was a lad of twenty
    And was working in High Street, Ken.,
I made quite a pile in a very little while—
    I was a bustle-maker then.
    Then there was work in plenty,
        And I was a thriving man;
But things have decayed in the bustle-making trade
    Since the bustle-making trade began.

I built bustles with a will then;
    I built bustles with a wit;
I built bustles as a Yankee hustles,
    Simply for the love of it.
    I built bustles with a skill then
        Surpassed, they say, by none;
But those were the days when bustles were the craze,
    And now those days are done.

I was a bustle-maker once, girls,
    Many, many years ago;
I put my heart in the bustle-maker's art,
    And I don't mind saying so.
  I may have had the brains of a dunce, girls;
    I may have had the mind of a muff;
I may have been plain and deficient in the brain,
    But I did know a bustle-maker's stuff.
  I built bustles for the slender;
    I built bustles for the stout;
I built bustles for the girls with muscles
    And bustles for the girls without.
  I built bustles by the thousands once
    In the good old days of yore;
But things have decayed in the bustle-making trade,
    And I don't build bustles any more.

  Many were the models worn once;
    But mine were unique, 'tis said;
No rival design was so elegant as mine;
    I was a bustle-maker bred.
  I was a bustle-maker born once—
    An artist through and through;
But things have decayed in the bustle-making trade,
    And what can a bustle-maker do?

  I built bustles to enchant, girls;
    I built bustles to amaze;
I built bustles for the skirt that rustles,
    And bustles for the skirt that sways.
  I built bustles for my aunt, girls,
    When other business fled;
But a bustle-maker can't make bustles for his aunt
    When a bustle-maker's aunt is dead.

  I was a bustle-maker once, girls—
    Once in the days gone by,

I lost my heart to the bustle-maker's art,
    And that I don't deny.
I may have had the brains of a dunce, girls,
    As many men appear to suppose;
I may have been obtuse and of little other use,
    But I could build a bustle when I chose.
I built bustles for the bulging;
    I built bustles for the lithe;
I built bustles for the girls in Brussels
    And bustles for the girls in Hythe.
I built bustles for all Europe once,
    But I've been badly hit.
Things have decayed in the bustle-building trade,
    And that's the truth of it.

                      PATRICK BARRINGTON

It's Very Unwise to Kill the Goose
(Sherlock Holmes)

It's very unwise to kill the goose that lays the golden
    eggs,
And in my case that goose consists of robbers, thugs
    and yeggs;
So every time I catch a thief, my natural enjoyment
Is tempered by the thought that I'm curtailing my
    employment.
It's an awkward situation that presents itself, you see.
While crime doesn't pay the criminal, it can and does
    pay me;
And so with contradictions my pathway is beset.
I want to put an end to crime—but not, I hope, quite
    yet.

It is my highest duty as a conscientious man
To aid Lestrade and Gregson in every way I can;
And yet if I succeed too well in teaching Scotland
    Yard,

I'm hoist (if I may coin a phrase) by means of my
    petard.
And with this painful prospect my waking dreams are
    linked—
The spectre of the hunter when his game becomes ex-
    tinct;
And so with mixed emotions my purpose I avow,
I want to put an end to crime—but not, I trust, just
    now.

'Twixt Scylla and Charybdis a narrow course I trace,
And try to smile as I cut off my nose to spite my face.
To vindicate the British law is my declared objective,
Yet doing so involves an end of Sherlock Holmes, de-
    tective.
But I must face the issue, carry on without a tremor,
Though inwardly impaled upon the horns of a di-
    lemma,
And of unfriendly Fortune I crave this single boon:
I want to put an end to crime—but not, I pray, too
    soon.

                  PHILIP H. RHINELANDER

The Englishman

St. George he was for England,
And before he killed the dragon
He drank a pint of English ale
Out of an English flagon.
For though he fast right readily
In hair-shirt or in mail,
It isn't safe to give him cakes
Unless you give him ale.

St. George he was for England,
And right gallantly set free
The lady left for dragon's meat
And tied up to a tree;

But since he stood for England
And knew what England means,
Unless you give him bacon
You mustn't give him beans.

St. George he is for England,
And shall wear the shield he wore
When we go out in armour
With the battle-cross before.
But though he is jolly company
And very pleased to dine,
It isn't safe to give him nuts
Unless you give him wine.

G. K. CHESTERTON

Sir Christopher Wren

Sir Christopher Wren
Said, "I am going to dine with some men.
If anybody calls
Say I am designing St. Paul's."

EDMUND CLERIHEW BENTLEY

"New King arrives in his capital by air . . ." —DAILY NEWSPAPER

Spirits of well-shot woodcock, partridge, snipe
Flutter and bear him up the Norfolk sky:
In that red house in a red mahogany book-case
The stamp collection awaits with mounts long dry.
The big blue eyes are shut which saw wrong clothing
And favourite fields and coverts from a horse;
Old men in country houses hear clocks ticking
Over thick carpets with a deadened force;

Old men who never cheated, never doubted,
Communicated monthly, sit and stare
At a red suburb ruled by Lady Liner
Where a young man lands hatless from the air.

JOHN BETJEMAN

J. S. Mill

John Stuart Mill,
By a mighty effort of will,
Overcame his natural bonhomie
And wrote "Principles of Political Economy."

EDMUND CLERIHEW BENTLEY

'Form Fours'

A Volunteer's Nightmare

If you're Volunteer Artist or Athlete, or if you defend
    the Home,
You sacrifice 'Ease' for 'Attention,' and march like a
    metronome;
But of all elementary movements you learn in your
    Volunteer Corps
The one that is really perplexing is known as the
    Forming of Fours.

Imagine us numbered off from the right: the Sergeant
    faces the squad,
And says that the odd files do not move—I never seem
    to be odd!
And then his instructions run like this (very simple in
    black and white)—
'A pace to the rear with the left foot, and one to the
    right with the right.'

Of course if you don't think deeply, you do it without
    a hitch;
You have only to know your right and left, and re-
    member which is which;
But as soon as you try to be careful, you get in the
    deuce of a plight,
With 'a pace to the right with the left foot, and one
    to the rear with the right!'

Besides, when you're thoroughly muddled the Ser-
    geant doubles your doubt
By saying that rules reverse themselves, as soon as
    you're 'turned about';
So round you go on your right heel, and practise until
    you are deft
At 'a pace to the front with the right foot, and one to
    the left with the left.'

In my dreams the Sergeant, the Kaiser, and Kipling
    mix my feet,
Saying 'East is left, and Right is Might, and never the
    twain shall meet!'
In my nightmare squad *all* files are odd, and their
    Fours are horribly queer,
With 'a pace to the left with the front foot, and one
    to the right with the rear!'

FRANK SIDGWICK

Peace

A Study

He stood, a worn-out City clerk—
    Who'd toiled, and seen no holiday,
For forty years from dawn to dark—
    Alone beside Caermarthen Bay.

He felt the salt spray on his lips;
  Heard children's voices on the sands;
Up the sun's path he saw the ships
  Sail on and on to other lands;

And laughed aloud. Each sight and sound
  To him was joy too deep for tears;
He sat him on the beach, and bound
  A blue bandana round his ears:

And thought how, posted near his door,
  His own green door on Camden Hill,
Two bands at least, most likely more,
  Were mingling at their own sweet will

Verdi with Vance. And at the thought
  He laughed again, and softly drew
That Morning Herald that he'd bought
  Forth from his breast, and read it through.

C. S. CALVERLEY

Message to General Montgomery

We've despatched, *pour la guerre,*
  A mackintosh pair
Of trousers and jacket, express;
  They are coming by air
  And are sent to you care
Of the Bishop of Southwark, no less.

So wherever you go
  From Pescara to Po,
Through mud and morasses and ditches,
  You undoubtedly ought
  To be braced by the thought
That the Church has laid hands on your breeches.

We think they'll suffice
  (As they should at the price)

To cover your flanks in the melee,
　　And avert the malaise
　　(In the Premier's phrase)
Of a chill in the soft underbelly.

　　According to Moss
　　(The outfitting Bros.)
'Twon't matter, so stout is their fibre,
　　If you happen to trip
　　And the mud makes you slip,
Like Horatius, into the Tiber.

　　And you'll find—so we hope
　　When you call on the Pope,
That his blessing's more readily given
　　On learning the news
　　That your mackintosh trews
Were brought down by a Bishop from Heaven.

H. F. ELLIS

London, 1944.

There Lived a King

There lived a King, as I've been told,
In the wonder-working days of old,
When hearts were twice as good as gold,
　　And twenty times as mellow.
Good-temper triumphed in his face,
And in his heart he found a place
For all the erring human race
　　And every wretched fellow.
When he had Rhenish wine to drink
It made him very sad to think
That some, at junket or at jink,
　　Must be content with toddy.
He wished all men as rich as he
(And he was rich as rich could be),

So to the top of every tree
  Promoted everybody.

Lord Chancellors were cheap as sprats,
And Bishops in their shovel hats
Were plentiful as tabby cats—
  In point of fact, too many.
Ambassadors cropped up like hay,
Prime Ministers and such as they
Grew like asparagus in May,
  And Dukes were three a penny.
On every side Field Marshals gleamed,
Small beer were Lords Lieutenant deemed,
With Admirals the ocean teemed
  All round his wide dominions.
And Party Leaders you might meet
In twos and threes in every street,
Maintaining, with no little heat,
  Their various opinions.

That King, although no one denies
His heart was of abnormal size,
Yet he'd have acted otherwise
  If he had been acuter.
The end is easily foretold,
When every blessed thing you hold
Is made of silver, or of gold,
  You long for simple pewter.
When you have nothing else to wear
But cloth of gold and satins rare,
For cloth of gold you cease to care—
  Up goes the price of shoddy.
In short, whoever you may be,
To this conclusion you'll agree,
When every one is somebodee,
  Then no one's anybody!

SIR W. S. GILBERT

Mad Dogs and Englishmen

In tropical climes there are certain times of day
When all the citizens retire
To tear their clothes off and perspire.
It's one of those rules that the greatest fools obey,
Because the sun is much too sultry
And one must avoid its ultry—violet ray.
Papalaka papalaka papalaka boo,
Papalaka papalaka papalaka boo,
Digariga digariga digariga doo,
Digariga digariga digariga doo.
The natives grieve when the white men leave their
         huts,
Because they're obviously definitely Nuts!

    Mad dogs and Englishmen
    Go out in the midday sun.
    The Japanese don't care to,
    The Chinese wouldn't dare to,
    Hindoos and Argentines sleep firmly from twelve to
         one.
    But Englishmen detest a—Siesta.
    In the Philippines there are lovely screens
    To protect you from the glare.
    In the Malay States there are hats like plates
    Which the Britishers won't wear.
    At twelve noon the natives swoon
    And no further work is done,
    But mad dogs and Englishmen
    Go out in the midday sun.

It's such a surprise for the Eastern eyes to see,
That tho' the English are effete,
They're quite impervious to heat.
When the white man rides every native hides in glee
Because the simple creatures hope he
Will impale his solar topee—on a tree.
Bolyboly bolyboly bolyboly baa,

Bolyboly bolyboly bolyboly baa,
Habaninny habaninny habaninny haa,
Habaninny habaninny habaninny haa,
It seems such a shame when the English claim the
       earth
That they give rise to such hilarity and mirth.

    Mad dogs and Englishmen
    Go out in the midday sun.
    The toughest Burmese bandit
    Can never understand it.
    In Rangoon the heat of noon
    Is just what the natives shun.
    They put their Scotch or Rye down—and lie down.
    In a jungle town where the sun beats down
    To the rage of man and beast,
    The English garb of the English Sahib
    Merely gets a bit more creased.
    In Bangkok at twelve o'clock
    They foam at the mouth and run,
    But mad dogs and Englishmen
    Go out in the midday sun.

    Mad dogs and Englishmen
    Go out in the midday sun.
    The smallest Malay rabbit
    Deplores this stupid habit.
    In Hong Kong they strike a gong
    And fire off a noonday gun
    To reprimand each inmate—who's in late.
    In the mangrove swamps where the python romps
    There is peace from twelve till two.
    Even caribous lie around and snooze,
    For there's nothing else to do.
    In Bengal, to move at all
    Is seldom if ever done,
    But mad dogs and Englishmen
    Go out in the midday sun.

NOEL COWARD

THE MALICIOUS MALE

When Adam day by day
Woke up in Paradise,
He always used to say
"Oh, this is very nice."

But Eve from scenes of bliss
Transported him for life.
The more I think of this
The more I beat my wife.

A. E. HOUSMAN

"Come, Come," Said Tom's Father

"Come, come," said Tom's father, "at your time of life,
  There's no longer excuse for thus playing the rake—
It is time you should think, boy, of taking a wife"—
  "Why, so it is, father,—whose wife shall I take?"

THOMAS MOORE

Elegy on Mrs. Mary Blaize

Good people all, with one accord,
  Lament for Madam Blaize,
Who never wanted a good word—
  From those who spoke her praise.

The needy seldom passed her door,
  And always found her kind;
She freely lent to all the poor—
  Who left a pledge behind.

She strove the neighbourhood to please,
  With manners wondrous winning;
And never followed wicked ways—
  Unless when she was sinning.

At church, in silks and satins new,
  With hoop of monstrous size;
She never slumbered in her pew—
  But when she shut her eyes.

Her love was sought, I do aver,
  By twenty beaux and more;
The king himself has followed her—
  When she has walked before.

But now her wealth and finery fled,
  Her hangers-on cut short all;
The doctors found, when she was dead—
  Her last disorder mortal.

235

Let us lament, in sorrow sore,
    For Kent Street well may say
That had she lived a twelvemonth more—
    She had not died to-day.

OLIVER GOLDSMITH

On Marriage

How happy a thing were a wedding,
    And a bedding,
If a man might purchase a wife
    For a twelvemonth and a day;
But to live with her all a man's life,
    For ever and for aye,
Till she grow as grey as a cat,
Good faith, Mr. Parson, excuse me from that!

THOMAS FLATMAN

Ballade of Charon and the River Girl

At first she thought it a fantastic dream:
    The hideous man of more than normal size,
The naked landscape, and the brackish stream
    That hardly stirred beneath the dismal skies.
    "I hope," she said, "you'll pardon my surmise,
But honestly I think there's something wrong;
    You weren't at Betty's. Did we meet at Di's?"
And Charon answered: "Now we shan't be long."

The boat crept on. She said, "Now, what's the scheme?
    Isn't it time you chucked your weird disguise?
Where are the cushions? Where's the fruit and cream,
    The gramophone, the ice, the cold game pies? . . .
    You domineering men, no one denies,
Intrigue a girl; and as we're going strong
    I may seem rather rude to criticise."
And Charon answered: "Now we shan't be long."

A sudden gasp; a quickly stifled scream . . .
   She saw the ugly Stygian night arise,
And Hell's red moon send forth a fiery gleam;
   She heard the lamentation and the cries
   Of all the damned who dream of Paradise,
And still the boat drew near that misty throng,
   "Charon!" she sobbed. "I thought all that was lies!"
And Charon answered: "Now we shan't be long."

Envoy

Prince, at that moment, much to his surprise,
She winked at him, and hummed a saucy song,
   And did a negro step, and rolled her eyes:
And Charon answered: "Now we shan't be long."

J. B. MORTON

Good Reasons

Two things make woman slow, we find,
   In going any place;
For first she must make up her mind
   And then her face.

KEITH PRESTON

Dirce

Stand close around, ye Stygian set,
   With Dirce in one boat conveyed!
Or Charon, seeing, may forget
   That he is old and she a shade.

WALTER SAVAGE LANDOR

The Difference

When man and woman die, as poets sung,
His heart's the last part moves,—her last, the tongue.

BENJAMIN FRANKLIN

MOMENTS MUSICAL

Now am I a tin whistle
Through which God blows,
And I wish to God I were a trumpet
—But why, God only knows.

SIR J. C. SQUIRE

Recipe for an Evening Musicale

Candles. Red tulips, sixty cents the bunch.
Two lions, Grade B. A newly tuned piano.
No cocktails, but a dubious kind of punch,
Lukewarm and weak. A harp and a soprano.

The Lullaby of Brahms. Somebody's cousin
From Forest Hills, addicted to the pun.
Two dozen gentlemen; ladies, three dozen,
Earringed and powdered. Sandwiches at one.

The ashtrays few, the ventilation meagre.
Shushes to greet the late-arriving guest
Or quell the punch-bowl group. A young man eager
To render "Danny Deever," by request.

And sixty people trying to relax
On little rented chairs with gilded backs.

PHYLLIS McGINLEY

Melodie Grotesque

The loud pianist summons from the dark
    Dim minor shapes of jungle oddities.
Here come the jackal and the lean aard-vark
    Stepping along the zebra-colored keys.

He musters lions bound with daisy chains,
    Dark panther puppies with delicious growls
Rolling among the basses he entrains,
    And seeks the angry tiger where it prowls.

He calls from out the distant caves of sound
    Strange beasts that snarl, desiring to be hid
Deep in the shadows of the night profound,
    That lurk beneath the black piano lid.

239

His twinkling fingers lure into the room
A savage cortege, dignified and slow;
He swerves to save from diatonic gloom
One lamb that gambols pianissimo.

PERSIS GREELY ANDERSON

Unfamiliar Quartet

The concert-hall creaked like a full-dress shirt
As the happy audience hugged its musical smart,
And waited to be titillatingly hurt
By the pelting of the over-ripe fruit of Art.

The violin wept its sugar, the saxophone
Howled like a mandrake raped by a lightning-stroke,
The 'cello gave a blond and stomachy groan—
And then the hard bugle spoke.

Sewing a wound together with brazen stitches,
Stitching a bronze device on the rotten skin,
And calling the elegant audience sons of bitches,
It ceased, and the sons of bitches
Applauded the violin.

STEPHEN VINCENT BENÉT

Opera in English?

Translated, won't the operatic word,
Outlandish and romantically blurred,
In clear-cut English seem a bit absurd?

Would it be fair to have this wished upon,
Say, "Caro nome," . . . or "E lucevan," . . .
Or "Mon coeur s'ouvre," . . . or "Mein lieber
Schwan"? . . .

Or have "Die Zauberflöte's" jumbled sense,
"Il Trovatore's" dim intelligence,
Made too apparent to the audience?

Or mar the alien, enchanted air
Of Pelléas' forest, or of Siegfried's lair
With tourist sounds of—English spoken there?

Or—cede to Billy Rose these distant zones,
And to the local Carmen he enthrones
Add Mignon, Thaïs and Brünnhilde Jones?—

To which the answer is perhaps: Why ask,
When singers make the language sound so queer
You wonder if it's Greek or Czech or Basque—
Or English—that has reached your puzzled ear?

BENJAMIN M. STEIGMAN

Theme Song for a Songwriters' Union

We are the Lovers of Local 1;
　　Ours, no easy chore:
Dreaming-Of-You is all we do
　　Daily from ten till four;
Now as we strike for a Tropical Moon
　　A-Shinin' on shorter hours,
For limited Love in the Month O' June
　　And rosier Rose-covered Bowers,
See to it, please, if we Roam In The Rain,
　　'Tisn't through Fields of Clover;
And order our rhyme but in no/4 time,
　　With time-and-a-half for over-.

AL GRAHAM

English Horn

The ENGLISH HORN I must reveal
Has no connection with John Peel;
In fact Old John would find it meaner
To play on than a vacuum cleaner.
Its tone would make his horses skittish
For it is neither horn—nor British.

Some call it—to increase this tangle—
The Cor Anglais—or horn with angle—
Concerning which I'm glad to state
The English Horn is long and straight.
Its misery and constant dwelling
On tragedy has caused a swelling
Just where the doleful note emerges;
Imbued with melancholy surges
This makes an English Horn cadenza
Sound fearfully like influenza.

                              LAURENCE McKINNEY

From "A Vigo-Street Eclogue"

The waits are whining in the cold
With clavicorn and clarigold;
They play them like a crumpled horn,
The clarigold and clavicorn.

                              SIR OWEN SEAMAN

To An Old Tenor

Melfort Dalton, I knew you well
With your frozen eyes and your spastic stance.
Ah, but your voice was clear as a bell
When you tenored the ladies into a trance;
The finest tenor in town you were,
Finest; but those were the days of yore,
Oh, but weren't you arrogant then,
Weren't you arrogant, Chanticleer,
When you told each hostess to go to hell:
"I'll sing what I like and I'll read the score"?
Little they knew; but I knew what you meant:
Yourself you first had to magnify
Before your notes unto Heaven were sent—
(Peacocks and tenors and G.P.I.)

I knew it, and that is the reason why
I now am recording the wonderful tale
Of how you received an offer to come,
Though your eyes and your legs were beginning to
    fail,
And sing at St. Joseph's Old Maids' Home,
And all the honors you gained therefrom.

We sat in the nearest respectable bar
Waiting the message of how you fared;
And, though we wished it, we were not for
Success overwhelming quite prepared.
Sitting we waited and tippled the ale;
In came the scout with the wonderful word
Of how they tittered and how you scored:
"Called back four times." And we roared, "Waes-hael!
Melfort has done it again, good Lord!"
We were not allowed in the Old Maids' Home;
And rightly so, for they might be scared;
But "Here, boy, here. Tell us all How Come?"
"He shuffled at first then he came to a stand.
He did not bow as a fav'rite should
(He knew that his balance was none too good)
But he stared with a visage inane and bland."
"But how did he merit such great applause?
Be more explicit, you poor recorder!"
"Once for singing, and thrice because
His dress revealed a quaint disorder."

Moral
(Non Nobis)

A moral lies in this occurrence:
Let those who have too much assurance
And think that public approbation
That comes from songs or an oration
Is due but to their own desert,
Remember Melfort Dalton's shirt.

OLIVER ST. JOHN GOGARTY

The Music Grinders

There are three ways in which men take
　　One's money from his purse,
And very hard it is to tell
　　Which of the three is worse;
But all of them are bad enough
　　To make a body curse.

You're riding out some pleasant day,
　　And counting up your gains;
A fellow jumps from out a bush,
　　And takes your horse's reins,
Another hints some words about
　　A bullet in your brains.

It's hard to meet such pressing friends
　　In such a lonely spot;
It's very hard to lose your cash,
　　But harder to be shot;
And so you take your wallet out,
　　Though you would rather not.

Perhaps you're going out to dine,—
　　Some odious creature begs
You'll hear about the cannon-ball
　　That carried off his pegs,
And says it is a dreadful thing
　　For men to lose their legs.

He tells you of his starving wife,
　　His children to be fed,
Poor little, lovely innocents,
　　All clamorous for bread,—
And so you kindly help to put
　　A bachelor to bed.

You're sitting on your window-seat,
　　Beneath a cloudless moon;

You hear a sound, that seems to wear
  The semblance of a tune,
As if a broken fife should strive
  To drown a cracked bassoon.

And nearer, nearer still, the tide
  Of music seems to come,
There's something like a human voice,
  And something like a drum;
You sit in speechless agony,
  Until your ear is numb.

Poor "home, sweet home" should seem to be
  A very dismal place;
Your "auld acquaintance" all at once
  Is altered in the face;
Their discords sting through Burns and Moore,
  Like hedgehogs dressed in lace.

You think they are crusaders, sent
  From some infernal clime,
To pluck the eyes of Sentiment,
  And dock the tail of Rhyme,
To crack the voice of Melody,
  And break the legs of Time.

But hark! the air again is still,
  The music all is ground,
And silence, like a poultice, comes
  To heal the blows of sound;
It cannot be,—it is,—it is,—
  A hat is going round!

No! Pay the dentist when he leaves
  A fracture in your jaw,
And pay the owner of the bear
  That stunned you with his paw,
And buy the lobster that has had
  Your knuckles in his claw;

But if you are a portly man,
  Put on your fiercest frown,
And talk about a constable
  To turn them out of town;
Then close your sentence with an oath,
  And shut the window down!

And if you are a slender man,
  Not big enough for that,
Or, if you cannot make a speech,
  Because you are a flat,
Go very quietly and drop
  A button in the hat!

OLIVER WENDELL HOLMES

To E. M. O.

Oakeley, whenas the bass you beat
  In that tremendous way,
I still could fancy at your feet
  A dreadful lion lay.
Askance he views the petulant scores,
But, when you touch a rib, he roars.

T. E. BROWN

Quatrain

A squeak's heard in the orchestra
  As the leader draws across
The intestines of the agile cat
  The tail of the noble hoss.

GEORGE T. LANIGAN

The Desired Swan-Song

Swans sing before they die—'twere no bad thing
Should certain persons die before they sing.

SAMUEL TAYLOR COLERIDGE

ONCE A-MAYING

I'm glad the sky is painted blue;
And the earth is painted green;
And such a lot of nice fresh air
All sandwiched in between.

ANONYMOUS

Where the verse, like a piper a-maying,
Comes playing—
And the rhyme is as gay as a dancer
In answer . . .

AUSTIN DOBSON

Corinna Goes a-Singing

(With Grace-Notes)

Spring

The year's at the spring, and the birds do sing
  'Hey ding-a-ding-ding' all choric,
And lover and lass through green corn pass,
  As of yore in the shire of Warwick:
Now under the trees (as Masefield sees)
  'The delicate deer troop shy-eyed,'
And 'half of the world a bridegroom is,
  And half' (says Watson) 'a bri-ide.'

Summer

Rising at five our farmers thrive
  Mens sana in corpore sano,
And the glebe new-tilled is drilled and filled
  With best Peruvian guano:
O'er pastures new in a mantle of blue
  The poet galumpheth free-heeled,
And Summer is i-comen, and bees are a-hummin',
  All over the clovery fie-ield.

Autumn

Now the harvest moon is plenilune,
  And hares retire at the double,
And close-time ends for Our Feathered Friends,
  And spaniels point in the stubble:
Under the star spins the brown eve-jar,
  And the moping owl 'tu-whoo' hoots,
And the poet asks Why, when the grass is dry,
  You walk through the fields in boo-oots?

Winter

When sponges freeze at thirty degrees,
  And the skater resembles Ole Bill,
The forespent plumber has dreams of summer
  And family men of the coal-bill:
Now poor Robin comes to look for crumbs,
  And even his bright eyes show woe;
And the chilblain numbs the housemaid's thumbs,
  For the stormy winds do blo-ow.

FRANK SIDGWICK

Lovers, and a Reflection

In moss-prankt dells which the sunbeams flatter
  (And heaven it knoweth what that may mean;
Meaning, however, is no great matter)
  Where woods are a-tremble, with rifts atween;

Thro' God's own heather we wonned together,
  I and my Willie (O love my love):
I need hardly remark it was glorious weather,
  And flitterbats wavered alow, above:

Boats were curtseying, rising, bowing,
  (Boats in that climate are so polite,)
And sands were a ribbon of green endowing,
  And O the sundazzle on bark and bight!

Thro' the rare red heather we danced together,
  (O love my Willie!) and smelt for flowers:
I must mention again it was gorgeous weather,
  Rhymes are so scarce in this world of ours:—

By rises that flushed with their purple favours,
  Thro' becks that brattled o'er grasses sheen,
We walked or waded, we two young shavers,
  Thanking our stars we were both so green.

We journeyed in parallels, I and Willie,
    In fortunate parallels! Butterflies,
Hid in weltering shadows of daffodilly
    Or marjoram, kept making peacock eyes:

Songbirds darted about, some inky
    As coal, some snowy (I ween) as curds;
Or rosy as pinks, or as roses pinky—
    They reck of no eerie To-come, those birds!

But they skim over bents which the millstream washes,
    Or hang in the lift 'neath a white cloud's hem;
They need no parasols, no goloshes;
    And good Mrs. Trimmer she feedeth them.

Then we thrid God's cowslips (as erst His heather)
    That endowed the wan grass with their golden
        blooms;
And snapt—(it was perfectly charming weather)—
    Our fingers at Fate and her goddess-glooms:

And Willie 'gan sing—(O, his notes were fluty;
    Wafts fluttered them out to the white-winged sea)—
Something made up of rhymes that have done much
        duty,
    Rhymes (better to put it) of 'ancientry':

Bowers of flowers encounted showers
    In William's carol—(O love my Willie!)
Then he bade sorrow borrow from blithe tomorrow
    I quite forget what—say a daffodilly:

A nest in a hollow, "with buds to follow,"
    I think occurred next in his nimble strain;
And clay that was "kneaden" of course in Eden—
    A rhyme most novel, I do maintain:

Mists, bones, the singer himself, love-stories,
    And all least furlable things got "furled";
Not with any design to conceal their glories,
    But simply and solely to rhyme with "world."

* * *

O if billows and pillows and hours and flowers,
    And all the brave rhymes of an elder day,
Could be furled together, this genial weather,
    And carted, or carried on wafts away,
Nor ever again trotted out—ay me!
How much fewer volumes of verse there'd be!

C. S. CALVERLEY

The Dick Johnson Reel

*(The old men say their grandfathers heard Dick
Johnson sing the chorus of this song in the timber-
lands of northern Summit County, Ohio.)*

Old Dick Johnson, gentleman, adventurer,
Braggart, minstrel, lover of a brawl,
Walked in the timber from Northfield to Hudson.
(Backward, forward and sashay all!)
Old Dick Johnson, joker and wanderer,
Poet, vagabond and beater of the track,
Sang a song of his bravery and prowess:
(Ladies go forward and gents go back!)

Chorus:

            Ripsi, rantsi,
            Humpsy, dumpsy;
            I, Dick Johnson,
            Killed Tecumseh!

Old Dick Johnson, fighter of the Indians,
Sang from Boston to the hills of Bath;
Sang the song of his muscle and his musket.
(Swing your partners and leave a path!)
The redskin sleeps where the wheat is growing,
But old Dick Johnson's ghost is free,
And it sings all night from Richfield to Twinsburg:
(All hands 'round with a one-two-three!)

Chorus:

Ripsi, rantsi,
Humpsy, dumpsy;
I, Dick Johnson,
Killed Tecumseh!

JAKE FALSTAFF

When Daffodils Begin to Peer

When daffodils begin to peer,
　　With heigh! the doxy over the dale—
Why, then comes in the sweet o' the year,
　　For the red blood reigns in the winter's pale.

The white sheet bleaching on the hedge—
　　With heigh! the sweet birds, O, how they sing!
Doth set my pugging tooth on edge,
　　For a quart of ale is a dish for a king.

The lark, that tirra-lyra chants,—
　　With heigh! with heigh! the thrush and the jay—
Are summer songs for me and my aunts,
　　While we lie tumbling in the hay.

WILLIAM SHAKESPEARE

PARODIES AT PAR

Behind a cloud his mystic sense,
Deep hidden, who can spy?
Bright as the night when not a star
Is shining in the sky.

HARTLEY COLERIDGE

If Gray Had Had to Write His Elegy in the Cemetery of Spoon River Instead of in That of Stoke Poges

The curfew tolls the knell of parting day,
  The whippoorwill salutes the rising moon,
And wanly glimmer in her gentle ray,
  The sinuous windings of the turbid Spoon.

Here where the flattering and mendacious swarm
  Of lying epitaphs their secrets keep,
At last incapable of further harm
  The lewd forefathers of the village sleep.

The earliest drug of half-awakened morn,
  Cocaine or hashish, strychnine; poppy-seeds
Or fiery produce of fermented corn
  No more shall start them on the day's misdeeds.

For them no more the whetstone's cheerful noise,
  No more the sun upon his daily course
Shall watch them savouring the genial joys,
  Of murder, bigamy, arson and divorce.

Here they all lie; and, as the hour is late,
  O stranger, o'er their tombstones cease to stoop,
But bow thine ear to me and contemplate
  The unexpurgated annals of the group.

There are two hundred only: yet of these
  Some thirty died of drowning in the river,
Sixteen went mad, ten others had D. T.'s,
  And twenty-eight cirrhosis of the liver.

Several by absent-minded friends were shot,
  Still more blew out their own exhausted brains,
One died of a mysterious inward rot,
  Three fell off roofs, and five were hit by trains.

One was harpooned, one gored by a bull-moose,
  Four on the Fourth fell victims to lock-jaw,
Ten in electric chair or hempen noose
  Suffered the last exaction of the law.

Stranger, you quail, and seem inclined to run;
  But, timid stranger, do not be unnerved;
I can assure you that there was not one
  Who got a tithe of what he had deserved.

Full many a vice is born to thrive unseen,
  Full many a crime the world does not discuss,
Full many a pervert lives to reach a green
  Replete old age, and so it was with us.

Here lies a parson who would often make
  Clandestine rendezvous with Claflin's Moll,
And 'neath the druggist's counter creep to take
  A sip of surreptitious alcohol.

And here a doctor, who had seven wives,
  And, fearing this *ménage* might seem grotesque,
Persuaded six of them to spend their lives
  Locked in a drawer of his private desk.

And others here there sleep who, given scope,
  Had writ their names large on the Scrolls of Crime,
Men who, with half a chance, might haply cope,
  With the first miscreants of recorded time.

Doubtless in this neglected spot is laid
  Some village Nero who has missed his due,
Some Bluebeard who dissected many a maid,
  And all for naught, since no one ever knew.

Some poor bucolic Borgia here may rest
  Whose poisons sent whole families to their doom,
Some hayseed Herod who, within his breast,
  Concealed the sites of many an infant's tomb.

Types that the Muse of Masefield might have stirred,
　　Or waked to ecstasy Gaboriau,
Each in his narrow cell at last interred,
　　All, all are sleeping peacefully below.

*　　　　*　　　　*　　　　*

Enough, enough! But, stranger, ere we part,
　　Glancing farewell to each nefarious bier,
This warning I would beg you to take to heart,
　　"There is an end to even the worst career!"

SIR J. C. SQUIRE

Listen, Pigeon, Bend an Ear

Listen, Pigeon, bend an ear
To the midnight ride of Paul Revere,
The only dude who was then alive
Who could cut a rug to the down beat jive!

The very first man in Boston town
Who got in the groove and rode on down!
He cracked to his pal, "If the redcoats blitz
I'll be down at the jukery, 'Rudy's Ritz.'
A light in the steeple will signal me,
One if by land, two if by sea."

He goes to the jukery to watch and wait
And cut a rug with a solid gate!
He snatches a quail with hep and class
And they go to town cooking with gas!

He ganders two glims up in the steeple!
"The redcoats are coming," he yells to the people,
Then he and his pigeon swing out in the street
Not missing a step or skipping a beat!

They spread the alarm both near and far
Yelling, "Solid Jackson eight to the bar!"

At Medford Bridge they switch their tune;
Like Frank Swoonatra they start to croon!

Windows fly up! heads fly out!
Corny citizens start to shout,
"Shut up!" "Cut it out!" "Let people sleep!"
"We'll call the cops!" "Go home, you creep!"
"The redcoats are coming," he croons,
"In their boats!"
"Lambsy divey and doazy doats!"

The nation was saved and is still alive
Just because Paul was hep to the jive!

H. W. HAENIGSEN

Autolycus' Song

Jog on, jog on the footpath way,
    And merrily hent[1] the stile-a.
A merry heart goes all the day,
    Your sad tires in a mile-a.

WILLIAM SHAKESPEARE

Autolycus' Song

(In Basic English)

Run on, run on, in a way causing shaking motion on
    the sidewalk
And in a bright way take a grip of the steps so placed
    that persons but not animals may get over or
    through-a;
A happy heart goes all the day,
Your unhappy becomes in need of rest in 5,280 feet-a.

RICHARD L. GREENE

---

[1] take.

Sing a Song of Sixpence

(Chaucerian)

Lordinges, I wol you singen of a grotë,
And of a pouche of reye also by rotë,
And eek of tweyë doseyn birdës blakë,
That weren in a pastee wel y-bakë:
So sonë thilkë pastee corven was,
Tho foulës al gan singen in that cas:
Me thinketh this so delicat it is;
A! kingës mowen ete of it, ywis!

The kingë to his countour-hous is goon,
To rekene of his penyes everichoon;
With-in hir propre bour the quenë setë,
Of breed with hony spraddë for to etë:
And in the gardin was the lavender [1] fresshë;
Ther-in she hangeth clothës newe y-wesshë,
Til sodeynly doun fleigh a papejay,
And plukked of hir nosë, weylaway!

FRANK SIDGWICK

1905

A. E. Housman and a Few Friends

When lads have done with labour
   in Shropshire, one will cry,
"Let's go and kill a neighbour,"
   and t'other answers "Aye!"

So this one kills his cousins,
   and that one kills his dad;
and, as they hang by dozens
   at Ludlow, lad by lad,

[1] Lavender is dissyllabic = 'laundress.'

each of them one-and-twenty,
  all of them murderers,
the hangman mutters: "Plenty
  even for Housman's verse."
                    HUMBERT WOLFE

Song of the Open Road

I think that I shall never see
A billboard lovely as a tree.
Indeed, unless the billboards fall
I'll never see a tree at all.
                    OGDEN NASH

To What Base Uses!

"Mrs. O—— now takes her daily dip at 5 in the
afternoon, instead of in the morning."
                    —*Newport Item*

This is the forest primeval.

This the spruce with the glorious plume
That grew in the forest primeval.

This is the lumberman big and browned
Who felled the spruce tree to the ground
That grew in the forest primeval.

This is the man with the paper mill
Who bought the pulp that paid the bill
Of the husky lumberjack who chopped
The lofty spruce and its branches lopped
That grew in the forest primeval.

This is the publisher bland and rich
Who bought the roll of paper which
Was made by the man with the paper mill
Who bought the pulp that paid the bill

Of the lumberjack with the murderous ax
Who felled the spruce with lusty hacks
That grew in the forest primeval.

This is the youth with the writing tool
Who does the daily Newport drool
That helps to make the publisher rich
Who ordered the stock of paper which
Was made by the man with the paper mill
Who bought the pulp that paid the bill
Of the husky Swede in the Joseph's coat
Who swung his ax and the tall spruce smote
That grew in the forest primeval.

This is the lady far from slim
Who changed the hour of her daily swim
And excited the youth with the writing tool
Who does the Newport drivel and drool
For the prosperous publisher bland and fat
Who ordered the virgin paper that
Was made by the man with the paper mill
Who bought the pulp that paid the bill
Of Ole Oleson the husky Swede
Who did a foul and darksome deed
When he swung his ax with vigor and vim
And smote the spruce tree tall and trim
That grew in the forest primeval.

This is the shop girl Mag or Liz
Who daily devours what news there is
Concerning the lady far from slim
Who changed the time of her ocean swim
And excited the youth with the writing tool
Who does the daily Newport drool
For the pursy publisher bland and rich
Who bought the innocent paper which
Was made by the man with the paper mill
Who bought the pulp that paid the bill

Of the Swedish jack who slew the spruce
That came to a most ignoble use—
The lofty spruce with the glorious plume—
The giant spruce that used to loom
In the heart of the forest primeval.

BERT LESTON TAYLOR

How Doth the Little Crocodile

How doth the little crocodile
   Improve his shining tail,
And pour the waters of the Nile
   On every golden scale!

How cheerfully he seems to grin,
   How neatly spreads his claws,
And welcomes little fishes in
   With gently smiling jaws!

LEWIS CARROLL

Ode to Himself

In the Manner of Robert Browning on the Occasion of the Author's Marriage

Licences? Yes. Poetic Licence,
   And Marriage Licences for the nonce,
And banns for whoso refuses my sense,
   And the click of the tomahawk on his sconce.

Marriage? By all means. And marriage banquets?
   Better and better. You catch my drift?
Put case you marry a wife: your lank wits
   And sober sages thrive ill on thrift.

From the celibate ranks if a colleague rat, you
    Regale him richly, as is most just,
While those who prefer to remain *in statu*
    Are not forbidden to share the bust.

O the overpotency of the muchness
    Of what men call marriage, and I call—what?
Nothing, be sure, that involves the suchness
    Of things that, being so, yet are not.

But I catch at a thought as it twinkles past me;
    So a boy flings cap at a butterfly,
And I pin it out in a poem to last me;
    He falls atop, crushes it; so not I.

Hands round! my friends, 'twere a thousand pities
    If you missed the point, as I'll stand bail
You mostly do in my lucid ditties.
    But how to avoid it?—accept a tale.

In the days of the Spanish Inquisition
    A certain Señor of ancient name
Enjoyed the responsible position
    Of sending victims to rack or flame.

One morning up gets my Don to his duty;
    "Heigh ho!" he yawned, "shall I boil or bake?"
Then they brought some maids of dazzling beauty
    Whose heresy had deserved the stake.

The dullest of men as well as the wittiest
    May find in St. Paul what serves his turn;
So "This one at least"—(and he picked the prettiest)
    "It is better to marry," says he, "than burn."

But he shortly found he had caught a Tartar,
    And his wife, ill-pleased to forgo her rights,
Enacted the rôle of Christian martyr
    For a brilliant run of ten thousand nights.

Who runs may read: you remark the moral?
   It's a thankless business your soul to vex
On behalf of persons who have no quarrel
   With the halter that hangs about their necks.

For benevolent schemes come oft to a deadlock,
   And well-meant overtures earn you frowning,
Whether one more bachelor's saved from wedlock,
   Or one more heretic's saved from browning.

Though the clan Mackay enlarge with rapture
   On the vanished glories of bygone years,
When marriage of souls was marriage by capture;
   Though Kuno contribute his crocodile tears;

Yet marry come up! And marry, the rest of you!
   For it still shall be as it still has been,
So I chant the nuptial hymn with the best of you,
   And I bang my head with my tambourine.

SIR WALTER RALEIGH

Einstein Among the Coffee-Cups
By T. S. Eli-t

Deflective rhythm under seas
   Where Sappho tuned the snarling air;
A shifting of the spectral lines
   Grown red with gravity and wear.

New systems of coördinates
   Disturb the Sunday table-cloth.
Celestine yawns. Sir Oliver
   Hints of the jaguar and sloth.

A chord of the eleventh shrieks
   And slips beyond the portico.
The night contracts. A warp in space
   Has rumors of Correggio.

Lights. Mrs. Blumenthal expands;
   Calories beyond control.
The rector brightens. Tea is served:
   Euclid supplanted by the sole.

LOUIS UNTERMEYER

Ballad

The auld wife sat at her ivied door,
   (Butter and eggs and a pound of cheese)
A thing she had frequently done before;
   And her spectacles lay on her aproned knees.

The piper he piped on the hill-top high,
   (Butter and eggs and a pound of cheese)
Till the cow said "I die," and the goose asked "Why?"
   And the dog said nothing, but searched for fleas.

The farmer he strode through the square farmyard;
   (Butter and eggs and a pound of cheese)
His last brew of ale was a trifle hard—
   The connexion of which with the plot one sees.

The farmer's daughter hath frank blue eyes;
   (Butter and eggs and a pound of cheese)
She hears the rooks caw in the windy skies,
   As she sits at her lattice and shells her peas.

The farmer's daughter hath ripe red lips;
   (Butter and eggs and a pound of cheese)
If you try to approach her, away she skips
   Over tables and chairs with apparent ease.

The farmer's daughter hath soft brown hair;
   (Butter and eggs and a pound of cheese)
And I met with a ballad, I can't say where,
   Which wholly consisted of lines like these.

Part II

She sat with her hands 'neath her dimpled cheeks,
  (Butter and eggs and a pound of cheese)
And spake not a word. While a lady speaks
  There is hope, but she didn't even sneeze.

She sat, with her hands 'neath her crimson cheeks;
  (Butter and eggs and a pound of cheese)
She gave up mending her father's breeks,
  And let the cat roll in her best chemise.

She sat, with her hands 'neath her burning cheeks,
  (Butter and eggs and a pound of cheese)
And gazed at the piper for thirteen weeks;
  Then she followed him out o'er the misty leas.

Her sheep followed her, as their tails did them.
  (Butter and eggs and a pound of cheese)
And this song is considered a perfect gem,
  And as to the meaning, it's what you please.
                                    C. S. CALVERLEY

You Are Old, Father William

"You are old, Father William," the young man said,
  "And your hair has become very white;
And yet you incessantly stand on your head—
  Do you think, at your age, it is right?"

"In my youth," Father William replied to his son,
  "I feared it might injure the brain;
But now that I'm perfectly sure I have none,
  Why, I do it again and again."

"You are old," said the youth, "as I mentioned before,
  And have grown most uncommonly fat;
Yet you turned a back-somersault in at the door—
  Pray, what is the reason of that?"

"In my youth," said the sage, as he shook his grey
    locks,
  "I kept all my limbs very supple
By the use of this ointment—one shilling the box—
  Allow me to sell you a couple?"

"You are old," said the youth, "and your jaws are too
    weak
  For anything tougher than suet;
Yet you finished the goose, with the bones and the
    beak—
  Pray, how did you manage to do it?"

"In my youth," said his father, "I took to the law,
  And argued each case with my wife;
And the muscular strength, which it gave to my jaw,
  Has lasted the rest of my life."

"You are old," said the youth, "one would hardly
    suppose
  That your eye was as steady as ever;
Yet you balanced an eel on the end of your nose—
  What made you so awfully clever?"

"I have answered three questions, and that is enough,"
  Said his father; "don't give yourself airs!
Do you think I can listen all day to such stuff?
  Be off, or I'll kick you down stairs!"

LEWIS CARROLL

Twinkle, Twinkle, Little Bat!

Twinkle, twinkle, little bat!
How I wonder what you're at?
Up above the world you fly,
Like a tea-tray in the sky.

LEWIS CARROLL

Song to Imogen

(In Basic English)

Listen, listen! The small song bird at the doorway of
  God's living place makes a whistling sound on a
  high note,
And Phoebus makes a start at getting up,
To give water to his horses at those waters coming up
  from the earth
That have the body stretched out parallel with the
  earth.
And Mary-buds getting their eyes open and shut
  quickly make a start at getting their gold eyes
  open.
With every thing that is good looking in a soft way
My sweet respected woman, get up!

RICHARD L. GREENE

An Ode to Spring in the Metropolis

(After R. Le G.)

Is this the Seine?
And am I altogether wrong
About the brain,
Dreaming I hear the British tongue?
Dear Heaven! what a rhyme!
And yet 'tis all as good
As some that I have fashioned in my time,
Like *bud* and *wood;*
And on the other hand you couldn't have a more pre-
  cise or neater
Metre.

Is this, I ask, the Seine?
And yonder sylvan lane,

Is it the *Bois?*
Ma foi!
Comme elle est chic, my Paris, my grisette!
Yet may I not forget
That London still remains the missus
Of this Narcissus.

No, no! 'tis not the Seine!
It is the artificial mere
That permeates St. James's Park.
The air is bosom-shaped and clear;
And, Himmel! do I hear the lark,
The good old Shelley-Wordsworth lark?
Even now, I prithee,
Hark
Him hammer
On Heaven's harmonious stithy,
Dew-drunken—like my grammar!

And O the trees!
Beneath their shade the hairless coot
Waddles at ease,
Hushing the magic of his gurgling beak;
Or haply in Tree-worship leans his cheek
Against their blind
And hoary rind,
Observing how the sap
Comes humming upwards from the tap-
Root!
Thrice happy, hairless coot!

And O the sun!
See, see, he shakes
His big red hands at me in wanton fun!
A glorious image that! it might be Blake's,
Or even Crackanthorpe's!
For though the latter writes in prose
He actually is a bard;

Yet Heaven knows
I find it passing hard
To think of any rhyme but *corpse*
For 'Crackanthorpe's.'

And O the stars! I cannot say
I see a star just now,
Not at this time of day;
But anyhow
The stars are all my brothers;
(This verse is shorter than the others).

O Constitution Hill!
(This verse is shorter still).

Ah! London, London in the Spring!
You are, you know you are,
So full of curious sights,
Especially by nights.
From gilded bar to gilded bar
Youth goes his giddy whirl,
His heart fulfilled of Music-Hall,
His arm fulfilled of girl!
I frankly call
That last effect a perfect pearl!

I know it's
Not given to many poets
To frame so fair a thing
As this of mine, of Spring.
Indeed, the world grows Lilliput
All but
A precious few, the heirs of utter godlihead,
Who wear the yellow flower of blameless bodlihead!

And they, with Laureates dead, look down
On smaller fry unworthy of the crown,
Mere mushroom men, puff-balls that advertise
And bravely think to brush the skies.

Great is advertisement with little men!
Moi, qui vous parle, L- G-ll-nn-,
Have told them so;
I ought know!

SIR OWEN SEAMAN

The Modern Nursery

I
W. H. Davies Simplifies the Simplicities He Loves

Earth does not lack
  Things beautiful;
The sheep, though **black**,
  Will give us wool.
The bird has wings,
  The child a toy—
Such little things
  Do give me joy.

The tree has leaves,
  The road has miles,
And nothing grieves
  Whene'er it smiles.
The crops have sun;
  The streams close by
Do ramble on,
  And so do I.

And happy then
  My lot shall be
While rook and wren
  Build in the tree;
While ring-doves coo,
  And lions roar,
As long as two
  And two are four.

II

Edgar A. Guest Considers "The Old Woman Who Lived in a Shoe" and the Good Old Verities at the Same Time

It takes a heap o' children to make a home that's true,
And home can be a palace grand or just a plain, old shoe;
But if it has a mother dear and a good old dad or two,
Why, that's the sort of good old home for good old me and you.

Of all the institutions this side the Vale of Rest
Howe'er it be it seems to me a good old mother's best;
And fathers are a blessing, too, they give the place a tone;
In fact each child should try and have some parents of his own.

The food can be quite simple; just a sop of milk and bread
Are plenty when the kiddies know it's time to go to bed.
And every little sleepy-head will dream about the day
When he can go to work because a Man's Work is his Play.

And, oh, how sweet his life will seem, with nought to make him cross,
And he will never watch the clock and always mind the boss.
And when he thinks (as may occur), this thought will please him best:
That ninety million think the same—including
                                          Eddie Guest.
                                          LOUIS UNTERMEYER

Mrs. Judge Jenkins

Being the only genuine sequel to *Maud Muller*

(Whittier)

Maud Muller all that summer day
Raked the meadows sweet with hay;

Yet, looking down the distant lane,
She hoped the Judge would come again.

But when he came, with smile and bow,
Maud only blushed, and stammered, "Ha-ow?"

And spoke of her "pa," and wondered whether
He'd give consent they should wed together.

Old Muller burst in tears, and then
Begged that the Judge would lend him "ten";

For trade was dull, and wages low,
And the "craps," this year, were somewhat slow.

And ere the languid summer died,
Sweet Maud became the Judge's bride.

But on the day that they were mated,
Maud's brother Bob was intoxicated;

And Maud's relations, twelve in all,
Were very drunk at the Judge's hall.

And when the summer came again,
The young bride bore him babies twain;

And the Judge was blest, but thought it strange
That bearing children made such a change;

For Maud grew broad and red and stout,
And the waist that his arm once clasped about

Was more than he now could span; and he
Sighed as he pondered, ruefully,

How that which in Maud was native grace
In Mrs. Jenkins was out of place;

And thought of the twins, and wished that they
Looked less like the men who raked the hay

On Muller's farm, and dreamed with pain
Of the day he wandered down the lane.

And, looking down that dreary track,
He half regretted that he came back;

For, had he waited, he might have wed
Some maiden fair and thoroughbred;

For there be women fair as she,
Whose verbs and nouns do more agree.

Alas for maiden! alas for judge!
And the sentimental,—that's one-half "fudge";

For Maud soon thought the Judge a bore,
With all his learning and all his lore;

And the Judge would have bartered Maud's fair face
For more refinement and social grace.

If, of all words of tongue and pen,
The saddest are, "It might have been,"

More sad are these we daily see:
"It is, but hadn't ought to be."

BRET HARTE

In Memory of Edward Wilson

Rigid Body (sings):

Gin a body meet a body
    Flyin' through the air,
Gin a body hit a body,
    Will it fly? and where?

Ilka impact has its measure,
   Ne'er a ane hae I,
Yet a' the lads they measure **me,**
   Or, at least, they try.

Gin a body meet a body
   Altogether free,
How they travel afterwards
   We do not always see.
Ilka problem has its method
   By analytics high;
For me, I ken na ane o' them,
   But what the waur am I?

              JAMES CLERK MAXWELL

Round

By Alfr-d Kr-ymborg

Worlds, you must tell me—
What?
What is the answer to it all?
Matter.

Matter, answer me—
What?
What are the secrets of your **strength?**
Molecules.

Molecules, be honest—
What?
What may be groping at your **roots?**
Atoms.

Atoms, I ask you—
What?
What have you hidden in your **hearts?**
Electrons.

Electrons, I charge you—
What?
What are you building in your wombs?
Worlds.

Worlds, you must tell me——

LOUIS UNTERMEYER

Of W. W. (*Americanus*)

The clear cool note of the cuckoo which has ousted
    the legitimate nest-holder,
The whistle of the railway guard despatching the
    train to the inevitable collision,
The maiden's monosyllabic reply to a polysyllabic
    proposal,
The fundamental note of the last trump, which is
    presumably D natural;
All of these are sounds to rejoice in, yea to let your
    very ribs re-echo with:
But better than all of them is the absolutely last chord
    of the apparently inexhaustible pianoforte player.

J. K. STEPHEN

Breathes There a Man

Breathes there a man with hide so tough
Who says two sexes aren't enough?

SAMUEL HOFFENSTEIN

PHYSICIANS & METAPHYSICIANS

When I the least belief bestow
On what such fools advise,
May I be dull enough to grow
Most miserably wise.

CHARLES SACKVILLE, EARL OF DORSET

Man may escape from rope and gun,
Nay, some have outlived the doctor's pill . . .

JOHN GAY

And in his dim, uncertain sight
Whatever wasn't must be right,
From which it follows he had strong
Convictions that what was, was wrong.

GUY WETMORE CARRYL

Ode to a Dental Hygienist [1]

Hygienist, in your dental chair
I sit without a single care,
Except when tickled by your hair.
I know that when you grab the drills
I need not fear the pain that kills.
You merely make my molars clean
With pumice doped with wintergreen.
So I lean back in calm reflection,
With close-up views of your complexion,
And taste the flavor of your thumbs
While you massage my flabby gums.
To me no woman can be smarter
Than she who scales away my tartar,
And none more fitted for my bride
Than one who knows me from inside.
At least as far as she has gotten
She sees how much of me is rotten.

EARNEST A. HOOTON

Two Men

There be two men of all mankind
    That I should like to know about;
But search and question where I will,
    I cannot ever find them out.

Melchizedek, he praised the Lord,
    And gave some wine to Abraham;
But who can tell what else he did
    Must be more learned than I am.

Ucalegon, he lost his house
    When Agamemnon came to Troy;

[1] *Peroration of address to the graduating class of Dental Hygienists, given at the Forsyth Dental Infirmary, Boston, July, 1942.*

But who can tell me who he was—
   I'll pray the gods to give him joy.

There be two men of all mankind
   That I'm forever thinking on:
They chase me everywhere I go,—
   Melchizedek, Ucalegon.
             EDWIN ARLINGTON ROBINSON

On Oculists

"The oculist prescribes me spectacles,"
   He says; "I hope the advice is sound." I think
A man as well might visit the Six Bells
   And ask mine host if throat should have a drink.
             SIR J. C. SQUIRE

Two Heads Are Better Than One

See, one physician, like a sculler, plies,
The patient lingers and by inches dies.
But two physicians, like a pair of oars,
Waft him more swiftly to the Stygian shores.
             JOSEPH JEKYLL

The Question Mark

Behold the wicked little barb
   Which catches fish in human garb
And yanks them back when they feel gay
   With "Will it last?" or "Does it pay?"

It fastens neatly in the gills
   Of those who have uncertain wills,
But even wily eels are caught
   Upon this bent pin of a thought.
             PERSIS GREELY ANDERSON

Case History

Omar is X-Rayed

Myself grown old do fearfully frequent
Grim hospitals and hear great argument
About me, but with luck have heretofore
Come out by the same door wherein I went.

ARTHUR W. BELL

Pocket and Steeple

The watch that near my midriff ticks
May run too fast, or run too slow,
Or even play rebellious tricks
And cease on any terms to go.
Yet will that old automaton,
The world at large, roll blandly on.

But let one public clock enact
Such tantrums, like a wayward wench,
The thing becomes—to be exact—
A shame, a hissing, and a stench.
There is no theme for soothing song
In public clocks—or men—gone wrong!

M. A. DEWOLFE HOWE

The Riddle

He told himself and he told his wife,
His boy and his dog the Facts of Life.
Guess who'd known them all along;
Guess who'd found them in a song;
Guess who knew he'd got them wrong.

RALPH HODGSON

I Do Not Love Thee, Doctor Fell

I do not love thee, Doctor Fell,
The reason why I cannot tell;
But this alone I know full well,
I do not love thee, Doctor Fell.

THOMAS BROWN

Medical Aid

Doctor Bottom was preparing to leave
After a visit to the Sykes farm.
Sid Sykes was down with a cold and fever.
The Doctor wasn't sure just what
It might develop into,
So he instructed Mrs. Sykes to keep a close watch.
Since the farm was five miles from the village
He didn't want to come again that day.
He gave Mrs. Sykes a clinical thermometer
And told her to take Sid's temperature
Toward night, and then, if it showed a rise,
To call him on the party wire.
—*If I don't hear from you, Mis' Sykes,*
I'll come up in the morning.

Mrs. Sykes had never seen any thermometer
Except the faded one that hung
Outside the kitchen door.
It had taken her some time to understand
The Doctor's explanation,
And even then she was uncertain.

The next morning, after his village calls,
The Doctor drove out to the Sykes farm.
Having heard nothing he supposed all was well.
The door into the bedroom was open

And as the Doctor came into the sitting room
He could see that the bed was empty.
It was made up all fresh and smooth
And there was no sign of Sid or of anyone else.
Bewildered, he crossed the sitting room
And went into the kitchen.
There he heard the regular swish of a washing machine
And the uneven puff of the gasoline engine.

—*Wall, as I was sayin'!* Mrs. Sykes leaned against the
     tub,
—*I ketched m'foot and dropped that glass tube.*
Then I WAS in a pickle.
Then I recollected that round thing with a face on it
That them city boarders gave Sid.
It hed a tube like the one you gave me
Only I couldn't get the whole thing
Into Sid's mouth.
She wiped her face with her apron and went on.
—*So I laid it onto Sid's chest.*
'Twa'n't long afore that hand pinted t' "Very Dry."
I went down cellar and fetched up a pi'cher o' cider
And gave it t' Sid.
She waved her hand toward the meadow.
—*And he's out there mowin' now.*

WALTER HARD

To the Terrestrial Globe

by a Miserable Wretch

Roll on, thou ball, roll on!
Through pathless realms of Space
     Roll on!
What though I'm in a sorry case?
What though I cannot meet my bills?
What though I suffer toothache's ills?

What though I swallow countless pills?
   Never *you* mind!
      Roll on!

Roll on, thou ball, roll on!
Through seas of inky air
   Roll on!
It's true I have no shirts to wear;
It's true my butcher's bill is due;
It's true my prospects all look blue—
But don't let that unsettle you:
   Never *you* mind!
      Roll on!

         [*It rolls on.*]
        SIR W. S. GILBERT

Psychoanalysts

The Old Mandarin was always pleased
When in his philosophical reading
He encountered the names of Deep Thinkers.
What an excellent name for a psychoanalyst
Is Schrenk-Notzing
For truly
They shrink from nothing.

        CHRISTOPHER MORLEY

Convalescence

I. The Nurses

The not-too-near slip softly by
Until I close a practice eye,
And then with instinct known as mother
They try to help me close the other.

II. The Fever Chart

Like Plimsoll lines on British hulls
My chart of temperature and pulse
Hangs from the bed, shows what I drink
And how much farther I can sink.

III. The Bed

My bed will fold up where I fold,
And arch its back, if all be told.
Providing angles as I choose,
My profiles run to "W's."

IV. The Visitors

The nurse looks round my clinic screen:
It's Mr. Jones or Mrs. Green.
Somehow my social self recurs;
I speak from strange interiors.

V. The Flowers

In slow recuperative hours
I cede the function of the flowers.
O keep them cold and crowd them in;
Reward them all with aspirin.

VI. The Letters

Letters are comforting to get.
Yes, I regret what they regret.
And I re-greet my dear regretters,
Livelier for Life & Letters.

VII. The Sneeze

I recommend for plain dis-ease
A good post-operandum sneeze;
You might as well be on the rack
When every stitch takes up its slack.

VIII. The Books

The books I have are made of lead—
They flatten me upon the bed.
A telegram is hard to hold:
Go easy on the Realms of Gold!

DAVID McCORD

Charity in Thought

To praise men as good, and to take them for such,
   Is a grace, which no soul can mete out to a tittle;—
Of which he who has not a little too much,
   Will by Charity's gage surely have much too little.

SAMUEL TAYLOR COLERIDGE

ROMANCE

Cats like milk,
And dogs like broo,
Lads like lasses weel,
And lasses lads too.

ROBERT BURNS

There is a love of the mind
That holds, never loosens,
More sweet than the bodily kind
And much less of a nuisance.

E. V. KNOX

Lady Jane

Sapphics

Down the green hill-side fro' the castle window
Lady Jane spied Bill Amaranth a-workin';
Day by day watched him go about his ample
        Nursery garden.

Cabbages thriv'd there, wi' a mort o' green-stuff—
Kidney beans, broad beans, onions, tomatoes,
Artichokes, seakale, vegetable marrows,
        Early potatoes.

Lady Jane cared not very much for all these:
What she cared much for was a glimpse o' Willum
Strippin' his brown arms wi' a view to horti-
        -Cultural effort.

Little guessed Willum, never extra-vain, that
Up the green hill-side, i' the gloomy castle,
Feminine eyes could so delight to view his
        Noble proportions.

Only one day while, in an innocent mood,
Moppin' his brow ('cos 'twas a trifle sweaty)
With a blue kerchief—lo, he spies a white 'un
        Coyly responding.

Oh, delightsome Love! Not a jot do *you* care
For the restrictions set on human inter-
-course by cold-blooded social refiners;
        Nor do I, neither.

Day by day, peepin' fro' behind the bean-sticks,
Willum observed that scrap o' white a-wavin',
Till his hot sighs out-growin' all repression
        Busted his weskit.

Lady Jane's guardian was a haughty Peer, who
Clung to old creeds and had a nasty temper;
Can we blame Willum that he hardly cared to
                    Risk a refusal?

Year by year found him busy 'mid the bean-sticks,
Wholly uncertain how on earth to take steps.
Thus for eighteen years he beheld the maiden
                    Wave fro' her window.

But the nineteenth spring, i' the Castle post-bag,
Came by book-post Bill's catalogue o' seedlings
Mark'd wi' blue ink at 'Paragraphs relatin'
                    Mainly to Pumpkins.'

'W. A. can,' so the Lady Jane read,
'Strongly commend that very noble Gourd, the
Lady Jane, first-class medal, ornamental;
                    Grows to a great height.'

Scarce a year arter, by the scented hedgerows—
Down the mown hill-side, fro' the castle gateway—
Came a long train and, i' the midst, a black bier,
                    Easily shouldered.

'Whose is yon corse that, thus adorned wi' gourd-leaves,
Forth ye bear with slow step?' A mourner answer'd,
' 'Tis the poor clay-cold body Lady Jane grew
                    Tired to abide in.'

'Delve my grave quick, then, for I die to-morrow.
Delve it one furlong fro' the kidney bean-sticks,
Where I may dream she's goin' on precisely
                    As she was used to.'

Hardly died Bill when, fro' the Lady Jane's grave,
Crept to his white death-bed a lovely pumpkin:
Climb'd the house wall and over-arched his head wi'
                    Billowy verdure.

Simple this tale!—but delicately perfumed
As the sweet roadside honeysuckle. That's why,
Difficult though its metre was to tackle,
           I'm glad I wrote it.

                SIR ARTHUR QUILLER-COUCH

'Twas at the Pictures, Child, We Met

'Twas at the pictures, child, we met,
  Your father and your mother;
The drama's name I now forget,
  But it was like another.

The Viscount had too much to drink,
  And so his plot miscarried,
And at the end I rather think
  Two citizens were married.

But at the opening of the play,
  By Fortune's wise design—
It was an accident, I say—
  A little hand met mine.

My fingers round that little hand
  Unconsciously were twisted;
I do not say that it was planned,
  But it was not resisted.

I held the hand. The hand was hot.
  I could not see her face;
But in the dark I gazed at what
  I took to be the place.

From shock to shock, from sin to sin
  The fatal film proceeded;
I cannot say I drank it in,
  I rather doubt if she did.

In vain did pure domestics flout
  The base but high-born brute;
Their honour might be up the spout,
  We did not care a hoot.

For, while those clammy palms we clutched,
  By stealthy slow degrees
We moved an inch or two and touched
  Each other with our knees.

No poet makes a special point
  Of any human knee,
But in that plain prosaic joint
  Was high romance for me.

Thus hand in hand and toe to toe,
  Reel after reel we sat;
You are not old enough to know
  The ecstasy of that.

A touch of cramp about the shins
  Was all that troubled me;
Your mother tells me she had pins
  And needles in the knee.

But our twin spirits rose above
  Mere bodily distress;
And if you ask me "Is this Love?"
  The answer, child, is "Yes."

And when the film was finished quite
  It made my bosom swell
To find that by electric light
  I loved her just as well.

For women, son, are seldom quite
  As worthy of remark
Beneath a strong electric light
  As they are in the dark.

But this was not the present case,
   And it was joy to see
A form as fetching and a face
   Magnetic as her knee.

And still twice weekly we enjoy
   The pictures, grave and gross;
We don't hold hands so much, my boy,
   Our knees are not so close;

But now and then, for Auld Lang Syne,
   Or frenzied by the play,
Your mother slips her hand in mine,
   To my intense dismay;

And then, though at my time of life
   It seems a trifle odd,
I move my knee and give my wife
   A sentimental prod.

Well, such is Love and such is Fate,
   And such is Marriage too;
And such will happen, soon or late,
   Unhappy youth, to you.

And, though most learned men have strained
   To work the matter out,
No mortal man has yet explained
   What it is all about.

And I don't know why mortals try;
   But if with vulgar chaff
You hear some Philistine decry
   The cinematograph,

Think then, my son, of your papa,
   And take the kindly view,
For had there been no cinema
   There might have been no you.

SIR A. P. HERBERT

Mournful Numbers

Where in the attic the dust encumbers
  Days that are gone,
I found a paper with telephone numbers
  Scribbled thereon.

Again I feel the tremendous wallop
  It gave to me
When I had a valid excuse to call up
  1503.

Again I feel the excuses springing,
  Just as of yore,
When I could no longer refrain from ringing
  9944.

Again I feel my old heart prickle
  As in my youth,
When I left the house to deposit a nickel
  In a sound-proof booth;

And I hear again a phantasmal titter,
  As I would coo
Passionately to the dark transmitter:
  "2342!"

My heart awakes, as if roused from slumber
  By a telephone bell;
Quick! I will call again the number
  Once loved so well!

I breathe the syllables recollected:
  "2342!"
But Central answers: "Disconnected!"
  How true! How true!

MORRIS BISHOP

Prose and Poesy:
A Rural Misadventure

They roamed between
　Delicious dells,
He had sixteen
　Ecstatic spells.

He said: "Yon herds!
　Yon stretch of fence!
Yon frequent birds!
　Immense! Immense!

"Yon blossoms shy,
　Yon blazing sun,
Yon wondrous sky—
　A1—! A1—!

"My own, my sweet,
　Do you not glow
With bliss complete?"
　She answered "No!"

He stopped. He eyed
　Her in a trance.
He almost fried
　Her with his glance.

Then walked he East
　And walked she West,
His wrath increased
　As he progressed.

For who would wed
　With such a one
When all is said
　And all is done?

T. R. YBARRA

The Tides of Love

Flo was fond of Ebenezer—
  "Eb," for short, she called her beau.
Talk of Tides of Love, great Caesar!
  You should see them—Eb and Flo.

T. A. DALY

The Scandalous Tale of Percival and Genevieve

Percival Wilberforce Henderson Crane
Was married and dwelt up in Bethlehem, Maine.
He attended the church, and was fond of his wife,
And he lived a respectable, virtuous life.
Now Genevieve Marguerite Valois Valence
Resided at Rouen, a city in France.
Her husband she loved in a manner insane,
For she never had heard about Percival Crane.
Each morning when Percival left for the day
He would kiss his wife fondly, then start on his way,
And at no other woman would Percival glance,
For he never had heard about Madame Valence.
Now Percival dreamed that through France he would
    tour
With his wife and his kids; but, alas, he was poor,
For his salary was small; so poor Percival Crane
Was obliged to stay home up in Bethlehem, Maine.
While Genevieve dreamed of a trip to the States,
But, alas, all her plans were upset by the Fates,
For her husband was poor, so she hadn't a chance
To travel from Rouen, a city in France.
So Percival still goes his virtuous way—
To church every Sunday, to business each day.
And at no other woman will Percival glance,
For he's never met Genevieve Valois Valence.

While Genevieve still leads a virtuous life.
Her husband she loves like a dutiful wife.
And no doubt she'll continue that way to remain,
For she's never met Percival Wilberforce Crane.

NEWMAN LEVY

Emily, John, James, and I

A Derby Legend

Emily Jane was a nursery maid—
    James was a bold Life Guard,
And John was a constable, poorly paid
    (And I am a doggerel bard).

A very good girl was Emily Jane,
    Jimmy was good and true,
And John was a very good man in the main
    (And I am a good man, too).

Rivals for Emmie were Johnny and James,
    Though Emily liked them both;
She couldn't tell which had the strongest claims
    (And *I* couldn't take my oath).

But sooner or later you're certain to find
    Your sentiments can't lie hid—
Jane thought it was time that she made up her mind
    (And I think it was time she did).

Said Jane, with a smirk, and a blush on her face,
    "I'll promise to wed the boy
Who takes me to-morrow to Epsom Race!"
    (Which *I* would have done, with joy).

From Johnny escaped an expression of pain,
    But Jimmy said, "Done with you!
I'll take you with pleasure, my Emily Jane."
    (And I would have said so too).

John lay on the ground, and he roared like mad
    (For Johnny was sore perplexed),
And he kicked very hard at a very small lad
    (Which *I* often do, when vexed).

For John was on duty next day with the Force,
    To punish all Epsom crimes;
Some people *will* cross, when they're clearing the
      course
    (I do it myself, sometimes).

      *   *   *   *

The Derby Day sun glittered gaily on cads,
    On maidens with gamboge hair,
On sharpers and pickpockets, swindlers and pads
    (For I, with my harp, was there).

And Jimmy went down with his Jane that day,
    And John by the collar or nape
Seized everybody who came in his way
    (And *I* had a narrow escape).

He noticed his Emily Jane with Jim,
    And envied the well-made elf;
And people remarked that he muttered "Oh, dim!"
    (I often say "dim!" myself).

John dogged them all day, without asking their leaves:
    For his sergeant he told, aside,
That Jimmy and Jane were notorious thieves
    (And I think he was justified).

But James wouldn't dream of abstracting a fork,
    And Jenny would blush with shame
At stealing so much as a bottle or cork
    (A bottle I think fair game).

But, ah! there's another more serious crime!
    They wickedly strayed upon
The course, at a critical moment of time
    (I pointed them out to John).

The crusher came down on the pair in a crack—
　　And then, with a demon smile,
Let Jenny cross over, but sent Jimmy back
　　(I played on my harp the while).

Stern Johnny their agony loud derides
　　With a very triumphant sneer—
They weep and they wail from the opposite sides
　　(And *I* shed a silent tear).

And Jenny is crying away like mad,
　　And Jimmy is swearing hard;
And Johnny is looking uncommonly glad
　　(And I am a doggerel bard).

But Jimmy he ventured on crossing again
　　The scenes of our Isthmian Games—
John caught him, and collared him, giving him pain
　　(I felt very much for James).

John led him away with a victor's hand,
　　And Jimmy was shortly seen
In the station-house under the grand Grand Stand
　　(As many a time I've been).

And Jimmy, bad boy, was imprisoned for life,
　　Though Emily pleaded hard;
And Johnny had Emily Jane to wife
　　(And I am a doggerel bard).

SIR W. S. GILBERT

To Lillian Russell

(A reminiscence of 18—.)

Dear Lillian! (The "dear" one risks;
"Miss Russell" were a bit austerer)—
Do you remember Mr. Fiske's
　　Dramatic Mirror

Back when—? (But we'll not count the years;
The way they've sped is most surprising.)
You were a trifle in arrears
    For advertising.

I brought the bill to your address;
I was the *Mirror's* bill collector—
In Thespian haunts a more or less
    Familiar spectre.

On that (to me) momentous day
You dwelt amid the city's clatter,
A few doors west of old Broadway;
    The street—no matter.

But while you have forgot the debt,
And him who called in line of duty,
He never, never shall forget
    Your wondrous beauty.

You were too fair for mortal speech,—
Enchanting, positively rippin';
You were some dream, and quelque peach,
    And beaucoup pippin.

Your "fight with Time" had not begun,
Nor any reason to promote it;
No beauty battles to be won.
    Beauty? You wrote it!

"A bill?" you murmured in distress,
"A bill?" (I still can hear you say it.)
"A bill from Mr. Fiske? Oh, yes . . .
    I'll call and pay it."

And he, the thrice-requited kid,
That such a goddess should address him,
Could only blush and paw his lid,
    And stammer, "Yes'm!"

Eheu! It seems a cycle since,
But still the nerve of memory tingles.
And here you're writing Beauty Hints,
    And I these jingles.

BERT LESTON TAYLOR

The Brewer's Man

Have I a wife? Bedam I have!
    But we was badly mated:
I hit her a great clout one night,
    And now we're separated.

And mornin's, going to my work,
    I meets her on the quay:
'Good mornin' to ye, ma'am,' says I;
    'To hell with ye,' says she.

L. A. G. STRONG

The Crier

Good folk, for gold or hire,
    But help me to a crier;
For my poor heart is run astray
After two eyes, that passed this way.
    O yes, O yes, O yes,
    If there be any man,
    In town or country, can
    Bring me my heart again,
    I'll please him for his pain;
And by these marks I will you show
That only I this heart do owe.

    It is a wounded heart,
        Wherein yet sticks the dart,
    Every piece sore hurt throughout it,
    Faith and troth writ round about it:

It was a tame heart and a dear,
    And never used to roam;
But having got this haunt, I fear,
    'Twill hardly stay at home.
For God's sake, walking by the way,
    If you my heart do see,
Either impound it for a stray,
    Or send it back to me.

MICHAEL DRAYTON

♂ and ♀

The glabrous girl and hispid boy
Make all the roses dance with joy:
The hispid wench and glabrous youth
Make even roses seem uncouth.
So to your proper sexes flee:
Glabrosity, hispidity!

W. CRADDLE

Dear, They Have Poached the Eyes You Loved So Well——

The limbs that erstwhile charmed your sight
Are now a savage's delight;
The ear that heard your whispered vow
Is one of many *entrées* now;
Broiled are the arms in which you clung,
And devilled is the angelic tongue: . . .
And oh! my anguish as I see
A Black Man gnaw your favourite knee!
Of the two eyes that were your ruin,
One now observes the other stewing.
My lips (the inconstancy of man!)
Are yours no more. The legs that ran
Each dewy morn their love to wake,

Are now a steak, are now a steak! . . .
O love, O loveliest and best,
Natives this *body* may digest;
Whole, and still yours, my *soul* shall dwell,
Uneaten, safe, incoctible . . .

RUPERT BROOKE

The Age of Wisdom

Ho, pretty page, with the dimpled chin,
  That never has known the barber's shear,
All your wish is woman to win,
This is the way that boys begin,—
  Wait till you come to Forty Year.

Curly gold locks cover foolish brains,
  Billing and cooing is all your cheer;
Sighing and singing of midnight strains,
Under Bonnybell's window panes,—
  Wait till you come to Forty Year.

Forty times over let Michaelmas pass,
  Grizzling hair the brain doth clear—
Then you know a boy is an ass,
Then you know the worth of a lass,
  Once you have come to Forty Year.

Pledge me round, I bid ye declare,
  All good fellows whose beards are grey,
Did not the fairest of the fair
Common grow and wearisome ere
  Ever a month was passed away?

The reddest lips that ever have kissed,
  The brightest eyes that ever have shone,
May pray and whisper, and we not list,
Or look away, and never be missed,
  Ere yet ever a month is gone.

Gillian's dead, God rest her bier,
  How I loved her twenty years syne!
Marian's married, but I sit here
Alone and merry at Forty Year,
  Dipping my nose in the Gascon wine.
                    WILLIAM MAKEPEACE THACKERAY

The Exchange

We pledged our hearts, my love and I,—
  I in my arms the maiden clasping;
I could not tell the reason why,
  But, oh! I trembled like an aspen.

Her father's love she bade me gain;
  I went, and shook like any reed!
I strove to act the man—in vain!
  We had exchanged our hearts indeed.
                    SAMUEL TAYLOR COLERIDGE

My Last Illusion

More years ago than I can state
  (Or would divulge if I were able)
It was my privilege and fate
  To worship the enchanting Mabel.

She was a maid of sweet fifteen;
  Blue-eyed and flaxen as a fairy
Was Mabel; as a rule I lean
  To something darker, but I vary.

And for a while the love-god smiled
  On our young selves, and all was jolly,
Till I was shamefully beguiled
  By one who bore the name of Molly.

For Molly's eyes were as black as ink,
    And Molly's hair was deepest sable;
It pains me even now to think
    How badly I behaved to Mabel.

But I was doomed to pay the price,
    For Molly proved both false and giddy;
We quarrelled once, we quarrelled twice,
    And I was jilted for a middy.

O bitter, bitter was my cup!
    I moved abroad like one demented;
I hardly cared for bite or sup
    Till I saw Mabel, and repented.

But Mabel's wrath was undisguised,
    She was distinctly stern and chilly;
I told her I apologized;
    I begged her not to be so silly.

I left no stone unturned to woo
    The suffrage of her tender mercies;
I wrote her letters not a few,
    And some extremely poignant verses;

Tears, vows, entreaties, all were vain:
    We parted with a final flare-up—
I only saw her once again,
    Just at the time she put her hair up.

Years waned, and still we ranged apart;
    But though in minor ways unstable,
Down in its deeps, my battered heart
    Has always hankered after Mabel;

And often, when I heard the name,
    It would begin to throb *con moto*
In homage to my boyhood's flame,
    And grief at having lost her photo.

That is all over now. To-night
   For one brief hour we came together,
And for that one brief hour you might
   Have knocked me over with a feather.

Perhaps the fault was mine. Perhaps,
   In nourishing a youth's Ideal,
I had forgotten how the lapse
   Of time would modify the Real.

Maybe the charms that won a boy's
   Young heart were there in full perfection,
But could no longer counterpoise
   My bias for a dark complexion.

But ah! what boots the abstract doubt?
   Seeing that she has wed Another,
What boots it that I thought her stout,
   And ominously like her mother?

'Tis but my last illusion fled,
   Perished—dissolved in idle folly;
The Mabel of my dreams is dead;—
   I wonder what became of Molly!

                        DUM-DUM

Tim the Dragoon

Be aisy an' list to a chune
That's sung of bowld Tim the Dragoon—
   Sure, 'twas he'd niver miss
   To be stalin' a kiss,
Or a brace, by the light of the moon—
                  Aroon—
Wid a wink at the Man in the Moon!

Rest his sowl where the daisies grow thick;
For he's gone from the land of the quick:
   But he's still makin' love
   To the leddies above,

An' be jabbers! he'll tache 'em the thrick—
               Avick—
Niver doubt but he'll tache 'em the thrick!

'Tis by Tim the dear saints'll set sthore,
And 'ull thrate him to whisky galore:
   For they've only to sip
   But the tip of his lip
An' bedad! they'll be askin' for more—
               Asthore—
By the powers, they'll be shoutin' 'Ancore!'
             SIR ARTHUR QUILLER-COUCH

Marital Tragedy

A modernist married a fundamentalist wife,
And she led him a catechism and dogma life.
             KEITH PRESTON

The Aeronaut to his Lady

'I
    Through
    Blue
Sky
Fly
    To
    You.
Why?

Sweet
    Love,
Feet
    Move
      So
      Slow!'
           FRANK SIDGWICK

A Letter of Advice

From Miss Medora Trevilian, at Padua, to Miss
Araminta Vavasour, in London.

> Enfin, monsieur, un homme aimable;
> Voilà pourquoi je ne saurais l'aimer.—Scribe.

You tell me you're promised a lover,
    My own Araminta, next week;
Why cannot my fancy discover
    The hue of his coat and his cheek?
Alas! if he look like another,
    A vicar, a banker, a beau,
Be deaf to your father and mother,
    My own Araminta, say 'No!'

Miss Lane, at her Temple of Fashion,
    Taught us both how to sing and to speak,
And we loved one another with passion,
    Before we had been there a week:
You gave me a ring for a token;
    I wear it wherever I go;
I gave you a chain,—is it broken?
    My own Araminta, say 'No!'

O think of our favourite cottage,
    And think of our dear Lalla Rookh!
How we shared with the milkmaids their pottage,
    And drank of the stream from the brook:
How fondly our loving lips faltered
    'What further can grandeur bestow?'
My heart is the same;—is yours altered?
    My own Araminta, say 'No!'

Remember the thrilling romances
    We read on the bank in the glen;
Remember the suitors our fancies
    Would picture for both of us then.

They wore the red cross on their shoulder,
  They had vanquished and pardoned their foe—
Sweet friend, are you wiser or colder?
  My own Araminta, say 'No!'

You know, when Lord Rigmarole's carriage
  Drove off with your cousin Justine,
You wept, dearest girl, at the marriage,
  And whispered 'How base she has been!'
You said you were sure it would kill you,
  If ever your husband looked so;
And you will not apostatize,—will you?
  My own Araminta, say 'No!'

When I heard I was going abroad, love,
  I thought I was going to die;
We walked arm in arm to the road, love,
  We looked arm in arm to the sky;
And I said 'When a foreign postilion
  Has hurried me off to the Po,
Forget not Medora Trevilian:
  My own Araminta, say "No!" '

We parted! but sympathy's fetters
  Reach far over valley and hill;
I muse o'er your exquisite letters,
  And feel that your heart is mine still;
And he who would share it with me, love,—
  The richest of treasures below—
If he's not what Orlando should be, love,
  My own Araminta, say 'No!'

If he wears a top boot in his wooing,
  If he comes to you riding a cob,
If he talks of his baking or brewing,
  If he puts up his feet on the hob,
If he ever drinks port after dinner,
  If his brow or his breeding is low,

If he calls himself 'Thompson' or 'Skinner,'
  My own Araminta, say 'No!'

If he studies the news in the papers
  While you are preparing the tea,
If he talks of the damps or the vapours,
  While moonlight lies soft on the sea,
If he's sleepy while you are capricious,
  If he has not a musical 'Oh!'
If he does not call Werther delicious;—
  My own Araminta, say 'No!'

If he ever sets foot in the City
  Among the stockbrokers and Jews,
If he has not a heart full of pity,
  If he don't stand six feet in his shoes,
If his lips are not redder than roses,
  If his hands are not whiter than snow,
If he has not the model of noses—
  My own Araminta, say 'No!'

If he speaks of a tax or a duty,
  If he does not look grand on his knees,
If he's blind to a landscape of beauty,
  Hills, valleys, rock, waters, and trees,
If he dotes not on desolate towers,
  If he likes not to hear the blast blow,
If he knows not the language of flowers—
  My own Araminta, say 'No!'

He must walk—like a god of old story
  Come down from the home of his rest;
He must smile—like the sun in his glory
  On the buds he loves ever the best;
And oh! from its ivory portal
  Like music his soft speech must flow!—
If he speak, smile, or walk like a mortal,
  My own Araminta, say 'No!'

Don't listen to tales of his bounty,
    Don't hear what they say of his birth,
Don't look at his seat in the county,
    Don't calculate what he is worth;
But give him a theme to write verse on,
    And see if he turns out his toe;
If he's only an excellent person,—
    My own Araminta, say 'No!'
                    WINTHROP MACKWORTH PRAED

Peadar Og Goes Courting

Now that I am dressed I'll go
Down to where the roses blow,
I'll pluck a fair and fragrant one
And make my mother pin it on:
Now she's laughing, so am I—
Oh the blueness of the sky!

Down the street, turn to the right,
Round the corner out of sight;
Pass the church and out of town—
Dust does show on boots of brown,
I'd better brush them while I can
—Step out, Peadar, be a man!

Here's a field and there's a stile,
Shall I jump it? wait a while,
Scale it gently, stretch a foot
Across the mud in that big rut
And I'm still clean—faith, I'm not!
Get some grass and rub the spot.

Dodge those nettles! Here the stream
Bubbling onward with a gleam
Steely white, and black, and grey,
Bends the rushes on its way—
What's that moving? It's a rat
Washing his whiskers; isn't he fat?

Here the cow with the crumpledy horn
Whisks her tail and looks forlorn,
She wants a milkmaid bad I guess,
How her udders swell and press
Against her legs—And here's some sheep;
And there's the shepherd, fast asleep.

This is a sad and lonely field,
Thistles are all that it can yield;
I'll cross it quick, nor look behind,
There's nothing in it but the wind:
And if those bandy-legged trees
Could talk they'd only curse or sneeze.

A sour, unhappy, sloppy place—
That boot's loose! I'll tie the lace
So, and jump this little ditch,
. . . *Her father's really very rich:*
He'll be angry—There's a crow,
Solemn blackhead! Off you go!

There a big, grey, ancient ass
Is snoozing quiet in the grass;
He hears me coming, starts to rise,
Wags his big ears at the flies:
. . . *What'll I say when*—There's a frog,
Go it, long-legs—jig, jig-jog.

He'll be angry, say—"Pooh, Pooh,
Boy, you know not what you do!"
Shakespeare stuff and good advice,
Fat old duffer—Those field mice
Have a good time playing round
Through the corn and underground.

But her mother is friends with mine,
She always asks us out to dine,
And dear Nora, curly head,
Loves me; so at least she said.

. . . Damn that ass's hee-hee-haw—
Was that a rabbit's tail I saw?

This is the house, Lord, I'm afraid!
A man does suffer for a maid.
. . . *How will I start?* The graining's new
On the door—Oh pluck up, do.
Don't stand shivering there like that.
. . . The knocker's funny—*Rat-tat-tat.*

JAMES STEPHENS

SHIRTSLEEVE PHILOSOPHY

Leave the flurry
To the masses;
Take your time
And shine your glasses.
OLD SHAKER VERSE

Intermission, Please!

What poet wrote these lovely lines?
What theme is this, from what sonata?
What king invented minus signs?
What's English for *persona grata*?

The aria we now shall hear
Is sung by basso, alto, tenor—?
What actress first played Chanticleer?
What's *Lebensraum*? What's *Sprachenkenner*?

Whichever way I turn the dial,
Somebody's asking someone something,
Somebody's learning is on trial,
Someone is being proved a dumb thing.

Someone is brilliant on the air
With repartee or quotes from Shaw,
Some marvel spots from Meyerbeer,
Some wit remembers canon law.

Where is the Yard? The Hook of Holland?
The Taj-Mahal? The Iron Lung?
What college sings the Song of Roland?
How do you tie a person's tongue?

The famous crowd the microphones
Primed with *bons mots* and information—
A movie star on postal zones,
A prince on pin-point carbonation.

Name four, name six, name three, name two.
Send the tin-foil, send in the bottle.
Send in your questions; we'll send you
A full Greek text of Aristotle.

I listen as they quip and quiz
And get a joke or get an answer:
What's the pluperfect tense of *Is*?
Whose head was carried by what dancer?

I listen to the poems and dates,
The facts, the whimsies, and the sparks,
The prompt mind that infuriates,
The quick recall, the bright remarks.

And as the quizzes end I go
(Sometimes I last but half-way through them)
To study hard until I know
So much I needn't listen to them.

IRWIN EDMAN

An Awful Responsibility

I am the captain of my soul;
    I rule it with stern joy;
And yet I think I had more fun,
    When I was cabin boy.

KEITH PRESTON

Lines Written in a Moment of Vibrant Ill-health

Things did not vibrate so when I was young;
    Nature preferred the steady note and long:
Wind among leaves, the yarded hounds at tongue,
    Suburban voices lift in sacred song,

And the submissive street-car's starting groan,
    The fishman's horn, the cry of the vegetable vendor,
The roll of iron-bound wheels, the screaming stone
    Of the knife-sharpener and umbrella-mender.

But now all rattles, beats, drums, bombinates.
    My ears are shaken with an incessant whir.
The air-drill chatters, the riveter palpitates.
    "Brrr!" goes the world; "Brr-rrr-rrr!"

Over my head the motors snore in space,
   Motors nose about on the parlor floor,
A motor crawls and mutters over my face;
   I don't think I can stand this very much more.

For after a while the clinching-nail unclinches,
   The gasket shudders on its uneasy bed,
The tie-plate ties no more, and the bolt flinches,
   And the nut tinily turns upon its thread.

MORRIS BISHOP

Commuter

Commuter—one who spends his life
In riding to and from his wife;
A man who shaves and takes a train
And then rides back to shave again.

E. B. WHITE

Text for Today

The syllables of Grief are small
   And bitter to the ear.
One little line can carry all
   That you must weep to hear.
One phrase can plunge you in the pit
   Of misery and doubt:
"Goodbye," perhaps; or "Please remit";
   Or "Better have it out."

But utterance as brief and shy
   Has Joy, for witness these:
"I love you"; "Check enclosed"; or "I
   Can find no cavities."

PHYLLIS McGINLEY

So This is Middle Age!

It's not the thickened midriff that I mind,
The shortened breath which says three sets of doubles
Will be enough (it *is* enough I find);
Shortcomings yes, but oh, such minor troubles
Compared with youth's smug deference polite
Which types one as a hoary oracle
To answer questions deep into the night
About events which youth regards historical.
You'd think that Coy or Brickley or Mahan
Were Hannibal, Ulysses, or Balboa;
While Dempsey, Tunney, and that Firpo man
Had boxed the compass with old skipper Noah;
The feline Lenglen and the pig-tailed Wills,
Whom only yesterday I saw do battle,
To youth, alas, seem older than the hills—
Skeletons the youngsters love to rattle.

Remind me, kids, when next you stop for tea,
I'll tell you what I heard Grant say to Lee!

FRANCIS WHITING HATCH

You Work and Work

You work and work, and keep on working,
While poets, even worse, are shirking;
Your hair falls out, your eyes grow bleary,
Your bones grow old, your outlook dreary;
But you never seek to break the fetters—
You go on filing useless letters.
Well, a day arrives, and it must be spring yet;
The birds, somehow, begin to sing yet;
The grass is green, the cows are mooing,
The flies are buzzing, the people shooing,
The air is fresh—it makes you tipsy—
And, all of a sudden, you turn gipsy.

So you come in late, you go home early;
The thought of the office makes you surly;
You come in later, you go home earlier;
The thought of the office makes you surlier;
You've worked enough; you've earned the leisure
To have some poor, but honest pleasure;
No desk, you think, should rise and quell you—
And what do you get? Do I have to tell you?

SAMUEL HOFFENSTEIN

Introspective Reflection

I would live all my life in nonchalance and insouci-
    ance
Were it not for making a living, which is rather a
    nouciance.

OGDEN NASH

The Dignity of Labor

Labor raises honest sweat;
Leisure puts you into debt.

Labor gives you rye and wheat;
Leisure gives you naught to eat.

Labor makes your riches last;
Leisure gets you nowhere fast.

Labor makes you bed at eight;
Leisure lets you stay up late.

Labor makes you swell with pride;
Leisure makes you shrink inside.

Labor keeps you fit and prime,
But give me leisure every time.

ROBERT BERSOHN

Policy

A suit of sheep's clothing
    I bought at the store;
To give to the wolf
    Who lives at my door.

CAROLYN WELLS

Man at Work

Man at work dictating letter,
Hums and haws and scratches cheek.
Girl with notebook understands him,
Writes it, waits for him to speak.

JOHN HOLMES

Enigma in Altman's

It is a strange, miraculous thing
    About department stores,
How elevators upward wing
    By twos and threes and fours,

How pale lights gleam, how cables run
    All day without an end,
Yet how reluctant, one by one,
    The homing cars descend.

They soar to Furniture, or higher,
    They speed to Gowns and Gifts,
But when the bought weighs down the buyer,
    Late, late, return the lifts.

Newton, himself, beneath his tree,
    Would ponder this and frown:
How what goes up so frequently
    So seldom cometh down.

PHYLLIS McGINLEY

Poem on a Slippery Sidewalk

Pious words are but a bubble
   in the mouths of those who think
that their walks may rightly double
   for a first-class skating-rink!

And how little do they matter—
   any sin or crime or vice
of the saintly souls who scatter
   sand or ashes on the ice!

                       KENNETH PORTER

Autobiography

Oh, both my shoes are shiny new,
   And pristine is my hat;
My dress is 1922. . . .
   My life is all like that.

                       DOROTHY PARKER

I Take 'Em and Like 'Em

I'm fonder of carats than carrots,
   And orchids are nicer than beans,
But life in a series of garrets
   Has made me receptive to greens.

                       MARGARET FISHBACK

Not a Cloud in the Sky

The Indians chant and dance about
To break a crop-destroying drought,
But I've a simpler means by far:
I only have to wash my car.

                       RICHARD ARMOUR

Early Rising

"God bless the man who first invented sleep!"
    So Sancho Panza said, and so say I:
And bless him, also, that he didn't keep
    His great discovery to himself; nor try
To make it—as the lucky fellow might—
A close monopoly by patent-right!

Yes; bless the man who first invented sleep
    (I really can't avoid the iteration),
But blast the man, with curses loud and deep,
    Whate'er the rascal's name, or age, or station,
Who first invented, and went round advising,
That artificial cut-off, Early Rising!

"Rise with the lark, and with the lark to bed,"
    Observes some solemn, sentimental owl;
Maxims like these are very cheaply said;
    But, ere you make yourself a fool or fowl,
Pray just inquire about his rise and fall,
And whether larks have any beds at all!

The time for honest folks to be a-bed
    Is in the morning, if I reason right;
And he who cannot keep his precious head
    Upon his pillow till it's fairly light,
And so enjoy his forty morning winks,
Is up to knavery; or else—he drinks!

Thomson, who sung about the "Seasons," said
    It was a glorious thing to *rise* in season;
But then he said it—lying—in his bed,
    At ten o'clock A.M.,—the very reason
He wrote so charmingly. The simple fact is,
His preaching wasn't sanctioned by his practice.

'Tis, doubtless, well to be sometimes awake,—
    Awake to duty, and awake to truth,—

But when, alas! a nice review we take
　Of our best deeds and days, we find, in sooth,
The hours that leave the slightest cause to weep
Are those we passed in childhood or asleep!

'Tis beautiful to leave the world awhile
　For the soft visions of the gentle night;
And free, at last, from mortal care or guile,
　To live as only in the angels' sight,
In sleep's sweet realm so cosily shut in,
Where, at the worst, we only *dream* of sin!

So let us sleep, and give the Maker praise.
　I like the lad who, when his father thought
To clip his morning nap by hackneyed phrase
　Of vagrant worm by early songster caught,
Cried, "Served him right!—it's not at all surprising;
The worm was punished, sir, for early rising!"

JOHN GODFREY SAXE

Money

Workers earn it,
Spendthrifts burn it,
Bankers lend it,
Women spend it,
Forgers fake it,
Taxes take it,
Dying leave it,
Heirs receive it,
Thrifty save it,
Misers crave it,
Robbers seize it,
Rich increase it,
Gamblers lose it . . .
I could use it.

RICHARD ARMOUR

Borrowing

(From the French)

Some of the hurts you have cured,
And the sharpest you still have survived,
But what torments of grief you endured
From evils which never arrived!

RALPH WALDO EMERSON

Abroad and at Home

As Thomas was cudgel'd one day by his wife,
He took to the street, and fled for his life:
Tom's three dearest friends came by in the squabble,
And sav'd him at once from the shrew and the rabble:
Then ventur'd to give him some sober advice;—
But Tom is a person of honour so nice,
Too wise to take counsel, too proud to take warning,
That he sent to all three a challenge next morning:
Three duels he fought, thrice ventur'd his life;
Went home, and was cudgel'd again by his wife.

JONATHAN SWIFT

I Stand Corrected

When I was happy in my youth
    I laid my state of mind to love,
But now, to tell the dismal truth,
    I see I didn't know whereof
I spoke. For I have lately found—
    With great dissatisfaction—that
Though love can make the world go round,
    It often makes the world go flat.

MARGARET FISHBACK

Complaint

How seldom, Friend! a good great man inherits
Honour or wealth, with all his worth and pains!
It sounds like stories from the land of spirits,
If any man obtain that which he merits,
Or any merit that which he obtains.

SAMUEL TAYLOR COLERIDGE

The Hardship of Accounting

Never ask of money spent
Where the spender thinks it went.
Nobody was ever meant
To remember or invent
What he did with every cent.

ROBERT FROST

Sentimental Journey

At breakfast a husband is cheery or blue.
    At dinner he's blue or he's cheery.
And when you've admitted these facts to be true,
    You've mastered the whole subject, dearie.

ELSPETH

Hug Me Tight

["Also, there was a charming hug-me-tight, finishing at the back in an amusing little bustle." —*Fashion Article.*]

About the fashions of the day
    I read some interesting notes
On every hue from grave to gay
    In frocks and furs, in hats and coats:

On this for noon and that for night,
  On lace to drape and silk to rustle,
And of a charming hug-me-tight
  With an amusing little bustle.

My Delia, if she has a fad,
  Is cracked on everything that's new;
However wild it be and mad
  She gets it, and it suits her too;
But, though she always cheers the sight
  And stimulates the red cor*pus*cle,
She hasn't got a hug-me-tight
  With or without its little bustle.

It may be that by being broke
  That once imprudent head is bowed,
Which ought to be a bitter stroke
  To one who does herself so proud;
But I'm the man to put things right;
  And, though to pay may prove a tussle,
I'll stand the girl her hug-me-tight
  Complete with its amusing bustle.

DUM-DUM

Why Tomas Cam Was Grumpy

If I were rich what would I do?
I'd leave the horse just ready to shoe;
I'd leave the pail beside the cow;
I'd leave the furrow beneath the plough;
I'd leave the ducks, tho' they should quack:
"Our eggs will be stolen before you're back";
I'd buy a diamond brooch, a ring,
A chain of gold that I would fling
Around her neck. . . . Ah, what an itch,
If I were rich!

What would I do if I were wise?
I would not debate about the skies;
Nor would I try a book to write;
Or find the wrong in the tangled right;
I would not debate with learned men
Of how, and what, and why, and when;
—I'd train my tongue to a linnet's song,
I'd learn the words that couldn't go wrong—
And then I'd say . . . And win the prize,
If I were wise!

But I'm not that nor t'other, I bow
My back to the work that's waiting now:
I'll shoe the horse that's standing ready;
I'll milk the cow if she'll be steady;
I'll follow the plough that turns the loam;
I'll watch the ducks don't lay from home:
—And I'll curse, and curse, and curse again
Till the devil joins in with his big amen;
And none but he and I will wot
When the heart within me starts to rot;
To fester and churn its ugly brew
. . . Where's my spade! I've work to do!

                              JAMES STEPHENS

Rarae Aves

Announce it here with triple leading
That once I heard a Noisy Wedding;
And accurately I recall
The day I saw a Sober Brawl.

I saw some burglars drive away
In a Low-Powered Car, the other day;
And yesterday, I'm pretty sure,
An Unknown Clubman died, obscure.

                              FRANKLIN P. ADAMS

Unsolved Mystery

We'd face, I'm sure, with more aplomb
  This season merry,
If we could tell which part is Tom
  And which is Jerry.

GEORGE RYAN

Just & Unjust

The rain it raineth on the just
  And also on the unjust fella;
But chiefly on the just, because
  The unjust steals the just's umbrella.

LORD BOWEN

Argument

Two stubborn beaks
Of equal strength
Can stretch a worm
To any length.

MILDRED WESTON

Résumé

Razors pain you;
Rivers are damp;
Acids stain you;
And drugs cause cramp.
Guns aren't lawful;
Nooses give;
Gas smells awful;
You might as well live.

DOROTHY PARKER

On Viewing a Florist's Whimsy at Fifty-Ninth and Madison

Consider, if you can, the heads
  That conjured up those grisly packs
Of elephants and dogs with beds
  Of pansies belching from their backs.

MARGARET FISHBACK

How Are You?

Don't tell your friends about your indigestion:
"How are you!" is a greeting, not a question.

ARTHUR GUITERMAN

TOBACCO & TROUT

Some sigh for this or that;
My wishes don't go far;
The world may wag at will,
So I have my cigar.

THOMAS HOOD

When in my pilgrimage I reach
The river that we all must cross
And land upon that farther beach
Where earthly gains are counted loss,

May I not earthly loss repair?
Well, if those fish should rise again,
There shall be no more parting there—
Celestial gut will stand the strain.

And, issuing from the portal, one
Who was himself a fisherman
Will drop his keys and, shouting, run
To help me land leviathan.

ANONYMOUS

Ode to Tobacco

Thou who, when fears attack,
Bidst them avaunt, and Black
Care, at the horseman's back
    Perching, unseatest;
Sweet, when the morn is gray;
Sweet, when they've cleared away
Lunch; and at close of day
    Possibly sweetest:

I have a liking old
For thee, though manifold
Stories, I know, are told,
    Not to thy credit;
How one (or two at most)
Drops make a cat a ghost—
Useless, except to roast—
    Doctors have said it:

How they who use fusees
All grow by slow degrees
Brainless as chimpanzees,
    Meagre as lizards:
Go mad, and beat their wives;
Plunge (after shocking lives)
Razors and carving knives
    Into their gizzards.

Confound such knavish tricks!
Yet know I five or six
Smokers who freely mix
    Still with their neighbours;
Jones—(who, I'm glad to say,
Asked leave of Mrs. J.)—
Daily absorbs a clay
    After his labours.

Cats may have had their goose
Cooked by tobacco-juice;
Still why deny its use
    Thoughtfully taken?
We're not as tabbies are:
Smith, take a fresh cigar!
Jones, the tobacco-jar!
    Here's to thee, Bacon!

C. S. CALVERLEY

Master and Man

Do ye ken hoo to fush for the salmon?
    If ye'll listen I'll tell ye.
Dinna trust to the books and their gammon,
    They're but trying to sell ye.
Leave professors to read their ain cackle
    And fush their ain style;
Come awa', sir, we'll oot wi' oor tackle
    And be busy the while.

'Tis a wee bit ower bright, ye were thinkin'?
    Aw, ye'll no be the loser;
'Tis better ten baskin' and blinkin'
    Than ane that's a cruiser.
If ye're bent, as I tak it, on slatter,
    Ye should pray for the droot,
For the salmon's her ain when there's watter,
    But she's oors when it's oot.

Ye may just put your flee-book behind ye,
    Ane hook wull be plenty;
If they'll no come for this, my man, mind ye,
    They'll no come for twenty.
Ay, a rod; but the shorter the stranger
    And the nearer to strike;
For myself I prefare it nae langer
    Than a yard or the like.

Noo, ye'll stand awa' back while I'm creepin'
    Wi' my snoot i' the gowans;
There's a bonny twalve-poonder a-sleepin'
    I' the shade o' yon rowans.
Man, man! I was fearin' I'd stirred her,
    But I've got her the noo!
Hoot! fushin's as easy as murrder
    When ye ken what to do.

Na, na, sir, I doot na ye're willin'
    But I canna permit ye;
For I'm thinkin' that yon kind o' killin'
    Wad hardly befit ye.
And some work is deefficult hushin',
    There'd be havers and chaff:
'Twull be best, sir, for you to be fushin'
    And me wi' the gaff.

SIR HENRY NEWBOLT

The Bait

Come live with me, and be my love,
And we will some new pleasures prove
Of golden sands, and crystal brooks,
With silken lines and silver hooks.

There will the river whispering run
Warmed by thy eyes, more than the sun;
And there the enamoured fish will stay,
Begging themselves they may betray.

When thou wilt swim in that live bath,
Each fish, which every channel hath,
Will amorously to thee swim,
Gladder to catch thee, than thou him.

If thou, to be so seen, beest loath,
By sun or moon, thou darkenest both,

And if myself have leave to see,
I need not their light, having thee.

Let others freeze with angling reeds,
And cut their legs with shells and weeds,
Or treacherously poor fish beset,
With strangling snare, or windowy net.

Let coarse bold hands from slimy nest
The bedded fish in banks out-wrest;
Or curious traitors, sleeve-silk flies,
Bewitch poor fishes' wandering eyes.

For thee, thou need'st no such deceit,
For thou thyself art thine own bait:
That fish, that is not catched thereby,
Alas! is wiser far than I.

JOHN DONNE

Patience

The firm resolve of Silas Sharp
To catch a more gigantic carp
Than hitherto had been recorded
Did not arise from any sordid
Desire for notoriety,
But merely from a wish that he
Might show a little son of his
How great a virtue patience is.

Each evening, therefore, he would take
The little fellow to a lake,
Where once a man had had a carp on
Which far out-tarponed any tarpon.

They dug upon the bank a pit
With camouflage concealing it;
And there they sat from day to day,
Waving the gnats and flies away;

And there they sat from week to week,
Restraining any wish to speak;
And there they sat from year to year,
Hoping the float would disappear.
"It will, my boy," cried Sharp each night,
"It will, you see if I'm not right."

At length the lad grew rather sick,
And slew his parent with a brick,
For which the judge, with angry frown,
Imposed a fine of half-a-crown.
"Patience," he said, "should rank among
The highest virtues of the young."

CAPTAIN E. E. NOTT-BOWER

Retrospect

They left behind the insistent strain
  Our capitalistic system knows:
  The Doctor almost comatose,
And Axel with a static brain.

And in the Nova Scotian wild,
  Well freed from phone and daily paper,
  They found that three-score years can caper;
That in the man is still the child.

They found the old is always new
  To seeing eye and hearing ear:
  The sandpeep, salmon, duck, and deer;
The squirrel's chatter, loon's halloo.

They found a wood-world life serene,
  That fits to quiet jibes and jokes;
  That fishes only when it smokes—
God bless the Lady Nicotine.

The Doctor felt again the blaze
  That shines in vain for city eyes;

The colors of the sunset skies;
  The little wood folk's silent ways;

Then sharpened up his pencil point,
    Uncorked again his pungent wit.
    Sometimes he made a pungent hit
Well filed to stick in Axel's joint.

Let Axel's lordly salmon grow
    As fish to fisher's yarns must stretch;
    Yet must the Doctor choose to sketch
How Axel jigged the gaspereau.

As little boys, with thumb at nose,
    For trite advice display contempt,
    And also show by their attempt
How true for them the vulgar pose,

So Axel when the Doctor roared
    Encased the noise in calm repose:
    Thrice is he armed whose manner shows
That tumult merely keeps him bored.

In other fields the Doctor walks,
    Kaleidoscopic is his mind;
    From cabbages to kings you'll find
Of many things he wisely talks,

Impatient of the fear-filled breed
    That quail before the things that be,
    His clear-eyed logic cannot see
Facts need be glozed for common need.

Yet strong within his sturdy frame
    Runs red his Presbyterian blood.
    Half pagan still he loves the mud
Because he knows from earth we came.

But stop—no friend dissects a friend—
    For still remains the unknown X.
    Why with analysis perplex—
I like the Doctor—that's the end:

Envoy

They had their trip and still are friends:
  Three weeks together is the test.
  "Jam served today" is still the best—
Though "Jam tomorrow" makes amends.

ROY DAVIS

Fishing in the Australian Alps

He said: I am a parson, but I take
My stand with modern thought,
And I love science deeply for the sake
Of that great truth all science still has taught,
(He cocked an eye along his fishing rod),
The love and the omnipotence of God.

Now take these hills—the oldest hills on earth,
Millions of years, they say,
And yet the Lord was present at their birth
And there was joy in heaven on that day
And—don't you think a white fly, white and thin,
(He cocked his eye again) will bring them in?

An ant and bee were struggling in the grass,
And soon the bee was out.
I wondered idly just how old God was
And where that love my friend was sure about,
And, turning from his quick sagacious eye,
Picked out with care my darkest fattest fly.

ERNEST G. MOLL

The Right Way to Fish

Mr. Wright went out to fish,
And he became a right angler;
He thought he'd try and catch a shark,
And he became a try angler.

He laughed to think how smart he was,
And he became a cute angler.
But he didn't see the shark
With its nose under his bark:
He was such an obtuse angler;
Until the creature tipped it over
When he became a wrecked angler.

From the WHITEHALL TIMES

Pernicious Weed

The pipe, with solemn interposing puff,
Makes half a sentence at a time enough;
The dozing sages drop the drowsy strain,
Then pause and puff, and speak, and pause again.
Such often, like the tube they so admire,
Important triflers! have more smoke than fire.
Pernicious weed! whose scent the fair annoys,
Unfriendly to society's chief joys,
The worst effect is banishing for hours
The sex whose presence civilizes ours.

WILLIAM COWPER

Ballade of a Summer Hotel

We're all inclined to bore our friends,
    And of their hobbies all men prate;
Whatever way one's fancy tends,
    One's apt to ride a rapid gait.
    Now, I like fish—please get this straight—
But every hour of every day
    I hear an argument on bait,
    And then, "How much did your bass weigh?"

All day they toil; on that depends
    The fish we eat in style sedate;

And when at last the sun descends
  They come with bass and perch in state.
  And yet, though caviling I hate,
It seems a monstrous price to pay
  To hear them argue as to bait,
  And then, "How much did your bass weigh?"

The early dawn each fisher sends
  With rod and line and hook and weight,
And when the lake with shadows blends
  He comes to tell what was his fate.
  Then these words follow soon or late,·
It doesn't matter what you say:
  First, some remarks about the bait
  And then, "How much did your bass weigh?"

Envoy

Prince, when the fisher at heaven's gate
  Admits them, as perchance he may,
Will they trade tips about the bait,
  And ask, "How much did your bass weigh?"
                                    JUNIA

A Song of Satisfaction on Completing an Overhauling of Fishing Tackle

My darling little fishing rods,
I count you by the score,
And if I am not careful
There'll be more, and more, and more.
You're all in good condition,
With all your ferrules tight;
My darling little fishing rods,
You fill me with delight.
There's a salmon rod by Leonard,
There's one by Thomas, too;

A half a dozen fly-rods,
Old greenheart—split bamboo.
Yes—they are made for trouting,
To fish both wet and dry;
That one by Payne, nine foot—two piece—
Can throw a pretty fly.
A battery of spinning-rods
For carp and stripèd bass—
Ah, no! we never spin for carp,
Corn puts *them* on the grass.
That one has been at Montauk Point—
Been drenched with flying foam;
That sturdy one with a hickory butt
Will bring the bluefish home.
And last, not least, that sweet quartet
Of smelt-poles—how I love 'em!
Oh, hurry up, September days,
When in the car I'll shove 'em.

Patience, my dears, it won't be long.
Soon we'll see April skies,
And *then!* by gum, God willing,
You'll get some exercise.

LESLIE P. THOMPSON

The Microscopic Trout and the Machiavelian Fisherman

A fisher was casting his flies in a brook,
  According to laws of such sciences,
With a patented reel and a patented hook
  And a number of other appliances;
And the thirty-fifth cast, which he vowed was the last
  (It was figured as close as a decimal),
Brought suddenly out of the water a trout
  Of measurements infinitesimal.

This fish had a way that would win him a place
    In the best and most polished society,
And he looked at the fisherman full in the face
    With a visible air of anxiety:
He murmured "Alas!" from his place on the grass,
    And then, when he'd twisted and wriggled, he
Remarked in a pet that his heart was upset
    And digestion all higgledy-piggledy.

"I request," he observed, "to be instantly flung
    Once again in the pool I've been living in."
The fisherman said, "You will tire out your tongue.
    Do you see any signs of my giving in?
Put you back in the pool? Why, you fatuous fool,
    I have eaten much smaller and thinner fish.
You're not salmon or sole, but I think, on the whole,
    You're a fairly respectable dinner-fish."

The fisherman's cook tried her hand on the trout
    And with various herbs she embellished him;
He was lovely to see, and there isn't a doubt
    That the fisherman's family relished him,
And, to prove that they did, both his wife and his kid
    Devoured the trout with much eagerness,
Avowing no dish could compare with that fish,
    Notwithstanding his singular meagreness.

And THE MORAL, you'll find, is although it is kind
    To grant favors that people are wishing for,
Still a dinner you'll lack if you chance to throw back
    In the pool little trout that you're fishing for;
If their pleading you spurn you will certainly learn
    That herbs will deliciously vary 'em:
It is needless to state that a trout on a plate
    Beats several in the aquarium.

GUY WETMORE CARRYL

Killarney

Oh Mr. Froude, how wise and good
    To point us out the way to glory,
They're no great shakes, those Snowdon Lakes,
    And all their pounders myth and story.
Blow Snowdon! What's Lake Gwynant to Killarney,
Or spluttering Welsh to tender blarney, blarney,
    blarney?

So, Thomas Hughes, sir, if you choose,
    I'll tell you where we think of going,
To swate and far o'er cliff and scar,
    Hear horns of Elfland faintly blowing;
Blow Snowdon! There's a hundred lakes to try in,
And fresh caught salmon daily, frying, frying, frying.

Geology and botany
    A hundred wonders shall diskiver,
We'll flog and troll in strid and hole,
    And skim the cream of lake and river.
Blow Snowdon! Give me Ireland for my pennies;
Hurrah! for salmon, grilse, and—Dennis, Dennis,
    Dennis!

CHARLES KINGSLEY

Haulage

An angler named Ezekiel Hutt
Once lost a fish on 4X gut.

He hooked a fish another day
On 3X gut. It got away.

"2X must be the gut for me,"
He said. It parted instantly.

He likewise failed to get one out
On "Medium Lake to Medium Trout."

A heavy fish saw fit to break
His "Extra Stout to Heavy Lake."

And so it was throughout the season;
He only just retained his reason.

But now he's steady as a rock;
He works a crane at Woolwich Dock.

CAPTAIN E. E. NOTT-BOWER

Tobacco

Tobacco is a dirty weed:
   I like it.
It satisfies no normal need:
   I like it.
It makes you thin, it makes you lean,
It takes the hair right off your bean,
It's the worst darn stuff I've ever seen:
   I like it.

GRAHAM LEE HEMMINGER

Pipes in the Sty

(A man in Georgia has taught his pig to smoke)

There lives a pig in Georgia's far land,
   A simple pig, of ordinary type
In no way different from the common brand,
   Except for his affection for a pipe.
     His owner taught him; why,
Is not apparent to the naked eye.

He may have lived apart, a lonely soul
   Remote from man, who felt the urgent need
Of one to play the fellow-smoker's *rôle*
   At evening, a companion of the weed;
     And, by some happy grace,
Fixed on the hog, from something in his face.

And they have smoked together, this queer pair;
   The silent man at peace, no more alone,
The hog reclining with seraphic air,
   And each engaged in musings of his own,
     United, pig and man;
A charmful fancy; beat it if you can.

Or has the blacker dream possessed his heart
   That, as the hog is fated at his end
To suffer smoking, it were well to start
   In life, and cure his unsuspecting friend,
     Adding, perhaps, to that
That in excess tobacco makes for fat?

No. That would rank him lower than the dog.
   O hog, by every pipe your lord has filled
You are immune; O happy, happy hog,
   Still shall you breathe, for all your portly build;
     For other hogs, the knife;
For you, long smokings and an unslit life.

DUM-DUM

TOMBSTONE & TWILIGHT

At Salisbury you strayed alone
Within the shafted glooms,
Whilst I was by the Verger shown
The brasses and the tombs.

COVENTRY PATMORE

'To me they—drat 'em!—never give
    A thought; they wander by,
An irritation while they live,
    A nuisance when they die.

'If there be one that needs lament
    The way these folks behave,
'Tis he whose holidays are spent
    In digging someone's grave,

'For when a person takes and dies,
    On Monday though it be,
They never hold his obsequies
    Till Sunday after three.

'And thus it fares through their delay,
    That I may not begin
To dig the grave till Saturday,—
    On Sunday fill it in . . . .'

DUM-DUM

Mary Anne Lowder

Here lies the body of Mary Anne Lowder,
She burst while drinking a Seidlitz powder.
Called from this world to her heavenly rest,
She should have waited till it effervesced.

ANONYMOUS

Here a Nit-Wit Lies

Here a nit-wit lies,
   Between myrtles serried.
Mourners, dry your eyes.
   He is better buried.

He from toe to crown
   Wooden like a tree was.
Never yet was clown
   Purer clown than he was.

Other fools have been
   Foolish for a season,
Yet at times have seen
   Glimmerings of reason.

He, the arch-fools' butt,
   Could do nothing clever,
But, conceiv'd a mutt,
   Stayed a mutt for ever.

No redeeming sparks
   From his brain rebounded.
His obtuse remarks
   Kept the world astounded.

Start his watch, and he
   Would be sure to stop it.
Give the fool a free
   Drink, and he would drop it.

Mourners, pass him by
　　Without word or mention.
Such a prodigy
　　Passes comprehension.

Here a nit-wit lies.
　　Let us not regret him.
When the dead shall rise
　　He'll forget to. Let him.

PATRICK BARRINGTON

One Down

Weight distributed,
　　Free from strain,
Divot replaced,
　　Familiar terrain,
Straight left arm,
　　Unmoving head—
Here lies the golfer,
　　Cold and dead.

RICHARD ARMOUR

Within this grave do lie,
Back to back, my wife and I;
When the last trump the air shall fill,
If she gets up, I'll just lie still.

ANONYMOUS

He Laughed Last

A Yankee country churchyard holds
The grave of a bygone town buffoon;
Chiseled on his marble slab,
"I expected this but not so soon."

FRANCIS WHITING HATCH

Here lies my gude and gracious Auntie
Whom Death has packed in his portmanty.

ANONYMOUS

Little Willie from his mirror
   Licked the mercury right off,
Thinking, in his childish error,
   It would cure the whooping cough.
At the funeral his mother
   Smartly said to Mrs. Brown:
" 'Twas a chilly day for Willie
When the mercury went down."

ANONYMOUS

In a Staffordshire Churchyard

Here lies father and mother and sister and I,
   We all died within the space of one short year;
They all be buried at Wimble, except I,
   And I be buried here.

ANONYMOUS

To the Memory of a Young Man

(A Hosier who had a Sweetheart named Hannah)

He left his hose, his Hannah, and his love
To sing Hosannahs in the world above.

ANONYMOUS

Here lies Johnny Cuncapod,
Have mercy on him, mighty God!
As he would do if he were God,
And you were Johnny Cuncapod.

ANONYMOUS

From the Greek Anthology

Bill Jupp lies 'ere, aged sixty year:
    From Tavistock 'e came.
Single 'e bided, and 'e wished
    'Is father done the same.

L. A. G. STRONG

Here lies John Auricular,
Who in the ways of the Lord walked perpendicular.

ANONYMOUS

He lived one hundred and five,
    Sanguine and strong;
A hundred to five,
    You live not so long.

ANONYMOUS

Here lies John Hill, a man of skill,
    His age was five times ten,
He ne'er did good, nor ever would,
    Had he lived as long again.

ANONYMOUS

On the Setting up of

Mr. Butler's Monument in Westminster Abbey

While Butler, needy wretch! was yet alive,
No generous patron would a dinner give:
See him, when starv'd to death and turn'd to dust,
Presented with a monumental bust!
The poet's fate is here in emblem shown,
He ask'd for bread, and he received a stone!

SAMUEL WESLEY, THE YOUNGER

Here lies the body of Sarah Sexton,
She was a wife that never vexed one.
I can't say as much for her on the next stone.

ANONYMOUS

Poor Martha Snell, she's gone away,
She would if she could, but she could not stay;
She'd two bad legs, and a baddish cough,
But her legs it was that carried her off.

ANONYMOUS

Here lies one who for medicine would not give
    A little gold, and so his life he lost:
I fancy now he'd wish again to live
    Could he but guess how much his funeral cost.

ANONYMOUS

This spot is the sweetest I've seen in my life,
For it raises my flowers and covers my wife.

ANONYMOUS

On a Puritanicall Lock-Smith

A zealous Lock-Smith dyed of late,
And did arrive at heaven gate,
He stood without and would not knocke,
Because he meant to picke the locke.

WILLIAM CAMDEN

Here lies the body of Jonathan Near
Whose mouth it stretched from ear to ear.
Tread softly, stranger, o'er this wonder,
For if he yawns, you're gone, by thunder!

ANONYMOUS

Our life is but a summer's day:
Some only breakfast, and away;
Others to dinner stay, and are full fed;
The oldest man but sups, and goes to bed.
Large his account who lingers out the day;
Who goes the soonest, has the least to pay.

ANONYMOUS

A Churchyard in Wales

Submite submitted to her heavenly king,
Being a flower of that eternal Spring,
Near three years old, she died in heaven to wait,
The year was sixteen hundred forty-eight.

ANONYMOUS

Reader, pass on!—don't waste your time
On bad biography and bitter rhyme;
For what I *am*, this crumbling clay insures,
And what I *was,* is no affair of yours!

ANONYMOUS

Mike O'Day

This is the grave of Mike O'Day
Who died maintaining his right of way.
His right was clear, his will was strong,
But he's just as dead as if he'd been wrong.

ANONYMOUS

Beneath this stone our baby lies,
It neither cries nor hollers,
It lived but one and twenty days,
And cost us forty dollars.

ANONYMOUS

Here lies the body of Jonathan Stout,
He fell in the water and never got out,
And still is supposed to be floating about.

ANONYMOUS

A Brewer

Here lies poor Burton,
   He was both hale and stout;
Death laid him on his bitter bier,
   Now in another world he hops about.

ANONYMOUS

Jersey

The manner of her death was thus:
She was druv over by a Bus.

ANONYMOUS

On the twenty-second of June
Jonathan Fiddle went out of tune.

Attributed to BEN JONSON

Here lies one Box within another;
   The one of wood
   Was very good;
We cannot say so much for t'other.

ANONYMOUS

Underneath this ancient pew
Lie the remains of Jonathan Blue;
His name was Black, but that wouldn't do.

ANONYMOUS

A bird, a man, a loaded gun,
No bird, dead man, thy will be done.

ANONYMOUS

On John Grubb

When from the chrysalis of the tomb,
I rise in rainbow-coloured plume,
My weeping friends, ye scarce will know
That I was but a Grubb below.

ANONYMOUS

Here lies the body of Ann Mann,
Who lived an old woman,
And died an old Mann.

ANONYMOUS

At Leeds

Here lies my wife,
Here lies she;
Hallelujah!
Hallelujee!

ANONYMOUS

Johnny Dow

Wha lies here?
I, Johnny Dow.
Hoo! Johnny, is that you?
Ay, man, but a'm dead now.

ANONYMOUS

On Mr. Partridge

Who Died in May

What! kill a partridge in the month of May!
Was that done like a sportsman? Eh, Death, eh?

ANONYMOUS

Epitaph on a Talkative Old Maid

Beneath this silent stone is laid
A noisy, antiquated maid,
Who, from her cradle talk'd till death,
And ne'er before was out of breath.
Whither she's gone we cannot tell;
For if she talks not, she's in ——!
If she's in ——, she's there unblest
Because she hates a place of rest.

BENJAMIN FRANKLIN

Here Ananias lies because he lied.
So he lies still, we all are satisfied.

F. W. MACVEAGH

ballade

outcast bones from a thousand biers
click us a measure giddy and gleg
and caper my children dance my dears
skeleton rattle your mouldy leg
this one was a gourmet round as a keg
and that had the brow of semiramis
o fleshless forehead bald as an egg
all men s lovers come to this

this eyeless head that laughs and leers
was a chass daf once or a touareg
with golden rings in his yellow ears
skeleton rattle your mouldy leg
marot was this one or wilde or a wegg
who dropped into verses and down the abyss
and those are the bones of my old love meg
all men s lovers come to this

these bones were a ballet girl s for years
parbleu but she shook a wicked peg
and those ribs there were a noble peer s
skeleton rattle your mouldy leg
and here is a duchess that loved a yegg
with her lipless mouth that once drank bliss
down to the dreg of its ultimate dreg
all men s lovers come to this

prince if you pipe and plead and beg
you may yet be crowned with a grisly kiss
skeleton rattle your mouldy leg
all men s lovers come to this

DON MARQUIS

John Bun

Here lies John Bun,
He was killed by a gun,
His name was not Bun, but Wood,
But Wood would not rhyme with gun, but Bun would.

ANONYMOUS

Here lies poor stingy Timmy Wyatt,
Who died at noon and saved a dinner by it.

ANONYMOUS

For Sir John Vanbrugh, Architect

Lie heavy on him, earth! for he
Laid many a heavy load on thee.

ABEL EVANS

Epitaph on an Unfortunate Artist

He found a formula for drawing comic rabbits:
   This formula for drawing comic rabbits paid.
So in the end he could not change the tragic habits
   This formula for drawing comic rabbits made.

ROBERT GRAVES

Egoism

I am anxious after praise;
I sometimes wish it were not so:
I hate to think I spend my days
Waiting for what I'll never know.

I even hope that when I'm dead
The worms won't find me wholly vicious,
But, as they masticate my head,
Will smack their lips and cry "Delicious!"

W. CRADDLE

Epitaph on Charles II

Here lies our Sovereign Lord the King,
   Whose word no man relies on,
Who never said a foolish thing,
   Nor ever did a wise one.

JOHN WILMOT, EARL OF ROCHESTER

A Dentist

Stranger! Approach this spot with gravity!
John Brown is filling his last cavity.

ANONYMOUS

Self-Composed Epitaph

On a Doctor by the Name of I. Letsome

When people's ill they come to I,
  I physics, bleeds, and sweats 'em;
Sometimes they live, sometimes they die;
  What's that to I? I Letsome.

Here lies old Jones,
Who all his life collected bones,
Till death, that grim and bony spectre,
That all-amassing bone collector,
Boned old Jones, so neat and tidy,
That here he lies all bona fide.

ANONYMOUS

Here Skugg lies snug
As a bug in a rug.

BENJAMIN FRANKLIN

On a Waiter

By and by
God caught his eye.

DAVID McCORD

Sir Roderic's Song

When the night wind howls in the chimney cowls, and
the bat in the moonlight flies,
And inky clouds, like funeral shrouds, sail over the
midnight skies—
When the footpads quail at the night-bird's wail, and
black dogs bay the moon,
Then is the spectres' holiday—then is the ghosts' high-
noon!

As the sob of the breeze sweeps over the trees, and the
mists lie low on the fen,
From grey tombstones are gathered the bones that
once were women and men,
And away they go, with a mop and a mow, to the revel
that ends too soon,
For cockcrow limits our holiday—the dead of the
night's high-noon!

And then each ghost with his ladye-toast to their
churchyard beds takes flight,
With a kiss, perhaps, on her lantern chaps, and a grisly
grim "goodnight";
Till the welcome knell of the midnight bell rings forth
its jolliest tune,
And ushers our next high holiday—the dead of the
night's high-noon!

SIR W. S. GILBERT

Grim death took little Jerry,
The son of Joseph and Sereno Howells,
Seven days he wrestled with the dysentery
And then he perished in his little bowels.

ANONYMOUS

On an Infant Eight Months Old

Since I have been so quickly done for,
I wonder what I was begun for.

ANONYMOUS

Here lies the man Richard,
    And Mary his wife,
Whose surname was Prichard:
    They lived without strife;
And the reason was plain,—
    They abounded in riches,
They had no care nor pain,
    And his wife wore the breeches.

ANONYMOUS

Essex, England

On Prince Frederick

Here lies Fred
Who was alive and is dead.
Had it been his father,
I had much rather;
Had it been his brother,
Still better than another;
Had it been his sister,
No one would have missed her;
Had it been the whole generation,
So much the better for the nation;
But since 'tis only Fred
Who was alive and is dead,
Why, there's no more to be said.

ANONYMOUS

It was a cough that carried him off,
It was a coffin they carried him off in.

ANONYMOUS

On a Newcastle Architect

Here lies Robert Trollope,
Who made yon stones roll up:
When death took his soul up
His body filled this hole up.

ANONYMOUS

Here lies I and my three daughters,
Killed by drinking Cheltenham waters;
If we had stuck to epsom salts,
We'd not been a-lying in these here vaults.

ANONYMOUS

Here lies the mother of children seven:
Four on earth and three in heaven;
The three in heaven preferring rather
To die with mother than live with father.

ANONYMOUS

A Geologist's Epitaph

For years he pried among the strata,
Collecting various sorts of data,
Uncovering many a fossil phiz;
We hope nobody digs up his.

JANE W. STEDMAN

Here lies returned to clay
Miss Arabella Young,
Who on the first of May
Began to hold her tongue.

ANONYMOUS

Here Lies Bill

Here lies Bill, the son of Fred.
He lied alive; he now lies dead.

OLIVER HERFORD

Epitaph On His Wife

Here lies my wife: here let her lie!
Now she's at rest—and so am I.

JOHN DRYDEN

An Undertaker's Advertisement

Why pay more for your funeral when
We've put away far better men,
Coffin and all, for twelve pounds and ten?

And this about your friends? Their pride?
Because the coffin's only dyed
To look like maple? You inside

May rest secure—our guarantee—
That no man ever made so free
As to scratch a coffin's lid to see!

ERNEST G. MOLL

On Peter Robinson

Here lies the preacher, judge, and poet, Peter
Who broke the laws of God, and man, and metre.

LORD JEFFREY

Merideth

Here lies one blown out of breath,
Who lived a merry life, and died a Merideth.

From the Greek Anthology

I saw no doctor, but, feeling queer inside,
Just thought of one—and naturally died.

Translated by HUMBERT WOLFE

TRICKY

I seen a dunce of a poet once, a-writin' a little book;
And he says to me with a smile, says he, "Here's a
* pome—d' you want to look?"*
And I threw me eye at the pome; say I, "What's the
* use o' this here rot?"*
"It's a double sestine," says he, lookin' mean, "and
* they're hard as the deuce, that's what!"*

GELETT BURGESS

"When Moonlike Ore the Hazure Seas"

When moonlike ore the hazure seas
    In soft effulgence swells,
When silver jews and balmy breaze
    Bend down the Lily's bells;
When calm and deap, the rosy sleap
    Has lapt your soal in dreems,
R Hangeline! R lady mine!
    Dost thou remember Jeames?

I mark thee in the Marble All,
    Where England's loveliest shine—
I say the fairest of them hall
    Is Lady Hangeline.
My soul, in desolate eclipse,
    With recollection teems—
And then I hask, with weeping lips,
    Dost thou remember Jeames?

Away! I may not tell thee hall
    This soughring heart endures—
There is a lonely sperrit-call
    That Sorrow never cures;
There is a little, little Star,
    That still above me beams;
It is the Star of Hope—but ar!
    Dost thou remember Jeames?

WILLIAM MAKEPEACE THACKERAY

Hubbub in Hub

Famous City of Boston,
    Accustomed to praise,
Again Fame has forced on
    Your forehead the bays.
Though narrow your vision,

Though broad be your A's,
Here comes a decision
    To last all your days—

Or at least for a while,
    For Mehl vanquished Venzke
    And Munski and Fenske
When Mehl won the mile.

In the land of the Cabot,
    The home of Revere,
They ran like the rabbit,
    They darted like deer.
Though Saltonstalls, Conants
    And others were near,
Such worthy opponents
    They could not but cheer—

Or at least they could smile
    When Mehl finished Fenske
    And Munski and Venzke
When Mehl won the mile.

LAURENCE McKINNEY

Lay of Ancient Rome

Oh, the Roman was a rogue,
He erat, was, you bettum,
He ran his automóbilis
And smoked his cigarettum,
He wore a diamond studibus,
An elegant cravattum,
A maxima-cum-laude shirt
And *such* a stylish hattum!

He loved the luscious hic-haec-hock
And bet on games and equi;
At times he won—at others, though,

He got it in the nequi.
He winked (quo usque tandem?)
At puellas on the Forum
And sometimes even made
Those goo-goo oculorum!

He frequently was seen
At combats gladiatorial
And ate enough to feed
Ten boarders at Memorial;
He often went on sprees
And said, on starting homus:
"Hic labor—opus est,
Oh, where's my hic—hic—domus?"

Although he lived in Rome,
Of all the arts the middle,
He was (excuse the phrase),
A horrid individ'l—
Oh, what a diff'rent thing
Was the homo (dative, hominy),
Of far-away B.C.
From us of Anno Domini!

                              T. R. YBARRA

To a Thesaurus

O precious codex, volume, tome,
    Book, writing, compilation, work
Attend the while I pen a pome,
    A jest, a jape, a quip, a quirk.

For I would pen, engross, indite,
    Transcribe, set forth, compose, address,
Record, submit—yea, even write
    An ode, an elegy to bless—

To bless, set store by, celebrate,
    Approve, esteem, endow with soul,
Commend, acclaim, appreciate,
    Immortalize, laud, praise, extol

Thy merit, goodness, value, worth,
    Expedience, utility—
O manna, honey, salt of earth,
    I sing, I chant, I worship thee!

How could I manage, live, exist,
    Obtain, produce, be real, prevail,
Be present in the flesh, subsist,
    Have place, become, breathe or inhale

Without thy help, recruit, support,
    Opitulation, furtherance,
Assistance, rescue, aid, resort,
    Favour, sustention and advance?

Alas! Alack! and well-a-day!
    My case would then be dour and sad,
Likewise distressing, dismal, grey,
    Pathetic, mournful, dreary, bad.

*   *   *   *

Though I could keep this up all day,
    This lyric, elegiac song,
Meseems hath come the time to say
    Farewell! Adieu! Good-bye! So long!

                FRANKLIN P. ADAMS

Lapsus Linguae

We wanted Li Wing
    But we winged Willie Wong,
A sad but excusable
    Slip of the tong.

                KEITH PRESTON

Unearned Increment

The Old Mandarin
Always perplexes his friend the Adjuster
At the Prune Exchange Bank
By adding his balances together
In the Chinese fashion.
For example: he once had $5000 in the bank
And drew various checks against it.
He drew $2000; thus leaving a balance of $3000.
He drew $1500; thus leaving a balance of $1500.
He drew $900; thus leaving a balance of $600.
He drew $600; thus leaving a balance of   000.
        ‾‾‾‾‾   ‾‾‾‾‾
        $5000. $5100.
Yet, as you see, when he adds his various balances
He finds that they total $5100
And the Old Mandarin therefore maintains
There should still be $100 to his credit.
They had to engage the Governor of the Federal Re-
    serve
To explain the fallacy to him.

                                    CHRISTOPHER MORLEY

O I C

I'm in a 10der mood today
   & feel poetic, 2;
4 fun I'll just—off a line
   & send it off 2 U.

I'm sorry you've been 6 o long;
   Don't B disconsol8;
But bear your ills with 42de,
   & they won't seem so gr8.

                                    ANONYMOUS

Sing a Song of the Cities

"Towanda Winooski? Gowanda!"
　　Rahway Setauket Eugene.
"Watseka? Ware! Tonawanda!"
　　Flushing Modesto De Queen.

"Wantagh Revere Petaluma!
　　Pontiac! Rye! Champaign!
Kissimmee Smackover! Yuma!"
　　Ossining, Waverly Kane.

"Rockaway! Homestead Tacoma!
　　Neenah Metuchen Peru!
Owego Moberly Homer!
　　Dover Andover Depew!"

MORRIS BISHOP

To an Egyptian Boy

Child of the gorgeous East, whose ardent suns
　　Have kissed thy velvet skin to deeper lustre
　　　　And given thine almond eyes
　　　　A look more calm and wise
　　Than any we pale Westerners can muster,
Alas! my mean intelligence affords
No clue to grasp the meaning of the words
　　Which vehemently from thy larynx leap.
How is it that the liquid language runs?
　　"Nai—soring—trif—erwonbi—aster—ferish—ip."

E'en so, methinks, did CLEOPATRA woo
　　Her vanquished victor, couched on scented roses
　　　　And PHARAOH from his throne
　　　　With more imperious tone
　　Addressed in some such terms rebellious Moses;

And esoteric priests in Theban shrines,
Their ritual conned from hieroglyphic signs,
    Thus muttered incantations dark and deep
To Isis and Osiris, Thoth and Shu:
    "Nai—soring—trîf—erwonbi—aster—ferish—ip."

In all my youthful studies why was this
    Left out? What tutor shall I blame my folly on?
        From Sekhet-Hetepu
        Return to mortal view,
    O shade of BRUGSCH or MARIETTE or CHAMPOLLION;
Expound the message latent in his speech
Or send a clearer medium, I beseech;
    For lo! I listen till I almost weep
For anguish at the priceless gems I miss:
    "Nai—soring—trîf—erwonbi—aster—ferish—ip."

To sundry greenish orbs arranged on trays—
    Unripe, unluscious fruit—he draws attention.
        My mind, till now so dark,
        Receives a sudden spark
    That glows and flames to perfect comprehension;
And I, whom no Rosetta Stone assists,
Become the peer of Egyptologists,
    From whom exotic tongues no secrets keep;
For this is what the alien blighter says:
    "Nice orang'; three for one piastre; very cheap."

H. W. BERRY

A False Gallop of Analogies

"The Chavender, or Chub."—IZAAK WALTON

There is a fine stuffed chavender,
    A chavender, or chub
That decks the rural pavender,
    The pavender, or pub,

Wherein I eat my gravender,
  My gravender, or grub.

How good the honest gravender!
How snug the rustic pavender!
From sheets as sweet as lavender,
  As lavender, or lub,
I jump into my tavender,
  My tavender, or tub.

Alas! for town and clavender,
  For business and for club!
They call me from my pavender
To-night; ay, there's the ravender,
  Ay, there comes in the rub!
To leave each blooming shravender,
  Each Spring-bedizened shrub,
And meet the horsy savender,
  The very forward sub,
At dinner at the clavender,
And then at billiards dravender,
  At billiards soundly drub
The self-sufficient cavender,
  The not ill-meaning cub,
Who me a bear will davender,
  A bear unduly dub,
Because I sometimes snavender,
  Not too severely snub
His setting right the clavender,
  His teaching all the club!

Farewell to peaceful pavender,
  My river-dreaming pub,
To sheets as sweet as lavender,
To homely, wholesome gravender,
And you, inspiring chavender,
  Stuff'd chavender, or chub.

             W. ST. LEGER

Triolets Ollendorfiens

Je suis le frère
Du bon cocher:
Où est sa mère?
Je suis le frère.
Tu es le père
Du jardinier:
Je suis le frère
Du bon cocher.

Où est mon canif?
J'ai perdu ma chatte.
Je veux du rosbif.
Où est mon canif?
J'ai tué le Juif.
Faut-il qu'on se batte?
Où est mon canif?
J'ai perdu ma chatte.

La belle cousine
Du fils de ma bru [1]
Vit dans ma cuisine,
La belle cousine!
Ta laide voisine
N'a jamais connu
La belle cousine
Du fils de ma bru.

J. K. STEPHEN

Aestivation

In candent ire the solar splendor flames;
The foles, languescent, pend from arid rames;
His humid front the cive, anheling, wipes,
And dreams of erring on ventiferous ripes.

[1] Daughter-in-law.

How dulce to vive occult to mortal eyes,
Dorm on the herb with none to supervise,
Carp the suave berries from the crescent vine,
And bibe the flow from longicaudate kine!

To me, alas! no verdurous visions come,
Save yon exiguous pool's confervascum,—
No concave vast repeats the tender hue
That laves my milk-jug with celestial blue!

Me wretched! Let me curr to quercine shades!
Effund your albid hausts, lactiferous maids!
O, might I vole to some umbrageous clump,—
Depart,—be off,—excede,—evade,—erump!

OLIVER WENDELL HOLMES

The Axolotl

"The axolotl
Looks a littl
Like the ozelotl,
Itl

"Drink a greatl
More than whatl
Fill the fatl
Whiskey bottl.

"The food it eatsl
Be no morsl:
Only meatsl
Drive its dorsl.

"Such an awfl
Fish to kettl!"
"You said a mawfl,
Pop'epetl!"

DAVID McCORD

The Modern Hiawatha

From "The Song of Milkanwatha"

He killed the noble Mudjokivis,
With the skin he made him mittens,
Made them with the fur side inside,
Made them with the skin side outside,
He, to get the warm side inside,
Put the inside skin side outside:
He, to get the cold side outside,
Put the warm side fur side inside:
That's why he put the fur side inside,
Why he put the skin side outside,
Why he turned them inside outside.

GEORGE A. STRONG

A Play on Words

Assert ten barren love day made
    Dan woo'd her hart buy nigh tan day;
Butt wen knee begged she'd marry hymn,
    The crewel bell may dancer neigh.
Lo atter fee tin vein he side
    Ant holder office offal pane—
A lasses mown touched knot terse sole—
    His grown was sever awl Lynn vane.

"Owe, beam my bride, my deer, rye prey,
    And here mice size beef ore rye dye;
Oak caste mean knot tin scorn neigh way—
    Yew are the apple love me nigh!"
She herd Dan new we truly spoke.
    Key was of noble berth, and bread
Tool lofty mean and hie renown,
    The air too grate testates, 't was head.

"Ewe wood due bettor, sir," she bald,
　"Took court sum mother girl, lie wean—
Ewer knot mice stile, lisle never share
　The thrown domestic azure quean!"
" 'Tis dun, no fare butt Scilly won—
　Aisle waist know father size on the!"
Oft tooth the nay bring porte tea flue
　And through himself into the see.

EUGENE FIELD

To His Godson Gerald C. A. Jackson

Aids to answering the first question in the Catechism

When C. J. G. Arden goes out in the garden,
　To play with the slugs and snails,
Their lives are imperilled by C. A. J. Gerald,
　Who treads on their backs and their tails.
Their tails and their backs on, treads G. C. A. Jackson,
　And each of them squirms and exclaims,
'Oh, G. A. J. Christopher, see how I twist over,
　Under your numerous names.'

A. E. HOUSMAN

History of Education

The decent docent doesn't doze:
He teaches standing on his toes.
His student dassn't doze—and does,
And that's what teaching is and was.

DAVID McCORD

The Up-Set

Joseph Moncure "Kid" March vs.
Robert "Farmer" Frost

One

Kid March had the stuff but his style was hard;
And he never got a chance at the Pulitzer Award.

Keen as a razor,
Tough as a strop,
He could write like a fool
And he knew when to stop.
His pace was swift
His plot was bold,
His last-line wallop
Would drop you cold.
Compact, terse, hard-boiled:
Tough?
I'll tell de woild.

His language was crude,
Colorful,
Rough:
With lines short,
But long enough.
Compact;
Neat.
He was light on his poetical feet.
(I'd like to show you
How bad he'd swear;
But it couldn't be printed in *Vanity Fair*.)
His stuff was modern.
He packed a punch.
But he didn't rate
With the Classical Bunch;

And whatever he wrote, you knew that he gave
Milton a shudder in his grave.
He was slick:
Quick:
Each effect was like a brick.

His poetry had the general mien
Of a sonnet written on a sewing-machine.
He got you nervous:
You never could tell
If his verse was prose, or what the hell.
The rhymes were cock-eyed—
The lines wouldn't scan—
But you couldn't lay it down once you began.
He'd warm up slow:
He'd let you go
For maybe a couple of pages or so.
Then he'd start.
One left—
One right—
And you'd keep on reading
The rest of the night.
Abrupt,
Emphatic,
His poems were always dramatic.

2

Then,
Sudden disaster:
A Boston pastor
Invoked the Senate's Clean Books law,
And hung a hot one on March's jaw.
They discovered his first book told the truth
And therefore endangered the morals of youth.
"Literature," Kid March pled.
"Obscene," the censor said.

Youth must be saved.
Mr. Sumner knew best.
"The Wild Party" was suppressed.

Two

Time out.
One year has passed:
Kid March has been released at last.
He is back to try to win his laurels
Without corrupting American morals.
Now he offers "The Set-Up,"
A dramatic recital,
To meet all comers for the Poetry title.

Three

The Hall of Fame was packed that night
With a public eager to see the fight
Between the challenger,
"Kid" March's book,
And "Farmer" Frost's "West-running Brook."
Battle of the Century!
Classic Collision!
Ten editions to a decision!

The huge Arena seemed dim,
Vast,
Filled with the shadows of the past.
The gathering crowd was vague and blurred.
Their judgment depended
On what they heard:
Newspaper ads;
Publicity stunts;
(The American public buys anything once.)
They only perused what the critics told them
And bought what the man in the bookstore sold them.

2

In the centre of the floor
The raised ring stood;
The light glared down from a metal hood.
The figures within it were ponderous,
Slow;
They crouched without exchanging a blow.
They didn't seem to do much fighting,
But that is the trouble with epic writing.

Around the ring,
Alert for news,
The critics were writing
Their reviews:
Each was preparing a pompous quotation
To bolster his critical reputation;
Each was prepared to sacrifice that
If a wise-crack happened to sound more pat.
They balanced their typewriters on their knees,
And they never raised their eyes
From the keys.
They didn't have to watch the racket.
They did their reviews right from the jacket.
Praising their friends;
Smug;
Secure:
The judges of American literature.

"Hey, buddy, I missed de opening bout.
How did dem two lightweights make out?"

"Who, dem?
Oh, fine.
Parker knocked out Hoffenstein!
One on the button in the third——"
"Aw, I knew dat Parker could lick dat bird!"

Shouts, calls,
Caterwauls:
"Come on, 'John Brown,'
Knock him down!"
Concerted yelling from one direction:
The Book-of-the-Month Club cheering section.

"Who's fighting now?"

"You kidding me? Say,
Dis here is Battling Steve Benét!"

"Yeh? Didn't he train wit' Guggenheim?"

"Sure, he handled him quite a time;
Two years in Yurrop——"

"Gees, he *oughta* be prime!"

Bowed;
A little cowed;
Several old timers sat in the crowd:
Markham, still leaning on the hoe
Which once had knocked them for a row;
And Masters, of a former age
When epitaphs were all the rage.
Dead;
Almost unread.
Forgotten by a younger set
Which had written nothing to forget.

"Who's Benét fighting?"

"Some old-time gink;
Sandburg, or some such name, I think.
It doesn't matter.
He don't rate.
I hear he had trouble to make the weight."

"Sure, Steve should be middle-weight champeen
With his epics of the American scene——"

Clang!

"There goes the bell!
Who's the announcer?"

"That's John Riddell!"

"Thee-ee decision, ladies and gents—
Thee-ee-ee decision is—
BENÉT!
He is now being matched to meet Millay
In this Arena, one year from to-day."

3

A happy shout.

"Good Morning, America" is carried out;
The crowd settles down for the final bout.
The ring is cleared,
The clamor has died.
Covici's elbow
Dug Kid March's side.

"Well—" he smiled.
"Here goes!
Come on, now—
On your toes!"

Friede lifted the bucket.
"Okay," he said.
Kid March strode down the aisle ahead.

A murmur arose from the gaping crowd;
They exchanged eager comments aloud:
"That's Kid March!
Did you read 'The Wild Party'?"

"Well, the Kid's looking pretty hearty!"

"I hear he uses Masefield's style——"

"Aw, he could beat Masefield by a mile!"

Suddenly
Frost appeared;
A few hoarse voices cheered.
Kid March stared at what he saw:
Granite shoulders;
New England jaw;
A Hardy form;
Plenty of meat;
Balanced securely
On classical feet;
Fists like sonnets,
Solid,
Sure.
Powerful lines
That would endure.

Something in March grew suddenly tight;
He knew he was in for a nasty fight.

4

The bell hammered,
Staccato,
Swift.
John Riddell's arm began to lift:

"LA-A-DEES—AN'
Gents . . ."
His voice roared out;
Echoed;
Immense:
In the vast arena
The words were lost.
". . . IN THIS CORNER—
FARMER FROST . . .!"

The Farmer bowed,
As stiff as starch.

". . . AND IN THIS CORNER—"
He bellowed:

". . . KID MARCH!"

Covici picked March's bathrobe up.
"All right, Kid—
Go get 'em, pup!"
The bell clanged.
Their gloves touched,
Brushed;
Around the ring the critics sat hushed.

5

They circled a moment,
Getting acquainted.
Kid March pretended to rhyme:
Feinted.
Frost raised his eyebrows
And shrugged unheeding;
He couldn't forget his Boston breeding.

The Kid
Crouched;
He
Pulled
His
Blows:
Then suddenly shot one full-length to the nose.

It caught Frost by surprise;
He glared at Kid March
And blinked his eyes.
They circled again;
Neither one led.
The Kid played the body;
Frost aimed at the head.
"Come on, now, Farmer!

Dis guy ain't nuttin'—
Shoot him a trilogy to de button!
Sock 'im wit' a landscape—
Put him away!
Just send him a quatrain:
A, B, B, A!"

Applause and jeers from the opposite faction:
•"You got him on plot, Kid—
Show us some action!"

6

Then suddenly,
Ominously,
Austere,
Farmer Frost uncorked an idea.

Kid March saw it coming;
He stood surprised.
His brain seemed dull,
Paralyzed.
He watched it coming
A hell of a while:
It sprang from the earth
In Vergilian style;
Started slow;
Gathered force;
Rose in a purely classical course.
March ducked too late
To save himself—!
It knocked him
For a five-foot shelf.

"Two . . .
"Three . . ."
He blinked his eyes and tried to see.
He seemed to be lying

On the floor:
He couldn't remember . . .
A voice droned *"Four . . ."*

His brain clicked.
Now he knew what it said:
They were counting editions
Over his head.
"Five . . ." said the voice,
Almost lost:
He had to get up
And get this Frost!

He crouched;
Sprang!
No time for rhymes now—
To hell with that!
He struck,
Hit something hard,
Slumped back against the ropes.

He glanced at his feet—
Then stared aghast—
He seemed to have won the fight at last!
Frost writhed there before him
In great agitation,
Clutching in both hands
His reputation.

The crowd rose:
Booed:
Clamored:
The bell hammered.
John Riddell sprang through the ropes once more,
And raised the Farmer's limp wrist from the floor.
He held it aloft;
Waved his hat;
Bowed.
His voice rang out above the crowd:

"Frost wins on a foul!
The judges' slips show it!
Kid March is ruled out—
He wasn't a poet!"

Four

And that is the tale of how Kid March lost
The critics' decision to Farmer Frost.
They declared Frost poet laureate,
And as for March,
He got the gate . .
As a matter of fact,
It was just as he'd planned,
For the whole gate totalled some fifty grand.
Which shows that it pays
To be a palooka:
Frost got the credit,
But March got the lucre.

2

And the moral is this: in American verse
The better you are, the pay is worse.

COREY FORD

THE UNFAIR SEX

I grieve about my fellow-men
For dark and dreary is their way.
But I remember, now and then,
That once a week they get their pay.

ELSPETH

In the Days of Crinoline

A plain tilt-bonnet on her head
She took the path across the leaze.
—Her spouse the vicar, gardening, said,
"Too dowdy that, for coquetries,
 So I can hoe at ease."

But when she had passed into the heath,
And gained the wood beyond the flat,
She raised her skirts, and from beneath
Unpinned and drew as from a sheath
 An ostrich-feathered hat.

And where the hat had hung she now
Concealed and pinned the dowdy hood,
And set the hat upon her brow,
And thus emerging from the wood
 Tripped on in jaunty mood.

The sun was low and crimson-faced
As two came that way from the town,
And plunged into the wood untraced. . . .
When separately therefrom they paced
 The sun had quite gone down.

The hat and feather disappeared,
The dowdy hood again was donned,
And in the gloom the fair one neared
Her home and husband dour, who conned
 Calmly his blue-eyed blonde.

"To-day," he said, "you have shown good sense,
A dress so modest and so meek
Should always deck your goings hence
Alone." And as a recompense
 He kissed her on the cheek.

THOMAS HARDY

A Reasonable Affliction

On his death-bed poor Lubin lies;
   His spouse is in despair;
With frequent sobs and mutual cries,
   They both express their care.

"A different cause," says Parson Sly,
   "The same effect may give:
Poor Lubin fears that he may die;
   His wife, that he may live."

              MATTHEW PRIOR

On Lady Poltagrue, a Public Peril

The Devil, having nothing else to do,
Went off to tempt My Lady Poltagrue.
My Lady, tempted by a private whim,
To his extreme annoyance, tempted him.

              HILAIRE BELLOC

Experience

Some men break your heart in two,
   Some men fawn and flatter,
Some men never look at you;
   And that cleans up the matter.

             DOROTHY PARKER

Wanted: One Cave Man with Club

Oh, for a man to take me out
And feed me fowl *or* sauerkraut
Without first asking *where* to dine.
If such there be, would he were mine!

             MARGARET FISHBACK

Take Me in your Arms,
Miss Moneypenny-Wilson

Take me in your arms, Miss Moneypenny-Wilson,
   Take me in your arms, Miss Bates;
Fatal are your charms, Miss Moneypenny-Wilson,
   Fatal are your charms, Miss Bates;
Say you are my own, Miss Moneypenny-Wilson,
   Say you are my own, Miss Bates;
You I love alone, Miss Moneypenny-Wilson,
   You, and you alone, Miss Bates.

Sweet is the morn, Miss Moneypenny-Wilson;
   Sweet is the dawn, Miss B.,
But sweeter than the dawn and the daisies on the lawn
   Are you, sweet nymphs, to me.
Sweet, sweet, sweet is the sugar to the beet,
   Sweet is the honey to the bee,
But sweeter far than such sweets are
   Are your sweet names to me.
Oh, bitter, bitter, bitter is the lemon to the fritter,
   Bitter is the salt to the sea,
And bitter, very bitter was my figure to the fitter
   Who fitted this suit on me;
Bitter to the sitter, when the crowds come and titter,
   Must the R.A.'s portrait be,
But bitterer by far than these bitternesses are
   Is your bitter scorn to me.

Moon of my delight, Miss Moneypenny-Wilson,
   Moon of my delight, Miss Bates;
Cold as you are bright, Miss Moneypenny-Wilson,
   Icily polite, Miss Bates;
Hear you not my voice, Miss Moneypenny-Wilson?
   Hear you not my voice, Miss Bates?
Are you deaf by choice, Miss Moneypenny-Wilson?
   Are you deaf by choice, Miss Bates?

Deaf to my cries, Miss Moneypenny-Wilson,
　　Deaf to my sighs, Miss B.;
Deaf to my songs and the story of my wrongs,
　　Deaf to my minstrelsy;
Deafer than a newt to the sound of the flute,
　　Deafer than a stone to the sea;
Deafer than a heifer to the sighing of a zephyr
　　Are your deaf ears to me.
Cold, cold, cold as the melancholy mould,
　　Cold as the foam-cold sea,
Colder than the shoulder of a neolithic boulder
　　Are the shoulders you show to me.
Cruel, cruel, cruel is the flame to the fuel,
　　Cruel is the axe to the tree,
But crueller and keener than a coster's concertina
　　Is your cruel, cruel scorn to me.

PATRICK BARRINGTON

His Hirsute Suit

A bristling beard was his peculiarity:
　　He kissed. She thought it smacked of insincerity,
　　And bridling up remarked with great severity,
'Such misdemeanours are, I trust, a rarity;
Also your face, besides its angularity,
　　Is hidden in a razorless asperity:
　　Were it not so, I call it great temerity—
Our walks in life are not upon a parity.'

Wherefore he shaved, to give his chin the purity
　　It knew ere he emerged from his minority.
The razor, naked, with no guard's security,
　　Slipped. Gizzard cut, he joined the great majority.
Where he will pass the æons of futurity—
　　Above—below—I can't say with authority.

FRANK SIDGWICK

Madeline at Jefferson Market
Night Court

If it wasn't for me and the likes of me
And what I choose to do,
What the hell, I'd like to know, would become of the
    likes of you?
Instead of tryin' "to save a soul"
You bums would hafta shovel coal!

MARGARET McGOVERN

Unfortunate Coincidence

By the time you swear you're his,
    Shivering and sighing,
And he vows his passion is
    Infinite, undying—
Lady, make a note of this:
    One of you is lying.

DOROTHY PARKER

Portrait of the Artist

Oh, lead me to a quiet cell
    Where never footfall rankles,
And bar the window passing well,
    And gyve my wrists and ankles.

Oh, wrap my eyes with linen fair,
    With hempen cord go bind me,
And, of your mercy, leave me there,
    Nor tell them where to find me.

Oh, lock the portal as you go,
　　And see its bolts be double. . . .
Come back in half an hour or so,
　　And I will be in trouble.

DOROTHY PARKER

Triolet on a Downhill Road

The older I grow
　　The meaner I get.
Don't tell *me*. I *know*
The older I grow.
Like peanuts and snow,
　　Like gossip and debt,
The older I grow
　　The meaner I get.

MARGARET FISHBACK

Gemini and Virgo

Some vast amount of years ago,
　　Ere all my youth had vanish'd from me,
A boy it was my lot to know,
　　Whom his familiar friends called Tommy.

I love to gaze upon a child;
　　A young bud bursting into blossom;
Artless, as Eve yet unbeguiled,
　　And agile as a young opossum:

And such was he. A calm-brow'd lad,
　　Yet mad, at moments, as a hatter:
Why hatters as a race are mad
　　I never knew, nor does it matter.

He was what nurses call a "limb";
  One of those small misguided creatures,
Who, tho' their intellects are dim,
  Are one too many for their teachers:

And, if you asked of him to say
  What twice 10 was, or 3 times 7,
He'd glance (in quite a placid way)
  From heaven to earth, from earth to heaven;

And smile, and look politely round,
  To catch a casual suggestion;
But make no effort to propound
  Any solution of the question.

And so not much esteemed was he
  Of the authorities: and therefore
He fraternized by chance with me,
  Needing a somebody to care for:

And three fair summers did we twain
  Live (as they say) and love together;
And bore by turns the wholesome cane
  Till our young skins became as leather:

And carved our names on every desk,
  And tore our clothes, and inked our collars;
And looked unique and picturesque,
  But not, it may be, model scholars.

We did much as we chose to do;
  We'd never heard of Mrs. Grundy;
All the theology we knew
  Was that we mightn't play on Sunday;

And all the general truths, that cakes
  Were to be bought at four a penny,
And that excruciating aches
  Resulted if we ate too many.

And seeing ignorance is bliss,
    And wisdom consequently folly,
The obvious result is this—
    That our two lives were very jolly.

At last the separation came.
    Real love, at that time, was the fashion;
And by a horrid chance, the same
    Young thing was, to us both, a passion.

Old Poser snorted like a horse:
    His feet were large, his hands were pimply,
His manner, when excited, coarse:—
    But Miss P. was an angel simply.

She was a blushing, gushing thing;
    All—more than all—my fancy painted;
Once—when she helped me to a wing
    Of goose—I thought I should have fainted.

The people said that she was blue:
    But I was green, and loved her dearly.
She was approaching thirty-two;
    And I was then eleven, nearly.

I did not love as others do;
    (None ever did that I've heard tell of;)
My passion was a byword through
    The town she was, of course, the belle of.

Oh sweet—as to the toilworn man
    The far-off sound of rippling river;
As to cadets in Hindostan
    The fleeting remnant of their liver—

To me was Anna; dear as gold
    That fills the miser's sunless coffers;
As to the spinster, growing old,
    The thought—the dream—that she had offers.

I'd sent her little gifts of fruit;
   I'd written lines to her as Venus;
I'd sworn unflinchingly to shoot
   The man who dared to come between us:

And it was you, my Thomas, you,
   The friend in whom my soul confided,
Who dared to gaze on her—to do,
   I may say, much the same as I did.

One night, I *saw* him squeeze her hand;
   There was no doubt about the matter;
I said he must resign, or stand
   My vengeance—and he chose the latter.

We met, we "planted" blows on blows:
   We fought as long as we were able:
My rival had a bottle-nose,
   And both my speaking eyes were sable,

When the school-bell cut short our strife.
   Miss P. gave both of us a plaister;
And in a week became the wife
   Of Horace Nibbs, the writing-master.

    *   *   *   *

I loved her then—I'd love her still,
   Only one must not love Another's:
But thou and I, my Tommy, will,
   When we again meet, meet as brothers.

It may be that in age one seeks
   Peace only: that the blood is brisker
In boys' veins, than in theirs whose cheeks
   Are partially obscured by whisker;

Or that the growing ages steal
   The memories of past wrongs from us.
But this is certain—that I feel
   Most friendly unto thee, oh Thomas!

And whereso'er we meet again,
  On this or that side the equator,
If I've not turned teetotaller then,
  And have wherewith to pay the waiter,

To thee I'll drain the modest cup,
  Ignite with thee the mild Havannah;
And we will waft, while liquoring up,
  Forgiveness to the heartless Anna.

C. S. CALVERLEY

Part Two

AFTER ALL

Some will have seen a star by day—
But few, I think, the Milky Way.

THE EDITOR

EXTRADUCTION

Let's put it this way: If you enjoyed your dinner in the main dining room, you might like to see what goes on in the kitchen. *After All* is a shelf of ingredients, largely unmixed but mixable. What it comprises was dictated entirely by the editor's personal whim and taste. Sources are given for certain verses in the book to assist the inquisitive reader in scouting out the original. Collateral and marginal reference to others may prove of more interest to the verse-fancier than to the lay reader, but no particular patron was previsioned. Where the editor has discovered two authors treating the same subject with nearly equal animation, the variant is likely to be quoted here. A few basic glossaries for dialect stuff were designed to be helpful; but care has been taken to avoid the pompous in this and any other use of the scholar's apparatus. You won't find the humdrum meaning of *prankt, malars, ywis,* etc., and such, for which a good dictionary is the cure. This is not a textbook, but a recipe for cheer.

After All itself was intended purely for sampling and for fun. If you are looking or hoping for a note on any particular verse-specimen, you have simply to leaf the pages until you come to a number corresponding to the page on which that verse is printed in the text. No number, no note. Short of a book of directions and a good cigar, this clears up the matter.

To shift the pliant metaphor: Good hunting, and tight lines!

D. T. W. McC.

i. *Sir W. S. Gilbert.* From *H.M.S. Pinafore,* i. "Wot cher!," the opening words of Albert Chevalier's famous music hall song—the chorus—would appear to be somewhat akin.

The Settlement of Rhode Island, 1874, by Charles T. Miller; taken from *Rhode Island in Verse,* edited by Mary Louisa Brown, 1936. Roger, of course, is Roger Williams. The next stanza explains the pun:

> The Indians thought it exceedingly cool,
>> And said we have neither chairs nor stool;
> So sit on the rock, you fussy old fool,
>> As all the rest of us do.

From *A Key into the Language of America,* by Roger Williams, 1643—seven years after the founding of Providence, R. I.:

> "What cheare Nétop? is the generall salutation
> of all English toward them, Nétop is friend."

xv. *beat feet.* Of course, reduplicated words are not the invention of the present younger generation. We think of *clap-trap, harum-scarum, hobnob,* etc., as old familiars. I am indebted to Mr. Harold Wentworth, author of the *American Dialect Dictionary,* for directing me to *A Dictionary of Reduplicated Words in the English Language* by Henry Benjamin Wheatley (London, 1866), which contains examples of about 600 such, including *handy-pandy, hanky-panky,* and many others better forgotten.

xvi. *"Sighted sub sank same."* An anonymous variation, reported orally, is

> Sighted Sub;
> Glub, glub!

1. *Plato. REPublic, 10;* Socrates speaking.

3. *Circumstance without Pomp.* Is there not a curious undertone in this very English verse, akin to the spirit of the Australian "Waltzing Matilda," included in the same section? See especially Mr. Ernest G. Moll's sympathetic note against page 13.

4. *How Pleasant To Know Mr. Lear.* Written for a young lady of his acquaintance, who had quoted to him the words of a young lady not of his acquaintance, "How Pleasant to know Mr. Lear!"

5. *Brown's Descent.* The author's final version.

8. *Miniver Cheevy.* Long before the promissory keel of this anthology was laid, a clipping of F.P.A.'s "The Conning Tower" containing the following parody was already in a private folder against the uncertain future.

MINIVER CHEEVY, JR.

Miniver Cheevy, Jr., child
   Of Robinson's renowned creation,
Also lamented and reviled
   His generation.

Miniver similarly spurned
   The present that so irked his pater,
But that langsyne for which he yearned
   Came somewhat later.

Miniver wished he were alive
   When dividends came due each quarter,
When Goldman Sachs was 205,
   And skirts were shorter.

Miniver gave no hoot in hell
   For Camelot or Troy's proud pillage;
He would have much preferred to dwell
   In Greenwich Village.

Miniver cherished fond regrets
   For days when benefits were boundless;
When radios were crystal sets,
   And films were soundless.

Miniver missed the iron grills,
   The whispered word, the swift admission,
The bath-tub gin, and other thrills
   Of Prohibition.

Miniver longed, as all men long,
　To turn back time (his eyes would moisten),
To dance the Charleston, play mah jong,
　And smuggle Joyce in.

Miniver Cheevy, Jr., swore,
　Drank till his health was quite imperiled;
Miniver sighed, and read some more
　F. Scott Fitzgerald.

D. F. PARRY

9. *Plain Language from Truthful James.* In the first edition of Bret Harte's poems (Ticknor & Fields, Boston, 1871), which contains this now venerable familiar, the words "Table Mountain, 1870" appear directly under the title. Editors usually omit it, and frequently retitle this best known of Bret Harte's verses, "The Heathen Chinee." "Further Language from Truthful James"—an excellent repeat performance—is also worth reading. A lasting parody is "The Heathen Pass-ee," by Arthur C. Hilton, which deals with cribbing in a Cambridge examination. It is included in *A Century of Parody and Imitation,* edited by Walter Jerrold and R. M. Leonard (Oxford, 1913) and in *Apes and Parrots,* an anthology of parodies collected by Sir J. C. Squire (Herbert Jenkins, Ltd., London, 1928). Squire's book is still for me the best—and likewise the most charming—collection of parodies in print. It was published in Cambridge, Mass., by Washburn & Thomas (now dissolved) in 1929. The only complaint might be that it does *not* contain Squire's own parody of Gray's "Elegy" in the voice of Edgar Lee Masters (see *Parodies at Par,* to the west of where you are now). Otherwise well worth owning.

13. *Waltzing Matilda.* Popular version. Mr. Ernest G. Moll, the Australian poet, has generously contributed the following note on this famous verse:

"The story of how *Waltzing Matilda* came to be written is recorded by an Englishman, Thomas Wood, who, during extensive travels in Australia, kept an eye out for anything in the nature of folk song. In Winton a local man told him: 'Banjo Paterson used to come and stay with old Robert McPherson, out at Dagworth Station, years ago. They were driving into Winton one day, in the buggy, along with McPherson's sister and Jack Lawton, the drover. He's told me the tale many a time. On the way they passed a man carrying his swag. "That's what we call *Waltzing Matilda* in these parts," said McPherson; and Banjo Paterson was so struck with the phrase that he got a piece of paper and wrote the verses there and then. When they got to Winton, his sister, who was a bit of a musician, wrote the tune; and they all sang it that night.'

"Though there have been some changes in music and words, they are singing it still—Australia's unofficial national anthem.

"The swagman is a familiar figure in the Australian landscape. To call him hobo or tramp is to do him a grave injustice. Like the snail he carries his house with him, but unlike the snail he is a great wanderer. His house is the blanket roll *(swag)*, which he carries on his back. In one hand he bears a tin can with a wire handle *(billy)*, a can blackened on the outside by the smoke of many fires and stained brown on the inside by the boiling of much tea. Sometimes, especially in hot country, he carries a canvas bag full of water. Hooked to the straps of his swag he has a bag *(tucker-bag)* for the food which he buys or begs or for which he does odd jobs to earn on the farms along his track. Though by reputation he is an honorable man, sometimes the desire for a little fresh mutton takes hold on him and then he takes hold of the sheep *(jumbuck)* that belongs to another. This gets him into trouble with the large landowner *(Squatter)*, and with the police, as the poem tells us.

"But the spirit of him? Like Lamb's borrower, he has risen above the hum-drum ways of the world; he has rejected the idea that man shall live by the sweat of his brow; he finds no call to burden himself with wife and child and home. The road is his home—all the roads in all Australia. He lights his campfire by the pools in dry creek-beds *(billabongs)*; in the heat of the day he rests in the shade of the gum trees *(coolibahs)*. He is free as a bird, and over a pipe in the evening he meditates on that freedom and knows that it is good. Perhaps that is why Australians celebrate him in song."

ERNEST G. MOLL

This is the original text as supplied by Mr. Moll from *Collected Verse of A. B. Paterson;* tenth collected edition, 1940, Angus & Robertson, Ltd., Sydney, Australia.

WALTZING MATILDA

(Carrying a Swag)

Oh! there once was a swagman camped in a Billabong,
    Under the shade of a Coolibah tree;
And he sang as he looked at his old billy boiling,
    "Who'll come a-waltzing Matilda with me?"

*   Who'll come a-waltzing Matilda, my darling,*
*   Who'll come a-waltzing Matilda with me?*
*   Waltzing Matilda and leading a water-bag—*
*   Who'll come a-waltzing Matilda with me?*

Down came a jumbuck to drink at the water-hole,
    Up jumped the swagman and grabbed him in glee;
And he sang as he stowed him away in his tucker-bag,
    "You'll come a-waltzing Matilda with me!"

Down came the Squatter a-riding his thoroughbred;
    Down came Policemen—one, two and three.
"Whose is the jumbuck you've got in the tucker-bag?
    You'll come a-waltzing Matilda with me."

But the swagman, he up and he jumped in the water-hole,
    Drowning himself by the Coolibah tree;
And his ghost may be heard as it sings in the Billabong
    "Who'll come a-waltzing Matilda with me?"

A. B. PATERSON

19. *The Fat-buttocked Bushmen. Malars,* not *molars,* is correct.

So far as the editor can ascertain across the barriers of friendship, most of the humorous verse written by Professor Hooton, the Harvard anthropologist, is marginalia to his current scientific work. Here, for example, is a fragment with an ancient background: *Homo modjokertensis* is the skull of a baby *Pithecanthropus erectus,* found in the Lower Pleistocene Djetis beds of Central Java in 1936. We may safely put small stock in the author's testimony that the verse comes from "a piece of paper picked up by the janitor of the Peabody Museum [of Harvard] in front of the show-case in which the cast of the skull is exhibited . . ."

Lines to Homo Somejerktensis

Young Pithy, from your Djetis bed,
You raise a scarcely human head,
With all its soft spots ossified
And sutures closed that should gape wide.
If you had lived to breed your kind,
It would have had the sort of mind
That feeds upon the comic strips
And reads with movements of the lips,
Equipped for general mastication
And not progressive education;
Instead of brows a bony torus,
And no ideals with which to bore us.

EARNEST A. HOOTON

24. *Ogden Nash.* Note for no particular reason: an antecedent of what is perhaps the most famous of all Nash verses (not included here) is in this fragment from *The Critic:*

A bumper of good liquor
Will end a contest quicker
Than justice, judge, or vicar.

RICHARD BRINSLEY SHERIDAN (1751-1816)

Mr. Franklin P. Adams in his introduction to *Innocent Merriment* cites as Mr. Nash's predecessors Thomas Hood, with "Our Village," and Sir W. S. Gilbert, with "Lost Mr. Blake." These are well known. Wrapped in the old miasmal mist is a quatrain by Rupert Brooke, which begins:

Would God I were eating plover's eggs . . .

There is one centipedal line in it. You can look it up, if you want to, in Edward Marsh's *Memoir* (John Lane, 1918). But this editor agrees with Mr. Adams that the Nashification of American verse undoubtedly owes nothing whatsoever to these prescient accidents of the past.

25. *The Flea.* Also "The Ape" and "The Goat." By the actor.

26. *M.* This seems to be a good place to explain that for financial reasons two poems by E. E. Cummings, selected with great care from the range of his collected work, had to be omitted. One of them, 24, belongs in this section—all about mice, little twitchy witches, little ghostthings, etc. I greatly regret this omission. Robert Benchley has somewhere referred to Mr. Cummings as the lower-case king. It would have been much easier in this book to have followed Mr. Cummings' practice and number each poem, and let the whole business go at that. Mr. Cummings doesn't bother with folios, either. Or tables of contents. He does other queer things. Forget about them. But don't forget about 24.

30. *The Kitten.* Ogden Nash has made the final condensation based on a relatively old theme—for even people anti-cat are apt to be partial to kittens. Oliver Herford, for example, in a little feline song modeled on Herrick concluded:

> And the Kittens of Today
> Will be Old Cats Tomorrow.

And long before Herford, Calverley in "Disaster" said:

> I had a kitten—I was rich
>   In pets—but all too soon my kitten
> Became a full-sized cat, by which
>   I've more than once been scratched and bitten . . .

31. *The Answers.* Animal and bird noises have attracted many others in the long, sweet meadow of verse. Wilson MacDonald has a nice one on crows—"The Black Crow"—in *Caw-Caw Ballads;* and T. E. Brown's "The Pessimist" begins:

> "Croak — croak — croak!
> Life's a pig-in-a-poke."
> "Indeed!" says the little Jackdaw.

Perhaps the most delightful stanza in Evoe's superb parody of Walter de la Mare—"The Last Bus," and a little too special to be pastured here—is the one which concludes:

> . . . Squabbles a squirrel; ululates a coot.

Cushlamachree! . . . *ululates* a coot!

And only the Great Counter knows how many hopefully humorous verses revolve upon what the owl says. To wit, nothing is quoted here.

32. *The Dromedary.* But the really cheerful bird:

THE COMMON CORMORANT

> The common cormorant or shag
> Lays eggs inside a paper bag
> The reason you will see no doubt
> It is to keep the lightning out
> But what these unobservant birds
> Have never noticed is that herds
> Of wandering bears may come with buns
> And steal the bags to hold the crumbs.
>
> ANONYMOUS

Taken from *The Poet's Tongue,* an unusual and rewarding anthology, chosen by W. H. Auden and John Garrett (G. Bell & Sons, Ltd., London, 1935). A volume somewhat complicated for the reader by an ingeniously difficult double-entry index. In *The Poet's Tongue* this charming verse appears unimpeded by commas as here. You will also find it (punctuated) in *Other Men's Flowers,* an anthology selected and annotated by A. P. Wavell—Field Marshal Viscount Wavell—(Putnam, 1945).

34. *Bowlines & Seascapes.* Out of the Second World War comes this American shipyard ballad. The author lives in Montana—the proof is elsewhere in this book—and the shipyard is one of Mr. Kaiser's on the Coast.

THE RIGGER

> He never heard of Newton's law
> Or tales of Archimedes old.
> He signals with a waving paw
> And guides the steel into the hold.

His hand-talk to the crane on top
Reads like the Army's semaphore,
And from the cloudlets gently drop
A dozen tons of steel and ore.

A bulkhead slipping from its boom
He heralds with a far-off "hey!"
And if you're deaf, or pinched for room,
Your carcass is a pool of whey.

Ye Okies, Arkies, men from Maine,—
'Twere better far to face a trigger,
Or tangle with a railroad train,
Than disregard the stealthy rigger!

WASHINGTON JAY McCORMICK

The word *Kurd* in "The Dromedary" and *whey* in "The Rigger" remind one of the pleasant last line of a quatrain called "Ethnology" by Henry William Hanemann:

But the Kurds have a whey of their own.

On another tack: Not all American admirers of the late Sir Thomas Lipton may be familiar with a couplet supplied, upon the occasion of one defeat, by Lady Tree, wife of the actor Sir Herbert Beerbohm-Tree. It is quoted in *The Sands of Time* by Walter Sichel (Hutchinson, London, 1923):

There is many a slipton
'Twixt the cup and the Lipton.

Still farther to windward: In the category of Whistler's famous query to Theodore Watts-Dunton when the latter took on the second surname—*"Theodore! What's Dunton?"* —belongs Mr. Sichel's remark about Sir Herbert: "He . . . added the wood to the fruit."

Algernon Charles Swinburne. A parody of Robert Browning. Swinburne himself was an excellent parodist. Not the least skillful of all examples which he committed to print is "Nephelidia," the famous one on his own alliterative, unfocused, mystical style. "His diffuseness is one of his glories," says T. S. Eliot.

From the depth of the dreamy decline of the dawn
   through a notable nimbus of nebulous moonshine . . .

Nor should "Salad," a Swinburne parody by Mortimer
Collins (1827-1876), be overlooked, if only for the ending,
thus:

> Anchovies, foam-born, like the lady
>   Whose beauty has maddened this bard;
> And olives from groves that are shady,
>   And eggs—boil 'em hard.

Above all, there is Arthur C. Hilton's "Octopus"—a parody
to end all Swinburne parodies. Two stanzas ought to prove
it:

> Strange beauty, eight limbed and eight handed,
>   Whence camest to dazzle our eyes?
> With thy bosom bespangled and banded
>   With the hues of the seas and the skies;
> Is thy home European or Asian,
>   O mystical monster marine?
> Part molluscous and partly crustacean,
>   Betwixt and between . . .
>
> Lithe limbs curling free as a creeper
>   That creeps in a desolate place,
> To enrol and envelop the sleeper
>   In a silent and stealthy embrace;
> Cruel beak craning forward to bite us,
>   Our juices to drain and to drink,
> Or to whelm us in waves of Cocytus,
>   Indelible ink! . . .

All three of the foregoing are included in *Apes and Parrots,*
edited by Sir J. C. Squire (elsewhere referred to).

37. *A Grain of Salt.* On the other hand:

THE SMUGGLER

O my true love's a smuggler and sails upon the sea,
And I would I were a seaman to go along with he;
To go along with he for the satins and the wine,
And run the tubs at Slapton when the stars do shine.

O Hollands is a good drink when the nights are cold,
And Brandy is a good drink for them as grows old.
There is lights in the cliff-top when the boats are home-
    bound,
And we run the tubs at Slapton when the word goes round.

The King he is a proud man in his grand red coat,
But I do love a smuggler in a little fishing-boat;
For he runs the Mallins lace and he spends his money free,
And I would I were a seaman to go along with he.

ANONYMOUS

Granted this is not a witty verse, yet some may find a
twinkle of humor in the brightness of its speech. It nearly
came out on the final sifting, but "to go along with he"
was one too much for I. What euphuist is not at the mercy
of the delightfully misplaced pronoun? See pages 159, 354.

38. *The Pacific Engagement.* From *Bungiana,* or an Assem-
blage of What-d'ye-call-em's (London, 1756). Reference is
to a somewhat farcical episode of the Seven Years' War:
Admiral Byng's surprising action with M. de la Galissonière
on May 20, 1756, when the former—"known to the Ad-
miralty for his hesitancy and want of initiative"—went to
relieve Minorca. Popular feeling in England demanded
that the Admiral's misconduct should be punished with
death. He was court-martialed and shot. *The Pacific Engagement* suggests that the French commander's conduct
in general was not considered much better than Byng's.
But Corbett in his *England in the Seven Years' War* (Vol.
1) calls the Marquis "probably the most capable officer in
the French Navy." Of Byng he says: "That he was a man
devoid of the character that makes a great commander is
certain, but the idea that he was not a scientific tactician
fully in touch with the developments of his time is as
certainly an error. The injustice done to him in this way
is no doubt due to the belief that naval tactics at this time
were stagnant, and Byng has been used to personify that
stagnation."

Coil down!

41. *Stephano's Song.* From *The Tempest,* ii,2. As to Shakespeare in general: If the reader has an itch for "An Old

Hare Hoar" (*Romeo and Juliet,* ii, 4) or more of the same, he is respectfully referred to the source. This collection has not a niche for more than two or three. I made up a little parcel of them all, but finally left it on the counter.

42. *Bridlewise.* It saddens me that I have not discovered, and do not know, any really amusing verses about dogs. There is one (strangely satiric) by E. B. White, but it wanted companions and was omitted. I had expected, when this collection was first planned, to devote a whole section to horses *and* dogs, but (with the exception noted) I have not found so much as one Dalmatian worthy to trail the coach. Even Charles E. Carryl's verses from *Davy and the Goblin* peter out before the end. But I still like the first two stanzas, though I wish they did not celebrate a pug— the middle syllable of *repugnant.*

> I had an educated pug,
>   His name was Tommy Jones;
> He lived upon the parlor rug
>   Exclusively on bones.
>
> And if, in a secluded room,
>   I hid one on a shelf,
> It disappeared; so I presume
>   He used to help himself. . . .

43. *The Famous Ballad of the Jubilee Cup.* For all I know—it isn't much—there may be somewhere a glossary to this remarkable verse. A friend of a friend is convinced that he discovers every year, in rereading it, at least one new sport. I have not attempted to count them all. The text is from the final revised edition of *Green Bays* (Oxford, 1930).

In this vein, D. B. Wyndham Lewis has written a Cavalier Song. You will find it in *A Treasury of British Humor,* edited by Morris Bishop (Coward-McCann, 1942). The opening lines are:

> Horse, boot, and saddle, and give it a rouse!
> Leap to the gaskins and swing at the chouse!
> Look to the surcingle, tighten the rein,
> Pause at the postern and gallop again!

51. *A Soldier of Weight.* The suggestion that a horse has a long memory appears also in a verse called "Over the Hills with Nancy," by Gelett Burgess, from *A Gage of Youth:*

> She has tightened her cinch by another inch,
>   She has shortened her stirrup strap,
> She is off with a whirl of horse and girl . . .

is the way this unorthodox race of the side-saddle era begins. It concludes:

> Oh, fair astride does Nancy ride,
>   And her spur she uses free,
> And it's little she cares for the gown she wears,
>   And it's little she cares for me.
>
> But the strawberry roan with the sharp backbone
>   That Nancy rode that day,
> He doesn't forget that Saturday yet,
>   When Nancy led the way!

The weary wayworn strawberry roan apparently left no memoirs, but Ribsy, the talking horse in *Davy and the Goblin,* arranged his history in popular form—in six canters. Here are perhaps the two happiest stanzas:

> As spry as a kid and as trim as a spider
>   Was I in the days of the Turnip-top Hunt,
> When I used to get rid of the weight of my rider
>   And canter contentedly in at the front.
>
> I never was told that this jocular feature
>   Of mine was a trick reprehensibly rude,
> And yet I was sold, like a commonplace creature,
>   To work in a circus for lodgings and food.

CHARLES E. CARRYL

62. *Infant Innocence.* Taken from *A.E.H.*, by Laurence Housman (Jonathan Cape, London, 1937). A note in square brackets at the foot of the poem says: "This was accompanied by a picture of a large fat bear, a nursemaid fleeing in the distance, and an empty perambulator."

65. *A Tonversation with Baby.* Quite in the mood of Mr. Bishop's much-praised "How to Treat Elves." I have chosen this one because it is less well known but just as good. They are both in *Spilt Milk*, by Morris Bishop (Putnam, New York, 1942).

69. *Crossing Boston Common.* The first, and self-sufficient, stanza of a four-stanza verse from *Pen Grins*, by Louise Dyer Harris (privately printed, Andover, Mass, 1941).

72. *Engineer's Yell.* Having lived in three separate university and college towns in the course of his extracurricular life, the editor was at some pains to discover if the colleges and universities of America could not yield a reasonable number of humorous verses about undergraduate life in general. To this end letters were dispatched to a great number of institutions the width and length of the continent. The result was disappointing. Most of the suggested verses which were funny were funny for local, and often obscure, reasons. All of the institutions were generously helpful; all were dubious of their contributions. Still, two or three good things did come to light. The reader will find them all in the section called *College & Curriculum.*

Oxford and Cambridge. "Oxford and Cambridge!" says Shane Leslie in a delightful book called *The End of a Chapter* (Heinemann, London, 1916); "Oxford and Cambridge! *quis separabit?* They are the sacred twins suckled by one *alma mater* . . . It is a divine truth that Cambridge men are Aristotelians and Oxford men Platonists . . ."

> Cambridge is a witty town
> And Oxford is a wise.

Here is one of the witty Aristotelians at work in rhyme and meter [1]:

"As you proceed from Clare, past the little lane and past a modern but unused entry, you come to a small, rather forlorn little triangle of a shrubbery, which Dr.

[1] From *Cambridge Past and Present*, by Brian W. Downs (Methuen & Co., Ltd., London).

Jowett (1752-1813), tutor of the College and Regius Professor of Civil Law, laid out in the year that Louis XVI was beheaded. It was a little larger in its prime—but not much. A wit of the day—Porson, some aver—commemorated the event and its consequence in a set of verses, surviving in a number of versions. The following has the air of a 'definitive text':—

> "A little garden little Jowett made
> And fenced it with a little palisade;
> And when this garden made a little talk
> He changed it to a little gravel walk;
> If you would know the mind of little Jowett
> This little garden don't a little show it."

75. *"Go tell your tale, Lord Lovell," she said.* Mention of "your grandmother of the hoary head" suggests the sinuous charm of this anonymous quatrain—the ultimate in rearrangement of an old and wonderful proverb:

> Teach not thy parent's mother to extract
>   The embryo juices of the bird by suction.
> The good old lady can that feat enact
>   Quite irrespective of thy kind instruction.

78. *Arac's Song.* From *Princess Ida.* At the end of the first line, stanza four, occurs the stage direction: *indicating leg pieces.* This, with *Removing cuirasses, Removing their brassets* (brassarts, armor for the upper arm), and another instructive line, has been re-removed in the interest of higher visibility.

From other Gilbert verses in this collection, the purely singable (less readable) repetitious choruses have been largely detached. The wounds would appear to have healed.

81. *Rev. Anthony C. Deane.* Born in 1870. Like the younger Milne, he belongs to the *Granta-Punch* family. The present verse is the last of the four stanzas which comprise "A Rustic Song" in *New Rhymes for Old* (John Lane, The Bodley Head, Ltd., London). The reader will also find it, and many other interesting things, in *Various Verses* (Methuen & Co., Ltd., London, 1925), Dr. Deane's self-

selection of his light verse. Practitioners in the craft will judge the preface sane and unfortunately true.

83. *The Intro.* Mr. Dennis provides a glamorous glossary for *The Sentimental Bloke,* the delightful Australian book from which "The Intro" and "Pilot Cove" are taken. Helpful, of course; though sometimes the picturesque language of revelation seems no more than tangential to the fact. It is given here verbatim, and you may possibly enjoy it for its own sake. Note that the words are arranged in the order in which they appear in "The Intro," with non-duplicated words from "Pilot Cove" added at the end. When a word has two or more meanings, only the relevant one is given. A few may be obvious. *Toff* is familiar enough to Americans from its use in England, but I like the glossarist's interpretation.

Smoodge, to bill and coo; *click,* a clique, also a "push"— a company of rowdy fellows gathered for ungentle purposes; *line up,* to approach, to accost; *brums,* tawdry finery (from Brummagem—Birmingham); *back the barrer,* to intervene without invitation; *bonzer,* adjective expressing the superlative of excellence; *chat,* to address tentatively; *tart,* a young woman (contraction of sweetheart); *chiack,* vulgar banter; *lurk,* regular occupation; *treat,* excessively [an American would say *flat*]; *tom,* a girl; *guyver,* make-believe; *Buckley's* (chance), a forlorn hope (cf. American *Chinaman's chance*); *mug,* a fool; *cove,* a chap or bloke; *orfis* (office), a hint; *Ribuck,* correct . . . an interjection signifying assent [okay, in plain American]; *work the oricle,* to secure desired results; *toff,* an exalted person; *done me block,* became flustered; *run the rabbit,* convey liquor from a small public house; *ole pot,* the male parent; *chuck orf,* to chaff; *spare me days,* a pious ejaculation; *cliner,* a young unmarried female; *it's a nark* [various explanations which I somehow fail to follow; it seems to mean "no go"]; *strike,* the innocuous remnant of a hardy curse; *cobber,* boon companion; *mash,* lover; *to do one's dash,* to reach one's Waterloo; *drop the bundle,* surrender; *Pilot Cove,* a clergyman; *finger,* an eccentric or amusing person; *chats* [obviously means "gives it to me straight," as used in "Pilot Cove"; the second equivalent of *chat* in the glossary is to "word"—

to accost with fair speech. This is perhaps a better interpretation of its meaning in "The Intro," but certainly does not apply to its use in "Pilot Cove."]; *chip,* to intervene; *mag,* to talk noisily; *snuff it,* to expire.

The Sentimental Bloke has enjoyed enormous popularity in Australia (pop. 7,137,000) where it was first published (Sydney) in October, 1915. My copy in the Platypus Series —indigenous title!—is dated 1925. I do not know how many copies have since been sold, but by then some 123,000 had been distributed after more than twenty printings. This could mean that the author was able to reach one out of every 50 of his countrymen. (I venture that no American or English poet can approach such a mark!) There was an American edition in 1916, which failed to take; but with new and blood relations between us and the people Down Under, some enterprising American publisher ought to try again. I am convinced that *The Sentimental Bloke* in its hundred-odd pages has more of the eternal values, not to mention humor, than most of the protein-fed or intellectualized literature about which the critics are shouting every day. The late E. V. Lucas (see his *Cloud and Silver*) tried to interest England in the book, and Mr. H. G. Wells apparently urged Mr. Dennis "to come and work in an older land." To this invitation Mr. Dennis wisely replied: "England has many writers: we in Australia have few, and there is big work before us." May it progress.

88. *Mia Carlotta.* Miss Jolanda Calabi of the Pittsburgh Symphony Orchestra once recited for me an Italian phonetic verse, something like the familiar *ragged rascal* alliteration which English-speaking people use to show their progressing mastery of the French "r." But the Italian fragment rhymes; the *ragged rascal* doesn't. Professor Rudolph Altrocchi of the University of California has rearranged it in verse form, though (as he says) the rhythm is poor. But the sound is good:

> Il re d'Inghilterra
> Dichiara la guerra
> Per mare e per terra
> Al re del Perù.

A little more of this and we'd be off into the French sausage tongue-twister, and more.

William Maginn in *The Odoherty Papers*, vol. 1 (see page 89) says: "A curious book might be written on mispronunciations. Is there a man in ten who calls Bolivar correctly? Every one almost is ready to rhyme him as

> Bold Simon Bolivar,
> Match for old Oliver, &c., &c.

Whereas it should be

> Few can deceive, or
> Baffle Bolivar."

See Byron, if you care to pursue the matter further.

89. *Brooklynese Champion.* Baron Ireland (Nate Salsbury) in "Take Nothing for Granite" is troubled by *coryougated, mispronounciations, ilyoustrated,* etc. Why not? And what's the matter with *athalete?*

90. *One Piecee Thing.* Quoted by Lewis Carroll as a chapter heading (Knot VI) in "A Tangled Tale." The editor is not informed as to how the author of *Alice in Wonderland* came by this absorbing fragment. It is possible but not likely that he wrote it himself.

If one takes to pidgin English, hopalong printee bottomside:

NURSERY SONG IN PIDGIN ENGLISH

> Singee a songee sick a pence,
>   Pockee muchee lye;
> Dozen two time blackee bird
>   Cookee in e pie.
> When him cutee topside
>   Birdee bobbery sing;
> Himee tinkee nicey dish
>   Setee foree King!
> Kingee in a talkee loom
>   Countee muchee money;
> Queeny in e kitchee,
>   Chew-chee breadee honey.

> Servant galo shakee,
> Hangee washee clothes;
> Cho-chop comee blackee bird,
> Nipee off her nose!
>
> WHO DONE HIM, HIM NO KNOW

91. *Sonnet on Stewed Prunes.* In Norse-American, how yuicily the "y" falls on the Norseless American ear! *Skol* means will or shall; *sum, as.* But New England is a long way from Wisconsin and Mansota, and about some other words in other verses by Mr. Kirk, ay yust ant ban too sure. But I *am* sure that *The Norsk Nightingale* (Small, Maynard, 1905) went through a good many printings, all of them deserved. Dodd, Mead controls the copyright today.

92. *Arthur H. Folwell.* From "Christmas at the Purple Bean."

Sir W. S. Gilbert. From *The Sorcerer,* i.

Bayard Taylor (1825-1878). From "Angelo Orders his Dinner," a Browning parody.

93. *The Pilgrims' Thanksgiving Feast.* More about the Pilgrims in "Thoughts for St. Stephen" in *Invective & Epigram,* page 178.

94. *Bacon and Eggs.* From the American side, Keith Preston celebrated another staple in two stanzas and two choruses. The first half brace is perhaps the better:

BALLAD OF BARLEY

'Twas barley gave the dander that drove Alexander on;
And barley built the burly boys who crossed the Rubicon,
And barley braced King Charlie, whom some call Charlemagne,
To do big things in Burgundy, and Germany, and Spain.

> Not beef alone made England great:
> If Britain bows to sloth,
> 'Tis that her sons neglect of late
> The British barley broth!

97. *The Cheese-Mites Asked.* Strong cheese apparently has

something funny about it, not including its smell. Here are the first two stanzas of a three-stanza verse by the late Stoddard King:

SONG OF SWITZERLAND

(Not to be sung at less than 5,000 feet altitude)

Some of the wealthy families of Switzerland possess cheeses more than a century old, which are served only on the most important occasions.—The Boston *Globe*.

The Swiss they are a hardy race, melodious in their shout-
    ings,
They climb up to the mountain tops and slide down on
    their outings;
And then they fortify themselves against the winter's cold
By masticating cheese that is a dozen decades old.
A dozen decades old (yodel)
A dozen decades old,
Long cheese, strong cheese, a dozen decades old.

The Swiss they are a gallant race, they have no taint of fear,
They hunt the wary edelweiss, the chamois and the beer;
But most of all they rise and shine when on the balmy
    breeze
They scent the rich aroma of a centenarian cheese.
A centenarian cheese (yodel)
A centenarian cheese,
There's nothing makes them gayer than a centenarian
    cheese.

100. *Far from Somewhere*. Alaska, wonderful region that it is, seems to have produced no gold significant to this mint. The name of Service suggests something, but a search through the sourdough brings nothing to light. Two parody fragments, however, in "The Rougherneck" by Christopher Ward (1868-1943) make me wish that there were more of the same. "The Rougherneck" is signed Robert W. Surface and appears in *Foolish Fiction* (Holt, 1925).

Lost with the lust of madness, shunned like curs accurst,
Gnashing their teeth in sadness, over the borders they burst,
Behold the men and their lemans, curst with a cruel cold,

Blowing their noses like demons, they ravish the Yukon's
  gold.

The second fragment is even shorter:

Oh, hark to the toot of the malamute that's known as Dan
  McGrew.
I'll bust the snoot of the damn galoot that stole my lady
  Lou.

103. *A Correction.* Sent from Franconia to George and Harriet Whicher in Amherst after Elinor Frost had written
that it was twenty below zero. That would be about 1916.

The American Traveller. Maine is a marvellous State, as
the Coffins and Robertses keep telling us. This corollary
verse (it is possible that the dates—if I knew them for certain—would alter the order) was written by a Canadian.
Some day perhaps another Canadian, preferably a fishing
doctor-poet, will do justice to that clinic of rivers on the
Gaspé: the Patapedia, Matapedia, and Cascapedia.

THE MAIDEN OF PASSAMAQUODDY

Sweet maiden of Passamaquoddy,
  Shall we seek for communion of souls
Where the deep Mississippi meanders,
  Or the distant Saskatchewan rolls?

Ah no—for in Maine I shall find thee,
  A sweetly sequestrated nook
Where the winding Skoodoowabskooksis
  Joins with the Skoodoowabskook.

There wander two beautiful rivers
  With many a winding and crook;
The one is the Skoodoowabskooksis;
  The other—the Skoodoowabskook.

Ah, sweetest of haunts! tho' unmentioned
  In Geography, Atlas, or Book,
How fair is the Skoodoowabskooksis
  When joining the Skoodoowabskook.

Our cot shall be close by the waters
　　Within that sequestrated nook—
Reflected in Skoodoowabskooksis
　　And mirrored in Skoodoowabskook!

*　　　*　　　*

Your food shall be fish from the waters,
　　Drawn forth on the point of a hook
From murmuring Skoodoowabskooksis,
　　On wandering Skoodoowabskook.

*　　　*　　　*

And you shall preside at the banquet
　　And I will wait on thee as cook;
And we'll talk of the Skoodoowabskooksis,
　　And sing of the Skoodoowabskook!

Let others sing loudly of Saco,
　　Of Quoddy, and Tatamagouche,
Of Kennebeccasis, and Quaco,
　　Of Merigonish, and Buctouche.

Of Nashwaak, and Magaguadaoique
　　Of Memmerimammericook,—
There's none like the Skoodoowabskooksis
　　Excepting the Skoodoowabskook.

JAMES DE MILLE

I have been unable to trace the source of the in some
respects pleasanter, and certainly shorter, variation of the
above which appeared in *Time*, June 19, 1944, page 10.
Its middle stanza runs this way:

Meduxnakik's waters are bluer,
Nepisiguit's pools are more black,
More green is the bright Oromocto,
And browner the Petitcodiac.
But colors more radiant in autumn
I see when I'm casting my hook
In the waves of the Skoodawabskooksis
Or perhaps in the Skoodawabskook.

JAMES DE MILLE

There is more of the sort in "Hiram Hover," a ballad
of New England life (after Whittier) by Bayard Taylor. He

starts off bravely with *Moosatockmaguntic,* rhyming it with *Skuntic,* trailing off into *Squeedunk . . . Pentucket.* But the epidemic of that particular disease has now been under control for a good many years. It was a virus.

107. *New England.* A delightful quatrain by E. A., which would be in this collection but for possible copyright complications (no fault of Mr. Untermeyer's), made its début in *From Another World* by Louis Untermeyer (Harcourt, Brace, 1939). It is called "Too Much Coffee."

Come to Britain. Sir A. P. Herbert for England; a native of Montana for the Bonanza:

In Montana

A Land of Contrasts

Oh, mountains loom the grandest in Montana
And summer air feels blandest in Montana
Moonshine kicks the strongest
Highways curve the wrongest
Winters last the longest

in Montana.

Women smile the fairest in Montana
Though busted hearts are rarest in Montana
Copper mines grow deepest
Forest trails the steepest
Leap-years come the leapest

in Montana.

Broncos ride the roughest in Montana
Cowhands are the toughest in Montana
Bunco games are bunker
Tires sink much sunker
Injuns get heap drunker

in Montana.

Christmases dawn whitest in Montana
Children's hearts beat lightest in Montana
Sugar beets grow sweetest
Lamb crops sound the bleatest
Meadowlarks tweet-tweetest

in Montana.

Biscuits bake the hardest in Montana
Hog meat comes the lardest in Montana
Bronchial tubes are wheezier
Orators sound breezier
Bankers are some easier

in Montana.

Chipmunks are the chippiest in Montana
Waitresses are flippiest in Montana
Handshakes are less clammy
Hotels not so crammy
Life flows freer, damme!

in Montana.

Bad men act the baddest in Montana
Pedagogues go maddest in Montana
Beefsteaks there are "juicer"
Papooses are papooser
Women run less looser

in Montana.

Wildlife roams the wildest in Montana
Flu bugs bite the mildest in Montana
Woodticks are the tickest
Politicians slickest
Cardsharps shuffle quickest

in Montana.

Fellowship is stronger in Montana
Funerals take longer in Montana
Grub-stakes are the surest
Latch-strings the securest
Pawn-shops grow the poorest

in Montana.

WASHINGTON JAY McCORMICK

110. *"Il est Cocu—le Chef de Gare!"* An engaging reference
to this ballade and the happily depressing history behind
it may be found in a little chapter called "Doom" in *Take
It to Bed* by D. B. Wyndham Lewis (Hutchinson & Co.,
London). Says Mr. Lewis in part:

"Sometime in the 1930's the Fraternelle des Chefs de
Gare Français, or whatever the stationmasters' union is

called, at length rebelled against having their marital in-
felicity sung to them by citizens poking their heads out of
railway carriages on every public holiday, and a couple
of these merry ones were hauled up before the beak at
Asnières, outside Paris, and fined. For behind all that gold-
braided pomp stationmasters are sensitive, and suffer like
other human beings in this vale of tears."

111. *On My Joyful Departure from the Same.* The title
has here been shortened by one word [City] to keep it on
a single line.

115. *Says I to Myself.* Imbedded as prose in one of his
delightful letters. I think this is its first appearance arranged
as verse. I hope so.

116. *Henry Aldrich.* A number of variants of this flavory
verse (one attributed to John Sirmond, 1589-1649) are current coin. So there *is* a choice, but it seems useless to go
into the matter here. Take it that the editor prefers the
one he has given. Aldrich was Dean of Christ Church,
Oxford.

To Mr. Paul V. Bacon I am indebted for a copy of the
Latin antecedent:

> Si bene commemini causae sunt quinque bibendi,
> Hospitis adventus, praesens sitis, atque futura,
> Vel vini bonitas, vel quaelibet altera causa.

Sir W. S. Gilbert. From *The Sorcerer,* i.

Louis MacNeice (1907-   ). From his "Bagpipe Music"
(*Selected Poems,* Random House, 1940). An arresting poem,
loosely written. The undercurrent of futility born of the
1930's is a little too much in it, though, to qualify it for a
collection of purely amusing things. Perhaps, like the in-
strument for which it is named, it has always had (though
I may admire it) a sobering, even saddening effect on me.

118. *Said Aristotle unto Plato.* "The Future of the Classics"
is a pleasant anonymous verse which you may find in *A
Whimsey Anthology,* collected by Carolyn Wells (Scribner's,
1906). Where Miss Wells discovered so many curious verses
dependent on queer spelling, freakish format, and other
obvious eccentricities, I cannot say. You can't wallow in it.

But her book is still one which the connoisseur of light
and humorous verse should have on his shelves. Some of
the sections are: Logical Whimseys, Shaped Whimseys,
Alphabetical Whimseys, Typographical Whimseys, Lipo-
grams, Alliterative Whimseys, Acrostics, Enigmas and Cha-
rades, Palindromes (lines which read backwards and for-
wards—as the Napoleonic, *Able was I ere I saw Elba*),
Catalogue Whimseys, Macaronic Poetry, Imitative Har-
mony, etc., etc. The quaint old days!

Where were we? Ah, yes, "The Future of the Classics"
—in part:

> No longer, O scholars, shall Plautus
>   Be taught us.
> No more shall professors be partial
>   To Martial.
>   No ninny
> Will stop playing "shinney"
>   For Pliny.
> Not even the veriest Mexican Greaser
>   Will stop to read Caesar.
> No true son of Erin will leave his potato
> To list to the love-lore of Ovid or Plato.
>   Old Homer,
>   That hapless old roamer,
> Will ne'er find a rest 'neath collegiate dome or
>   Anywhere else . . .

Incidentally, the marriage of *Plato* and *potato* fascinated
this anonymous author too. Also the creator of archy &
mehitabel:

> How often when they find a sage
>   As sweet as Socrates or Plato
> They hand him hemlock for his wage,
>   Or bake him like a sweet potato!
>
>   DON MARQUIS

And Irwin Edman: see stanza seven of "Intermission,
Please!" in the section called *Shirtsleeve Philosophy*, page
312, for *Aristotle, bottle*.

Drinking. An affection for Edward Thomas (1878-1917)
does not diminish with the years because he shows little

humor in his writing. In *Richard Jefferies: His Life and Work* he could quote (Innkeeper speaking):

> My liquor is good, my measure is just;
> Then pray excuse, I cannot trust.
> Pray be seated and call away
> For what you will, and I'll obey.
>
> There's one thing more I do desire:
> That you'll not stand before the fire,
> Nor on the table attempt to sit
> Unless a quart you pay for it. . . .

119. *Down in a Wine Vault.* The first four stanzas of a verse in *The Old Soak.* Try Sonnets XX & XXI, same vat.

124. *Two Gentlemen of Soho.* "Shakespeare," said Carolyn Wells in her introduction to *A Parody Anthology* (Scribner's, 1904), "with the exception of one or two of his most hackneyed speeches, is rarely parodied; doubtless owing to the fact that his harmonious work shows no incongruities of matter or manner, and strikes no false notes for the parodists to catch at." Perhaps so. In general, Shakespearean parodies make for dull and boring reading. But not this one. "Two Gentlemen from Soho" originally enjoyed almost simultaneous publication in *The London Mercury* and *The Atlantic Monthly* (May, 1927). All in all, it is still the best *tonal* parody of Shakespeare that one editor, at least, has ever read.

127. *Habitant.* I could wish there were space in this collection to include all the verses of a Habitant song called "Credo du Pêcheur." I would add the lovely music too. I first and last heard it sung by guides north of the St. Lawrence, in the Province of Quebec, much too long ago. This is the third verse and chorus, to the best of my French-Canadian syntax[1]:

[1] The French-Canadian of river and lake is often not too sure of his letters. My frien' Professor Arthur F. Whittem, who obligingly touched up a spot or two in the stanzas beyond, tells me of a Laurentide road-sign attempting to sell fish to the transients:

POIZON A VANDRE

Je crois en vous, les gros poissons:
Brochets, baleines, minnows, truites;
Et j' vous compose même des chansons,
Avant que vos têtes soient cuites.

Jamais, jamais, je vous le dis:
J' n' vous f'rai de mal, mes bons apôtres;
Mordez, mordez, en étourdis,
Car j' voudrais bien en prendre d'autres.

136. *Merry Old Souls.* Napoleon was a merry old soul.
Here is a stanza all about him, impressed from a verse by
Newman Levy called "Outline of History, by H. G. Wells."
Mr. Levy's condensation, paradoxically enough, deserves
the full treatment here, but space forbids. The reader will
find it in *Gay But Wistful* (Knopf, 1925).

. . . Napoleon, though little, had a large and lofty bean.
When but an unknown corporal, he married Josephine.
But when to fame he rose at length,
He said: "I'll have to play through strength.
I've only honors in my hand, so I'll discard my queen.". . .

142. *"The Art of Our Necessities Is Strange."* This title is
from *King Lear,* iii, 2. So Forrest Izard. Thus Al Graham:

FOLKS, I GIVE YOU SCIENCE!

Scientist discovers new chemical curiosity called Dry Water.
—*News Item.*

Now Science is a dandy thing—explaining, as it can,
The ultra ray, the Milky Way, and prehistoric man;
Supplying dope on dopes, as well as dope on protoplasm;
And helping rid a dog of fleas, when-as-and-if he has
'em. . . .

Again, it wields a magic wand in diagnosing ills,
In easing varied aches and pains with ointments, salves,
and pills;
It tells us how electric current lights a little lamp,
And what the watt is all about, and what the ohm, and amp.

Yes, Science is a dandy thing; and now it lets us know
That Wet is not the only kind there is of H_2O;

And so, with water on our minds (a sort of arid brain-juice),
Let's drink a toast to Science here—in good old-fashioned
   rain-juice!

147. *The Human Race.* Another introduction to this most
illusive and allusive of all subjects might be found in the
closing four lines of "Rose Is a Rose," a translation from
the Chinese by Christopher Morley.
   Rose is a Rose! Attar boy!

> The aphis, for roses,
>   Is part of the plan,
> And Sin presupposes
>   Existence of Man.

I wish I loved the Human Race. The title is: "Wishes of
an Elderly Man;" the subtitle, "Wished at a Garden Party,
June, 1914."

152. *"A Christian Is a Man Who Feels."* From "Exit God,"
by Gamaliel Bradford (1863-1932), the third, fourth, and
sixth (last) stanzas make a nice antiphonal to Mr. Ybarra's
philosophy:

> Now Hell has wholly boiled away
>   And God become a shade.
> There is no place for him to stay
>   In all the world he made.

> The followers of William James
>   Still let the Lord exist,
> And call him by imposing names,
>   A venerable list. . . .

> I sometimes wish that God were back
>   In this dark world and wide;
> For though some virtues he might lack,
>   He had his pleasant side.

154. *Incense & Nonsense.* Through the kindness of Mr.
John L. Sweeney, I have come upon the following fragment of engaging rhythm. Mr. Maxwell E. Foster, who recited it to him, has approved the present text.

Who tarried in Jericho
Until their beards did grow,
Judas Iscariot, Captain Marryat, and Harriet Martineau.

Mr. Sweeney also led me to the following couplet, composed in a dream—as he puts it—by the late Arthur T. Hadley (1856-1930), President of Yale University. Its symmetrical beauty, you may agree, depends on what Mr. Sweeney aptly calls the "accident of shift."

Timbuctoo, with the stress on the Timbuc
-too with the stress on the Timbuc too.

Writing down one's impressions of verses composed in a dream is apt to be disappointing. Noted in the night, they take on a queer complexion in the morning, and very few fragments that I have ever heard recited or reported suggest the intrinsic genius of what Mr. Hadley preserved. A few such, out of my own experience, lie somewhere in a neglected journal, but not many of them ever came to rhyme. The only one still somewhat to my fancy is:

The muted malted dilutors are moving in next door . . .

157. *The Owl and the Pussy-Cat.* "Mr. Lear," says Sir Edward Strachey, Bart., in the ninth edition of *Nonsense Songs and Stories* (Frederick Warne and Co., London, 1894) —"Mr. Lear was delighted when I showed to him that this couple were reviving the old law of Solon, that the Athenian bride and bridegroom should eat a quince together at their wedding."

159. *The Bees' Song.* How delicate is the humor of this gentle verse—one of the true visibles—not to be got at or more than half appreciated unless the printed page is before the reader. "Z" is a pretty letter in almost any typeface, Roman or italic. A misfortune, perhaps, that it was not given to be one of the common consonants. But its very uncommonness here lends freshness to the texture of the de la Mare spelling.

As to some of the same rhymes in their "s" state, inspect "The Song of Quoodle" (unfortunately not in this book) by G. K. Chesterton. De la Mare, incidentally, was not the first to spell roses with a "z". Edward Lear in "His Garden":

And if you voz to see my rozziz
As is a boon to all men's nozziz . . .

The beauty and dignity of the letter "Z" is never better shown than in I Chronicles, iv and vi, on such a page as you will find in the Pepys Bible, printed in Cambridge by John Field, 1660.

T. E. Brown also has an echo of this bee business in a verse called "The Pazons" (parsons), which may be found in *Poems of T. E. Brown* (Macmillan). Says z, with his wonderful tongue for the sound of uncommon common speech:

What's the gud of these Pazons? They're the most despard
      rubbage go'n',
Reg'lar humbugs they are. Show me a Pazon, show me a
      drone!
Livin' on the fat of the land, livin' on the people's money
The same's the drones is livin' on the beeses honey.

And why isn't Brown (Sir Arthur Quiller-Couch's schoolmaster) read today? "The Pessimist" belongs in every anthology of light verse, but you will look for it in vain. The stanzas called "In the Coach" (Anglo-Manx dramatic lyrics) are long delights in flexible concertina lines and fresh rhythms. Here, for example, from "The Christening":

> Did you put it in the papers?
> No, no! What capers!
> No, no!
> Splendid though!
> Upon my life—
> *Catharine, wife*
> *Of Mounseer*
> *Eddard Creer,*
> *Esqueer,*
> *Otherwise dadaa,*
> *Of a son and heer!*
> hip-hip-hip-hip, hooraa!

> Bless my sowl! am I draemin'?
> He'll make a seaman
> Will yandhar lad—
> Aw, the glad! . . .

> Go, Jemmy, they're lyin' quite handy,
> A bottle of rum and another of brandy,
> In the starboard locker theer—
> And, Jemmy! there's a taste of gin—
> Aw, navar fear!
> Tell the chaps to finish it—
> All the kit—
> And listen—tell ould Harper
> We'll take and warp her
> Inside
> On the morning's tide—
> About hafe-past four'll be time to begin—
> My gough! but we'll have a chrizzenin'!

Thus ending in Z . . . And this man is known to the public solely for

> A garden is a lovesome thing, God wot!

As to that, Jim White to whom this book is dedicated used to make it his special business to ruin verses for me, viz.:

> And a small cabin build there, *of beer and skittles* made . . .

In this instance

> A garden is a *wotsome* thing . . .

The reference to Yeats brings to mind a number of parodies of "The Lake Isle of Innisfree." Of the two or three genuinely good ones, these four lines by Frank Sidgwick from "Imaginary Conversation" in *Some Verse* (Sidgwick & Jackson, London, 1915) deserve to be better known:

> Yeats (in despair):

> I will arise and go now, and go to Charing Cross,
>   And a small cabman hire there, of grey and mottled face;
> Twelve brown pence will I give him and one for the poor
>   old hoss,
>   And drive alone to a fly-blown place.

162. *Incidents in the Life of My Uncle Arly*. It seems likely that Poe's Raven dipped his beak into this one. But it is still pure Lear at its best.

Admirers of "The Akond of Swat" will do well to look up *The Book of Canadian Poetry,* edited by A. J. M. Smith (University of Chicago Press, 1943). There, on pages 125-126 is "A Threnody," little known in the United States, by George T. Lanigan (1846-1886). Lanigan, founder of the newspaper that is now the Montreal *Star,* was born in the year in which *The Book of Nonsense* was first published. Mr. Smith suggests that "A Threnody," beginning

> What, what, what,
> What's the news from Swat?

—quite a funny verse, too—was known to Lear "in a little book of American humorous verse in Walter Scott's *Canterbury Poets,* which had been published in the eighties." That Lear got his inspiration from Lanigan seems wholly unlikely, for in his *Journal* for July 27, 1873 (San Remo), he records that he had just finished "The Ahkond of Swat" —carefully retaining the "h". Lanigan, incidentally, spells it *Ahkoond.*

Passionate lovers of Lear may care to examine "The Scroobious Pip," an unfinished verse, to be found in a limited edition of *Nonsense Songs & Laughable Lyrics,* published in the U.S.A. (with a foreword by Philip Hofer) by the Peter Pauper Press, 1935. Many of Lear's fanciful words are common to two or more of his poems: *runcible, Gromboolian plain, the hills of the Chankly Bore,* the *Jumblies,* for example. *Scroobious* appears in at least two of the limericks: "There was an Old Person of Philæ," and "There was an old person of Grange."

165. *Antigonish.* This admired quatrain was originally an untitled verse in a play called *The Psyco-ed,* written for an undergraduate English course at Harvard about the year 1899. In 1910 Mr. Mearns "put the play on with a group of college students. It made gay headway for many months." In 1922 F.P.A. printed the quatrain in "The Conning Tower" (then appearing in the New York *World*).

Undoubtedly many readers of "Antigonish" have reflected at least once in their several minds on the curious title of this sturdy little verse. Those familiar with the Nova Scotian town of that name may have suspected a possible relation-

ship. A word from Mr. Mearns—as of October 1, 1944—
disperses the clouds: he chose "Antigonish" as a title because at the moment the papers were carrying daily stories
of a haunted house in a village called Antigona or Anti-
gonia. "The ghost was always missing when the reporters
came.

"Gelett Burgess [he continues] insists that 'Antigonish'
is a new nonsense form, and he ought to know . . . He
understood instantly that my formula was to state what
seems impossible but which, in fact, is a common truth of
human experience. The 'man who wasn't there,' I happen
to know, is a terrifying reality to women whose mate does
not appear but is so permanently in their thoughts as they
ascend the stair that it would be natural for them to cry
out, 'I wish to God he'd stay away!' (one of the many versions of that last line). So, you see, it is a quatrain of
female frustration. The very word Antigonish carries the
suggestion of agony."

THE LADY WITH TECHNIQUE

As I was letting down my hair
I met a guy who didn't care;
He didn't care again today—
I *love* 'em when they get that way!

HUGHES MEARNS

" 'The Lady with Technique' is woman's understanding
laugh at man's pretense of self-sufficiency. Adam's fall is
evidence enough that the male is the easier victim. 'The
woman did give it me to eat.' "

When the original "Antigonish" appeared in "The Conning Tower" in 1922, it was an instant success and enjoyed
wide popularity by word of mouth, undergoing many variations in the process. According to its author, it reached
England in the 1930's, and was quoted by Chesterton and
other prominent writers. "Because of that," says Mr.
Mearns, "a small controversy arose there over authorship.
Claire Leighton used it as a chapter heading a year or so
ago. She said she thought it was a folk bit like Mother
Goose."

Here is another Mearns. Let's not explain it.

The Perfect Reactionary

As I was sitting in my chair
I *knew* the bottom wasn't there,
Nor legs nor back, but *I just sat,*
Ignoring little things like that.

HUGHES MEARNS

Aunt Eliza. Harry Graham, a British author who made his pen name into a pun (Col. D. Streamer) because he was a captain in the famous Coldstream Guards (joining in 1895), put his fireplace verses into a volume called—with something close to another pun—*Ruthless Rhymes for Heartless Homes* (1901). Contrariwise, one American editor of a popular collection of light verse still in active circulation refers obviously to a *Colonel* D. Streamer, and treats Graham as a separate individual, with verses indexed under each.

Graham's most famous verse is probably the one called "Tender-Heartedness." I can remember learning it as a youngster—by oral report—the first line running:

Little Willie, in the best of sashes, etc., etc.

Here, however, is the authorized text:

Billy, in one of his nice new sashes,
Fell in the fire and was burnt to ashes;
Now, although the room grows chilly,
I haven't the heart to poke poor Billy.

What influence! What persistence! *Time* for February 28, 1944, reported that London's weekly *Time & Tide* "offered prizes for the best wartime ruthless rhyme." Three of the six prize winners were:

Willie in his roguish way
Tipped Grandpa on the fire one day.
Mother said "My dear, that's cruel!
But of course it *does* save fuel—"

Tommy for his evening game
Set his sister's hair aflame;
Wardens shouted at the sight
"Wretched Boy—*PUT OUT THAT LIGHT!*"

Dad, a Home Guard, when in liquor,
Missed his target—killed the Vicar;
With more practice, like as not,
Dad may be a better shot.

168. *The Great Auk's Ghost*. Extinction has a definite
charm for the light verse clan. Apparently there is something funny about simply being extinct. The very name
of the dodo is funny. (Mr. Hodgson has one called "The
Final Dodo.") The roc[1] is funnier still, probably because
its "k" is extinct as well. Carolyn Wells wrote a verse on
the extinctness of the Moa of New Zealand—first I'd heard
of it. It ends:

> . . . So I've essayed
> To sing thy cherished name, oh, Moa!
> Cherished too likely, I'm afraid,
> By nobody but me and Noah.

The passenger pigeon and, more restrictedly, the heath
hen of Martha's Vineyard (freshly extinct) seem to have
passed unnoticed. Too tragic, maybe. If you like this sort
of thing, turn to pages 135 and 146. The eg of the roc is
out of stoc; if not, I beg your pardon, eg.

169. *Jabberwocky*. The object of the following transcription
is not to glossarize the lines which you learned as a child
(and glossarized for yourself) but to prove that the *sound*
of Basic English translations of verse (see pages 257 and
267) is older than Basic English. First of all, you must
know that Carroll himself explained some of the strange
words in "Jabberwocky," *e. g.*:

Brillig—the time of broiling dinner; that is, the close
of the afternoon.

Tove—a species of badger which lived chiefly on cheese.

Wabe—the side of a hill.

Borogove—an extinct kind of parrot. They had no wings,
beaks turned up, and made their nests in sundials; lived
on veal.

Wherefore, in Lewis Carroll's Basic preview: "It was
evening, and the smooth active badgers were scratching

[1] Funniest, perhaps, for never having existed.

and boring holes in the hillside; all unhappy were the
parrots, and the green turtles squeaked out." Q. E. D.

Jabberwocky—word and verse—is old hat to most of us,
but sentiment (a fighting word in the midriff of the
twentieth century) constrained me to put it in. We are
all of us weak in various ways. But the *French* Jabberwocky is a different matter. It would be here had I been
successful in locating the author, Mr. Frank L. Warrin, Jr.
Has it lost any freshness since the dandy day some years
ago when it appeared so unexpectedly in *The New Yorker?*
I trust not. Of course not. Impossible. *O jour frabbegeais!*
This is the way it would begin if I could print it:

LE JASEROQUE
(The Jabberwock)

Il brilgue: les tôves lubricilleux
Se gyrent en vrillant dans le guave,
Enmîmés sont les gougebosqueux,
Et le mômerade horsgrave . . .

See page 149 for a reference to Jabberwock, Alice, and
the future.

Were this not such a large book, I might not have found
excuse for the omission of "The Walrus and the Carpenter."
This, of course, is the most famous verse about oysters—
in fact, time and tide have produced no succulent com-
petitors. In some way the static, unpragmatic life of the
oyster lends an enchantment which writers of light verse
find irresistible. There are two words for him in Horace
But perhaps Pistol discovered the true poetry in him:

Why, then the world's mine oyster
Which I with sword will open.

Sir A. P. Herbert has written at least two oyster verses, both
of them good. One is early Herbert and one appeared in
Punch but a few years ago, and I wish he would put it
into a book. I don't think he has. John G. Saxe contrived
a sonnet to a clam. The late Stoddard King should have
written a verse about the agile and wonderful geoduc, the
superquahog of the Pacific shores of his adopted State of
Washington. Perhaps he did. There's a Nash oyster, too.

In the first of the two volumes of the fabulous *Odoherty Papers* of William Maginn (Redfield, 1855), Mrs. M'Whirter's Chant celebrates the Irish species of oyster called the Powldoodies of Burran. But Powldoodies, says a footnote, "went out of fashion, and Carlingford oysters came in." Nevertheless,

Some people eats their Powldoodies quite neat just as they
    came out of the sea,
But with a little black pepper and vinegar some other
    people's stomachs better agree;
Young ladies are very fond of oyster pates, and young
    gentlemen of oyster broth,

But I think I know a bit of pasture that is far better than
    them both:
For whenever we want to be comfortable says I to the
    Doctor—my dear man,
Let's have a few scalloped Powldoodies, and a bit of tripe
    fried in the pan,

  Chorus—Oh! the Powldoodies of Burran,
          The green green Powldoodies of Burran,
          The green Powldoodies, the clean Powldoodies,
          The gaping Powldoodies of Burran.

Even A. E. Housman produced an oyster poem, the best stanza of which seems to be:

    The oyster is found in the ocean
      And cucumbers grow on the land;
    And the oyster is slightly the moister,
      As most people well understand.

No one, however, seems to have written about horse-radish, which is half an oyster to me.

171. *The Suicide's Grave.* This amusing little parody of Gilbert may fade when America's musical war is over, but then the back-scene meaning of a good deal of him is not too clear today to Americans—or perhaps even today to the English. There is a conscious suggestion of evanescence in the third stanza.

Petrillo

What musical numbers float over the breeze,
 Singing Trillo, Petrillo, Petrillo!
The sweet little woodwinds, in several keys,
 Play Trillo, Petrillo, Petrillo.
But where are the rest of the musical crew,
And what shall the listening multitudes do
Who crave something more than the metrical coo
 Of Trillo, Petrillo, Petrillo?

Now I feel just as sure as I'm sure that my name
 Isn't Trillo, Petrillo, Petrillo,
That sweetness and light are not quite the whole game   •
 Of Trillo, Petrillo, Petrillo,
For still there are spaces in music for which
Some others than Trillo can set the right pitch,
Though I doubt if they ever can grow quite so rich
 As Trillo, Petrillo, Petrillo.

But as to the name that so limpidly flows
 In Trillo, Petrillo, Petrillo,
Now take it in full, and observe how it goes—
 It's Caesar, James Caesar Petrillo.
And Caesar, remember, is nothing but Czar,
And Czars, on the market, have dropped below par—
They drop very fast, and they drop very far,
 O Trillo, James Caesar Petrillo!

August, 1942.   GILBERTULUS

177. *Emerson.* Henry David Thoreau (1817-1862), referred to enthusiastically as a humorist by no less a humorist than E. B. White, occasionally fooled with light verse, though not much more successfully than Emerson. Much as I admire the sage who once unfairly said of his younger Concord friend, "I am very familiar with all his [Thoreau's] thoughts—they are my own quite originally drest," I find it hard to smile at the frequently reprinted "Fable." It is not included in these pages. I don't know that any of us would smile at this of Thoreau's, taken from "Ktaadn":

> A quart of arbor vitae
> To make him strong and mighty.

But it does come clean like a sliver shaved from one of his own surviving cedar pencils here on my desk.

On reading over the above, I find it confusing. I forget what I was aiming at. I am too tired to fix it up now. It will have to wait for another edition.

178. *Thoughts for St. Stephen.* Take a look at "The Pilgrims' Thanksgiving Feast" in *Epicures & Feeders,* page 93.

179. *The Artist.* One in particular:

> A Pre-Raphaelite
> Had to have things right.
> The patient redhead, Elizabeth Siddal,
> Lay in the bathtub up to her middle
> (But richly gowned)
> To show what she would look like drowned.
> At last she sneezed: Oh Mr. Millais,
> Do I 'ave to welter 'ere all day?
> It's enough to congeal ya:
> Posing for Ophelia.

CHRISTOPHER MORLEY

The Artist. Father Feeney, somewhat more specifically:

> Though art be on vacation,
>   The studio remains;
> The well of inspiration
>   Is backing out of drains.
>
> Come, let us daub, my crazys,
>   Surrealize the thrill
> Of soapsuds on the daisies
>   And skylarks in the swill.
>
> Ours not to reason whether
>   Surprise surpasseth wonder,
> When man hath joined together
>   What God hath rent asunder.

LEONARD FEENEY, S.J.

180. *Engraved on the Collar of His Highness' Dog.* For the purpose of this collection it was difficult to cope with Pope. He fits well in an anthology of light verse, though he has

not often enjoyed the luck of being skillfully selected. But
he does not seem to fit in here. Better than a few links of
heroic couplets, however, is this extract from Lytton Strachey's masterly essay on Pope (The Leslie Stephen Lecture
at Cambridge, 1925). He is quoting from the youthful poet
(the *Pastorals*):
  "The lines flow on with the most transparent limpidity—

  "But see, the shepherds shun the noon-day heat,
  The lowing herds to murm'ring brooks retreat,
  To closer shades the panting flocks remove;
  Ye Gods! and is there no relief for love?

Everything is obvious. The diction is a mass of *clichés;* the
epithets are the most commonplace possible; the herds low,
the brooks murmur, the flocks pant and remove, the retreats
are green, and the flowers blush. The rhythm is that of a
rockinghorse; and the sentiment is mere sugar. But what a
relief! What a relief to have escaped for once from *le mot
propre,* from subtle elaboration of diction and metre, from
complicated states of mind, and all the profound obscurities
of Shakespeare and Mr. T. S. Eliot! How delightful to have
no trouble at all—to understand so very, very easily every
single thing that is said!"

A. Pope wrote a parody on "The House that Jack Built"—
"The Domicile of John"—full of long words: albulactic,
saponaceous, muricide, exosculate, eumenidal, lethiferous,
latebrose, etc. But memorable lines are strewn the length
of it, like the outcrop of country rock in a New England
landscape:

  The old mordaceous rat that dared devour
    Antecedaneous ale in John's domestic bower . . .

  E'en as he kissed the virgin all forlorn
    Who milked the cow with implicated horn . . .

  The loud cantankerous Shanghai comes at last,
    Whose shouts aroused the shorn ecclesiast . . .

Note, however, as Mr. Harold Wentworth, switching his
syllabic radar into action, has pointed out: this is *a* Pope,

not *the* Pope. Many of those implicated words are not in
the Pope concordance—were not born as early as 1744, the
year the Master died.

Pope?
Nope.

But who was *A.* Pope? Equally possibly, who *is*? I wish I
knew. Carolyn Wells knew—I am sure.

A good thing that Sir Thomas Browne died six years
before Alexander Pope was born. Or is there nothing of his
murmurous, poetic prose, once removed—even in parody?
I like to fancy the transmitted—transmuted—influence. Or,
conversely, would it not be pleasant to live to see the fruit
of influence, were one Sir Thomas? Yes, it would. What did
Oliver Herford say?

If only I had not been born so soon,
Or if you had not gone to press so late . . .

181. *To R. K.* Stephen in his few, brief days achieved something of the stature of the great Calverley, whom he resembles in many respects, not the least of which is facility
with Latin. In his own words,

Vivat J. K. Stephanus,
Humilis Poeta!

As to this verse, remembered chiefly for the closing couplet
—in which his premature misjudgment of Kipling tapers
off into wonderful nonsense—it appears today as virtually
the sole support of his fame. "Who can . . . forget [asks
Shane Leslie] the memory of J. K. Stephen, the flower of
King's [College, Cambridge], who died young and mad,
leaving behind him two memorable lines desirous of a
better country . . ."

Frank Sidgwick in *More Verse* (Sidgwick & Jackson, London, 1921) parodies him thus:

J.K.S. So there yet may come a season which shall rid us
from the curse
That the converse of a poet should be deadlier than
his verse;

Then shall rudyards cease from kipling—(pardon if
    myself I quote)—
And no haggards ride hagridden by the fear of
    Woman's Vote.

182. *My Bishop's Eyes*. A companion piece (in which the
Bishop is speaking, as he well deserves to speak) is this
anonymous quatrain:

> Tell my Priests, when I am gone,
> O'er me to shed no tears,
> For I shall be no deader then
> Than they have been for years.

183. *Warning*. Epigram referring to an Indiana road, *circa*
1839. Might be Vermont in the spring. I wish it were.

184. *Life & Letters*. It is possible, nay probable, that more
light verse than poetry is written purely for gain. I question,
however, if *humorous* verse is written primarily for gain.
The impulse to be funny in rhyme generally precedes all
thought of reward—however pure, however sordid. So much
the better. Mr. Ybarra in his *Young Man of the World*
explains the light verse attitude in a few shameless stanzas,
the first of which actually clatters with loose change:

> There's a beautiful check at the end of this verse:
> I see it three stanzas away,
> And bag it I will for the good of my purse
> If Luck is my partner today.

Christopher Morley. Samuel Hoffenstein looks at this truism
from a different point of view:

> How much we pay to say, *"Je suis,"*
> *"Ich bin,"* or *"Sum,"* or even *"Me"!*
> SAMUEL HOFFENSTEIN

185. *The Canadian Authors Meet*. Others have plied these
shallow waters, but none (I think) so skillfully, and with
so little splashing, as Mr. Scott. A Canadian, as you may
imagine. Professor of Constitutional Law at McGill, as you
may not imagine.

189. *Book and Bookplate.* From "The Laureate":

> Who would not be
> The Laureate bold,
> With his butt of sherry
> To keep him merry,
> And nothing to do but to pocket his gold?
>
> WILLIAM E. AYTOUN (1813-1865)

And speaking of Horace, there are no translations from Horace in this collection. Beyond the fact that I have always found most of them laborious, or at least tenuous, they seem to me to belong in the category of light verse and not in the category of purely humorous or witty verse. But I respect the translator: *Juxta fluvium puteum fodit.* Readers of light verse would probably welcome a creative (not scholarly) anthology of Horace in which the wisest— and only the wisest—translation is used for each of the Odes (omitting the Satires). The editor would not have much difficulty in performing his happy task, for many of the gilded names in light verse are signed to translations or parodies of the Odes: Calverley, Stephen, Eugene Field, Sir Arthur Quiller-Couch, Sir Owen Seaman, Franklin P. Adams, Keith Preston, and Louis Untermeyer, for example. Such a collection would clear away the flaccid stuff in English and American literature which tends to cloud rather than to clarify the genius that was Horace; and for those who have none of his language would set him (in Leonard Bacon's phrase) "at ease with Gods and Men and Things."

191. *Fate and the Younger Generation.* There would be an Aldous Huxley here somewhere, if the choice did not narrow down to the obvious "Fifth Philosopher's Song." You can find it in many places. I wish he had written more verse and not gone out with that first dry wave of cicadas.

194. *To Minerva.* A famous quatrain by Miss Millay, the antithesis of this—though the subject is not literary—was omitted for financial reasons. Admirers of it (the poet herself, says her agent, is not among them) may care to look at a dandy Hoffenstein parody (omitted for similar reasons).

It appears on page 193 of *Poems in Praise of Practically Nothing* (Boni & Liveright, 1928).

198. *Thoughts.* C_2H_5OH—ethyl alcohol to those who have no chemistry.

199. *As I Was Laying on the Green.* An unauthorized version, prettier to my fancy—and a little more logical with *playing* in the first line—is this:

> As I was playing on the green
> A little book it chanced I seen.
> Carlyle's *Essay on Burns* was the edition;
> I left it laying in the same position.

But any way you look at it, this is a funny sermon on education. The essential charm, of course, lies in the wonderful last line and in the genius of that phrase, "in the same position."

200. *Us Potes.* If anyone germane to this collection as a whole belongs in the division called *Life & Letters* it is Franklin P. Adams. American light verse in general owes a great debt to a number of able column conductors in various newspapers from Boston to Spokane. But the king conductor was F.P.A., whose daily stint was putting life and letters together as if they were inseparable. Were I to list the number of contributors to *What Cheer* who first or early appeared in "The Conning Tower," my point would be driven home. Mr. Adams always was and is the craftsman. He held the standards of verse writing as high as anyone could hold them, and I for one pay tribute to him here for his many years of exemplary and beneficent service to a small but healthy field of American literature.

205. *Commercial Candour.* Looking back on it all, I can think of no excuse whatsoever for having omitted Chesterton's "A Ballade of Suicide." But it's in lots of places—quite possibly in your head. I hope so.

212. *Limericks.* When I think of Edward Lear, I think of him as a magic presence in my own childhood, and in wonder and admiration. His voice is still young—still supreme in the faraway world cf nonsense. Indeed, this

other planet of electronics and gadgets continues to twirl
so beautifully in the outer void that I doubt if the old
master, in his innocence and withdrawal, will ever be
successfully challenged. As if there were or could be a
challenger! His letters alone (so sadly neglected) could
give him immortality.

But there is one corner of his little shop where I am
still the reluctant customer. I do not care much for his
pioneering limericks—largely because they repeat the first-
line rhyme-word for the fifth. Sometimes they repeat more
than that. Take the best offending example:

> There was a Young Lady of Ryde,
> Whose shoe-strings were seldom untied;
>   She purchased some clogs
>   And some small spotty dogs,
> And frequently walked about Ryde.

Except for the pun involving walk and Ryde, this fifth
line has been completely fifth-columned. Lear's limericks
for me are thus a series of lost opportunities. The single
example which I can quote with pleasure—and that in the
main for the masterful use of the word *partially*—is:

> There was on Old Man who supposed
> That the street door was partially closed;
> But some very large Rats ate his coats and his hats,
> While that futile Old Gentleman dozed.

See note against page 218.

213. *"A flea and a fly in a flue."* Some thirty-five years ago
I first heard (and learned by heart) this sad little song—
but not in limerick form. What I learned was:

> A flea and a fly flew up in a flue.
> Said the flea to the fly, "Oh, what shall we do?"
>   "Let us flee," said the fly,
>   "Let us fly," said the flea;
> So they fluttered and flew up a flaw in the flue.

Somehow that early version is a speck more musical to my
ear, though judgment may be colored by familiarity and
sentiment.

214. *Anonymous.*[1] This word in anthologies is frequently abbreviated *Anon.* In pages where it must occur several times in succession—as in this section of limericks—the effect of the repeated contraction would be to scatter a handful of unwanted periods like canary seed on the floor of the cage. Without a period, the four letters resemble a familiar dramatic adverb—Anon, and on, and on, and on. For every reason, therefore, *Anonymous* is written out the length and breadth of this happy, happy book.

Mr. Newman Levy, concerned with *Ibid* and *Anon.* Lovers of ibids—both the wire-haired and plumed varieties—will look to the rookery which Mr. Frank Sullivan shuffled together in an issue of *The New Yorker* not long after the appearance of Mr. Van Wyck Brooks' *New England: Indian Summer.* He called it "A Garland of Ibids." Mr. Levy:

> Now Ibid's works run more to prose,
> Statistics and the like.
> With poetry Anon just flows
> Like water o'er a dike.
> Though critics may dispute their claims,
> Yet when we're dead and gone,
> Still bright will shine the deathless names
> Of Ibid and Anon.

215. *"When you go to a store in Ascutney . . ."* This and the limerick following are Vermont, of course.

217. *My Face.* Why so hard to keep a good limerick from falling into the clutches of anonymity? It is something like signing your name to a tea leaf or a coffee bean. For that reason it seems only fair in this instance to reprint the note which Anthony Euwer has set against "My Face" in his Oregonian *Rhymes of Our Valley:*

"The limerick 'My Face' was first published in the Pittsburgh *Index* about '98, one of a series, and accompanied with a drawing of a bulldog. It was reprinted later in a small volume *The Smile on the Face of the Tiger* and afterwards in *The Home Book of Verse* [Stevenson] published by Henry Holt. After his nomination for the Presidency, it was used on a number of occasions by Woodrow

[1] "Most modest of all men of genius, Mr. Anon.," says W. de la M.

Wilson, at which time it found its way into numerous
papers and periodicals throughout the country. After many
vicissitudes and having been attributed to various sources,
it is here given for the first time in some years [1916] under
its rightful authorship."

"A tutor who tooted a flute." Nothing compulsory, reader,
but you might care to glance at the note against page 318.

218. *"There was a young man of Sid. Sussex."* This limerick, like "The Vulture and the Husbandman," elsewhere
mentioned, is taken from *The Light Green,* of which only
two issues were published, both in 1872. According to my
informant, Mr. W. G. Constable, Curator of Paintings at
the Boston Museum of Fine Arts, "The writer of the two
issues was Arthur Clement Hilton, who produced them
while he was an undergraduate at Cambridge, as a parody
on a periodical published at Oxford at the time, called
The Dark Blue . . . a highly aesthetic and lugubrious
publication. This accounts for the general tenor of *The
Light Green.* These copies of mine are, alas, only the re-
prints of 1890, and the original editions are practically un-
obtainable . . . Oddly enough, Hilton took Orders; less
surprisingly, he died young . . . The 'Sid' in 'Sid. Sussex'
is short for Sidney in Sidney Sussex, the Cambridge College
founded with money bequeathed by Frances, Lady Sussex,
daughter of Sir William Sidney, whose two names the title
commemorates."

The limerick in question is taken from No. 2 of *The
Light Green,* "and is one of a series of seven limericks and
a parody of 'The Jumblies,' the whole headed 'Nonsense
Verses by Edward Leary.' The limericks have perhaps some
claim to distinction in that the fifth line ends with a different word rhyming with the end words of the first and
second lines; and is not, as with Lear, a repetition of the
last word of the first line. [See note against page 212.]
Whether Hilton was responsible for this innovation, I don't
know, but he must have been pretty early in the field."

See also note against page 9.

"There was an old fellow of Trinity." A traditional lim-

erick, revived in 1942 by Christopher Morley in his novel *Thorofare* (Harcourt, Brace, 1942).

221. *Rudyard Kipling.* From "Kitchener's School" (1898). Stanza 5, line 4.

229. *Message to General Montgomery.* There is an interesting story behind this verse—verse, incidentally, attributed to General A. E. Nye, Vice Chief of the Imperial General Staff, when *Time* published four stanzas of it in its issue of December 27, 1943. A letter to the editor from the War Office in London (August 18, 1944) puts the matter straight: "During the fighting in Italy, General Montgomery wired home and asked for a mackintosh suit. We did our best to find him a suitable garment, and in the end purchased a mackintosh coat and trousers at two different establishments, making the hybrid garment which General Monty frequently can be seen wearing. When it came to despatching the parcel, the only person going to Italy was found to be—somewhat to our surprise—the Bishop of Southwark whom we immediately telephoned and invited to take the parcel. This he did, accompanied by the attached poem of which, I may say, at the time he was not aware."

The verse first came to my attention in a copy sent me by an American Army captain stationed in England. The text used in this book is exactly as authorized by the War Office, Whitehall, London. I am indebted particularly to Major Peter B. Earle, G. S., Military Assistant to the Chief of the Imperial General Staff, for his courtesy and promptness in solving the mystery of authorship.

Out of Italy, whence was dispatched that message to the General, comes this brief "Ode of Lament," written by a Ranger for *The Stars and Stripes:*

> God gave the pig
> A mighty snout
> With which to dig
> And root about.
> And claws like iron
> He gave the mole
> With which to burrow
> And dig his hole.

But God forgot
In the human riggin',
To provide a tool
For foxhole diggin'.

RANGER RANDOLPH JECK

Italy, 1944.

230. *There Lived a King.* From *The Gondoliers*, ii. In this
and other Gilbert pieces the promotional refrains have been
omitted. They go better with the music. See Edward Lear's
"The Owl and the Pussy-Cat" (page 157) for the reversal of
all this. In the familiar and happy music[1] by Geo. Ingraham, the repeated Lear endings have been dropped to the
advantage of both verse and music.

232. *Mad Dogs and Englishmen.* A prohibitive fee asked by
his music publisher in the United States prevented the in-
clusion of the words for Mr. Coward's "The Stately Homes
of England." Words divorced from their legally wedded
music are never entirely satisfactory as verse unless they
were written without reference to the accenting demands
of musical notation. Gilbert perhaps is the best example
of the librettist whose verse reads as well as it sings. Mr.
Coward, being both librettist and composer, knows all the
tricks of both trades, and the resulting art is completely
fused. For this reason the bare stanzas of "Mad Dogs and
Englishmen"—but to a lesser extent than those of "The
Stately Homes of England"—contrive a certain unevenness
of rhythm which disappears altogether when the verses are
sung. Thus "The Stately Homes of England" in that opening line of the chorus has a long uplifting, accented first
syllable in *England* which, once you know it musically,

[1] There are several other musical settings of this marvelous
verse, but Mr. Ingraham's, published in 1886 (G. Schirmer, copyright), is touched with original delight. Lear himself set the
poem to music, but the score was never written down, and
most tragically perished with him. Lear had no voice, yet his
singing could make people cry. Once, in 1851, when he was
singing "Home they brought her Warrior" at a large party,
Archbishop Tait, then Bishop of Carlisle, said to him: "Sir, you
ought to have half the Laureateship."

carries over into any reading of the line and makes it a prettier affair than it was when Felicia Hemans uttered the poem from which the parody stems:

> The Stately homes of England!
> How beautiful they stand,
> Amidst their tall ancestral trees,
> O'er all the pleasant land!

Moral: If you write both words *and* music, music is the controlling factor. Additional moral: Writing words *for* music is an art in itself. It requires a knowledge of vowel and consonant values which even the best of light verse writers may not understand. The converse of this is why the editor has not culled a few verses from the text of first-rate musical comedies such as *Of Thee I Sing*. They just don't read as well as they sing.

Incidentally, Evoe is the author of a quatrain parody of Mrs. Hemans' stanza—earlier, I think, than Mr. Coward's verse of the same title. Here it is:

THE STATELY HOMES OF ENGLAND

> The stately homes of England
> How beautiful they stood
> Before their recent owners
> Relinquished them for good. . . .
>
> E. V. KNOX

That will be all for now.

238. *Sir J. C. Squire*. The title of the quatrain is "A Fresh Morning."

239. *Melodie Grotesque*. This also:

LENGTHY SYMPHONY

> The opus rises to fortissimo
> While I, once more, resign myself to fate,
> Hemmed in quite hopelessly by row on row
> Of music lovers, hushed, insatiate.
> I know it is a sacrilege to sigh—
> The end is nearing, in all likelihood—
> But one affrighted piccolo and I
> See no way out of this enchanted wood.
>
> PERSIS GREELY ANDERSON

241. *Theme Song for a Songwriter's Union.* See note against "The Suicide's Grave," page 171.

242. *From a Vigo-Street Eclogue.* A musical line by Sir Owen which occasionally crosses the idle mind tinkles sweetly in a Herrick verse of his, "To Julia under Lock and Key," involving a "circumvolving zonulet". (*Zonulet!* Mencken, what a sound!)

> . . . to hear
> About her limb so lithe and lank
> My Julia's ankle-bangle clank.

246. *To E.M.O.* ". . . You may remember the notable boast some time ago of the organist of Londonderry (Ulster) Cathedral? 'I could play jazz all week on the cathedral organ without doing it any harm,' he growled; reminding us forcibly at the time of Tennyson's lines:

> "Seated one day at the organ
> I jumped as if I'd been shot,
> For the Dean was upon me, snarling
> 'Stainer—and *make it hot*.'

> "All week I swung Stainer and Barnby,
> Bach, Gounod, and Bunnett in A;
> I said, 'Gosh, the old bus is a wonder!'
> The Dean, with a nod, said 'Okay.' "
>
> D. B. WYNDHAM LEWIS

247. *Once a-Maying.* From Milton's "L'Allegro," line 20.

248. *Corinna Goes a-Singing.* Were there an aptitude test for Are You Fit to Read Humorous Verse? this could stand as Question No. 1. For skill, symmetry, enchantment, and celestial aura, about as good as they co-ome.

252. *"When daffodils begin to peer."* From *The Winter's Tale,* iv, 3. Autolycus singing.

257. *Autolycus' Song.* From *The Winter's Tale,* iv, 2.

Autolycus' Song (in Basic English). Acknowledgment should here be made to *The Basic Dictionary* by C. K. Ogden (Kegan Paul, Trench, Trubner & Co., Ltd., London, 1939).

Some months after Mr. Greene wrote his Basic parodies, Sir A. P. Herbert contributed some others to *Punch*. Such an example of what the anthropologists call converging evolution is repeated frequently in the history of light verse which, far more than poetry, depends on timely and quickly dated subjects. Several similar examples are cited in the length of these notes—and would not be cited if the editor thought for a moment that in any case Author A knew what Author B was up to. He has been guilty of the same thing himself in all innocence.

258. *A. E. Housman and a Few Friends.* D. B. Wyndham Lewis speaks somewhere of the "sombre surprise of Hugh Kingsmill contemplating a Shropshire Lad:

> "What, still alive at twenty-two,
>   A clean upstanding chap like you?"

The whole Kingsmill affair—equal to, or perhaps better than, Humbert Wolfe's fine parody—is in *A. E. H.* by Laurence Housman (Jonathan Cape, London), page 180. Who could forget:

> But bacon's not the only thing
>   That's cured by hanging from a string.

And this is a good one by the distinguished editor of *Punch:*

Mr. A. E. Housman on the Olympic Games

> I pluck the white hibiscus,
>   And muse upon the day
> When John would hurl the discus
>   A thousand yards away,
> When javelins could beguile 'em
>   Down under Breedon Hill,
> And Tom would take the pilum
>   And cast it back to Bill.

E. V. KNOX

See note about this editor and author against page 285.

259. *Song of the Open Road.* Parodies gain by being brief. Poems largely remembered for a single arresting line, how-

ever, are not apt to be good parody subjects as a whole. But Myron Stuart Kaufmann (1921-　) has done wonders with the opening of Carl Sandburg's famous "Fog":

> The fog comes
> on little cat feet . . .

Mr. Kaufmann:

> The frogs come
> on little flat feet . . .

A single-stanza Byron parody of durable delight is based on the middle four lines of the familiar

> So we'll go no more a-roving
> So late into the night . . .

> For the sword outwears its sheath,
> And the soul wears out the breast,
> And the heart must pause to breathe,
> And Love itself have rest . . .

This is it:

> For the sword outwears its sheath,
> And the soul wears out the breast,
> And the coat outwears the pants
> Till there's nothing left but the vest.
>
> THEODORE MORRISON

To What Base Uses. Of the many Hiawatha parodies, few have deserved survival. I am plagued by the first line of one, however, and I wish I could recall what it is, or even what the second line is. The first line (as I remember it) runs:

> This is the forest's prime evil . . .

Another ghost which rises occasionally from the mists of limbo involves the word *prim,* not *prime.* It is the beginning of a Wordsworth parody which likely has something to do with Sherlock Holmes or one of his lineal descendants:

> A primrose by the river's brim
> No simple primrose was to him . . .

Chesterton in "Citizenship" rings this one:

> A Primrose in the social swim
> A Mr. Primrose is to him,
> And he is nothing more.

Mark A. DeWolfe Howe contributes still another, "On hearing William Primrose, formerly of the London String Quartette, play (with the Boston Symphony Orchestra) the solo viola part in Berlioz's *Harold in Italy:*

> A Primrose by the orchestral brim
> A fiddling Primrose was to him—
> But he was something more!

Etc.

261. *Ode to Himself.* In the literature of parody there are several good ones on Robert Browning. He is easy to parody, for his poetry is full of the raisins of digression. By all odds the greatest imitation of him, and a wonderful verse in its own right, is Calverley's "The Cock and the Bull." You will find it in many collections—Franklin P. Adams' *Innocent Merriment,* for example. But it needs a good reading knowledge of Browning to yield all that is in it; and since Browning is out of fashion, I pass it by. A simpler parody—and still excellent by all standards of the craft—is Sir Walter Raleigh's. In hilarious mood, the one by Yeatman and Sellar (*q.v.*). Browning lovers should not overlook another fine one, "The Flight of the Bucket," by Kipling. Jack and Jill is the subject. As Kipling says, he

> Who wrote "Sordello" finds no subject tough.

See Carolyn Wells' *A Parody Anthology,* elsewhere gratefully referred to.

The clock-work interior of "The Cock and the Bull" suggests a remarkable satire-parody called "Homage to Ezra Pound," which appeared in *The Nation* for February 21, 1942. It was written by Gilbert Highet. Much more than in Calverley's case, Ezry's misery is for specialists, but here is some of it—and very funny. "The well-oiled fire-engine" is a critical quotation from T. S. Eliot, referring to Pound's admired technique.

. . . And there sat the well-oiled fire-engine
    all ready to strain its gutmost
       eek ow ouf honk honk
    unable to think, but ready to quote and paraphrase
      in six languages
    including Provençal. . . .
      ei didl didl
      li chat e li fidl
         it took a man like Ezra to kill Provençal poetry
           for us. . . .

And he had learnt all he could
    not a hell of a lot
    στεῖραν βοῦν=sterile bulls, that was a good one,
      Canto I
    a significant bit of bull
    Cimbrorumque minas=Welsh coal mines, meant
      to be funny, maybe?
    pretty damn funny, anyway
    QUAINT like all his Chinese and Greeks and
      Romans
    they appear QUAINT to Homer Pound's boy from
      the backwoods
the Idaho poeta. . . .

And his temper was never good, you get eccentric liv-
      ing in Rapallo and loving
BEAUTY
    the Emperor is at Ko
    but No
    silken strings shiver no longer, clashing of smilax,
      dark
    nuts on the dry bough, nuts on wet earth, nuts
it's lonesome too being the only one who understands
                      Caius Properzius,
                 'Alkaios,
           Li Pu,
      all great guys,
    an' I *know* 'em, see?

Uncle Ezry on the Acropopopoulos, the rube at his
    grocery stove
gignetei colon
: . . . .   GILBERT HIGHET

264. *Ballad*. After Jean Ingelow (1820-1897).

265. *You Are Old, Father William*. Unlike Edward Lear's,
many of Carroll's most famous verses are parodies. For
instance, "How doth the little crocodile" and " 'Tis the
Voice of the Lobster" are parodies of Dr. Watts; "Twinkle,
Twinkle, Little Bat" touches Jane Taylor, and "You Are
Old, Father William" is after Southey's "The Old Man's
Comforts," beginning familiarly

    You are old, Father William, the young man cried.

Southey is here forgotten and his imitator remembered. But
the anthologists usually wash their hands at this point (see,
for example Carolyn Wells' excellent collection, *A Parody
Anthology*, or the notes in *A Century of Parody and Imitation*, and in *A Book of Light Verse*, edited by R. M. Leonard
—both mentioned elsewhere). Southey is not the *only* one
forgotten, for "You Are Old, Father William" is a *double*
parody—not a secret but a fact seldom pointed out. Will it
bore you if I point it out? Isaac Bickerstaffe, who is thought
to have died twenty years before Carroll was born, was the
author of "An Expostulation":

    When late ı attempted your pity to move,
        What made you so deaf to my prayers?
    Perhaps it was right to dissemble your love,
        But—why did you kick me downstairs?

In turn, Carroll's verses, and "You Are Old, Father William" in particular, have been widely parodied *ad nauseam*.
But there is something charmingly humorous in this fragment from *The Norsk Nightingale* by William F. Kirk (see
also page 91 and the glossary note against that page):

    "Yu ban old, Fader Olaf," a young geezer
        say, "yure hair it ban whiter sum snow;
    Ay lak yu to tal me how yu keep so young."
        "By Yudas! Ay ant hardly know . . ."

Lewis Carroll figures in Leonard Bacon's speculative sonnet on page 149.

266. *Twinkle, Twinkle, Little Bat.* A parody of Jane Taylor (1783-1824).

267. *Song to Imogen (in Basic English).* See note against "Autolycus' Song" (in Basic English), page 257.

An Ode to Spring in the Metropolis (After R. Le G.). R. Le G. is Richard Le Gallienne (1866-   ).

271. *Edgar A. Guest.* Here is a pretty stanza (the first) from "Mary and the Lamb," by Frank Dempster Sherman (1860-1916). The humor creeps in at the end:

> Mary,—what melodies mingle
>   To murmur her musical name! . . .
> About her an ancient tradition
>   A romance delightfully deep
> Has woven in juxtaposition
>   With one little sheep . . .

How dextrous that swanny Swinburne line:

> *Has woven in juxtaposition.*

273. *In Memory of Edward Wilson.* James **Clerk Maxwell** is probably unique among the great scientists of history who dabbled in light verse. Charles Lutwidge Dodgson (Lewis Carroll) was a mathematician, but his stature is measured by *Alice* and not by some famous equations. Benjamin Franklin was more the moralizer than the entertainer. Maxwell (he is more modernly indexed as Clerk-Maxwell) wrote a considerable amount of poetry as well as light verse—some thirty-eight pages of it are in the *Life,* somewhere referred to. A good deal of the light stuff is mathematical in texture; much of it just good-natured banter about meetings, lectures, and other communal affairs of the professional world of science. But the "Song of the Edinburgh Academician" (1848) is a minor classic of its kind, with the refrain:

> Dear old Academy,
> Queer old Academy,

> A merry lot we were, I wot,
> When at the old Academy.

And my favorite lines:

> Let pedants seek for scraps of Greek,
> Their lingo to Macadamize . . .

But anyone with Scottish blood is probably biased. The verse which provides the excuse for this note has been in anthologies before; though not, I think, in a very recent one. It is surely needless to add that it is a parody of Burns.

275. *Of W. W. (Americanus).* See by all means (methods, procedures, stratagems) E. B. White's "A Classic Waits for Me," page 200.

Carolyn Wells once said: "Of all the poets, Tennyson has probably been parodied the most; followed closely in this respect by Edgar Allan Poe. After these, Browning, Swinburne, and Walt Whitman; then Moore, Wordsworth, Longfellow, and Thomas Campbell." Miss Wells was in a position to know, for *A Parody Anthology* (Scribner's, 1904) is still an authority in the field. I cannot quarrel with her evidence, but it seems to me that Whitman is higher than this on the list. Certainly most of the Whitman parodies are vapid and futile, but a number of them are first rate. No single line has ever quite set him off so well as this by an unrecorded poet:

> Divinely tanned and freckled; gloriously unkempt . . .

Here is one of my favorites, also by an Englishman:

IMAGINARY CORRESPONDENCE
Walt Whitman to Austin Dobson

I who have walked splay-footed in hobnailed boots,
I who have written at large in sesquipedalian lines,
I am eager for juxtaposition of mutual antagonisms.
The formule of splay-footedness is the formule of sesqui-
    pedalian lines;
But your formule, camerado, is the formule of varnished
        pumps and minuets;
You have minced through life, minion camerado,
You have minced with Q. Horatius Flaccus, Proverbs in
    Porcelain,

Beaux in Brocade, and Roses in Bonnets.
Juxtapose yourself, I beg;
Exude me the efflux of your eighteenth-century soul;
Lilt me a lyric, lisp in numbers, curt and compt;
Exude to me, minion to monster, pump to hobnail;
By return mail exude!

FRANK SIDGWICK

It seems proper and fitting to say here that Housman
appears to be the most parodied poet since Tennyson,
Whitman, Browning, and Swinburne. See note against page
258.

276. *John Gay.* The Beggar's Opera. The opera that made
Gay rich and Rich gay unfortunately yields nothing further
for this collection. *Quaerenti cella vacua.*

In this section, had I known of it in time, a place would
have been found for the following verse. It was first recited
to me by my surgeon friend—a classicist, incidentally—Dr.
Fred B. Lund. He says that *he* heard it recited some decades
ago by a Mr. Schlesinger, a young London surgeon who was
then visiting Boston. Mr. Schlesinger is presumably the author. It is on Dr. Lund's responsibility that I publish the
verse, glad of the chance to honor its grace and felicity. I
only wish that I knew the author's whole name and could
thank him for a courtesy which I trust he would grant.
How much I admire

How I regret the changes taking place. . . .

To The Parotid Gland

(By a Sufferer from the Mumps)

O dainty gland, whose lobulated grace
Adorns in health, unnoticed, my zygoma,
How I regret the changes taking place
Within your fair parenchyma and stroma.

Well you performed your lubricating mission;
Helped me to chew the bitter with the sweet.
How I regret the laudable ambition,
Born as you watched the passers on the street!

Never, you swore, should British-bred parotid
Yield to a Yankee gland the premier place,
And holding to that thought, when once you'd got it,
Straightway you started swelling on my face.

But O, ye Gods! Why should I have to suffer?
Why should my temperature mount, bit by bit?
Just because you, you patriotic duffer,
Wanted to teach the Yankees how to spit!

285. *Robert Burns.* From "Gude'en to You, Kimmer."
E. V. Knox. The present editor of *Punch* usually signs
his contributions EVOE. In debasic American this is often
mispronounced Evo or Evoy. As a matter of fact, it is a
Latin word *(evoe* or *euhoe)* from the Greek εὐοῖ, a shout
of joy at the festivals of Bacchus. In old-school English
phonetics it combines the sound of Mr. Knox's primary
initials: Eevee, with the accent on the first syllable.

292. *Prose and Poesy: A Rural Misadventure.* It is curious
(perhaps faulty) that in my reading of light verse I can
recall but one other poet who has used "A1" as a rhyme.
This was James Russell Lowell in a stanza of "The
Courtin' ":

> He was six foot o' man, A 1,
>   Clear grit an' human natur',
> None couldn't quicker pitch a ton
>   Nor dror a furrer straighter.

It was, incidentally, something of a struggle to decide to
omit "The Courtin' " from this collection. In the last analysis, however, it seems clearly to belong in the light verse
category rather than in the purely humorous. The reader
will find it in many anthologies, such as Burton Stevenson's
The Book of Home Verse; and in *A Book of Light Verse,*
edited in 1910 by R. M. Leonard (Oxford University Press).

296. *To Lillian Russell.* Is there, after all, so very much dif-
ference between British and American verse of this sort?
Compare Bert Leston Taylor's approach with that of Sir
A. P. Herbert (page 288) in " 'Twas at the Pictures, Child,
We Met." The tone is much the same, the informality is
charming, and the humor wherever it occurs is effortless.

299. ♂ *and* ♀ are the biological signs for male and female, respectively. Another poet who has used them in a title before Mr. Craddle is the physicist, James Clerk Maxwell (*q.v.*): "Valentine by a Telegraph Clerk ♂ to a Telegraph Clerk ♀"; *The Life of James Clerk Maxwell,* by Lewis Campbell and William Garnet; Macmillan (London, 1884), pages 408-409.

Dear, They Have Poached the Eyes You Loved So Well—. "The fourth line," said Brooke in a letter concerning this sonnet (see *Rupert Brooke: A Memoir,* by Edward Marsh; John Lane, 1918), "would have to be

And all my turbulent lips are *maître-d'hôtel—*"

But it wasn't, as it turned out. I have used the tentative first line of the unwritten sonnet as the title of the (by him) untitled sonnet which he *did* write. The whole business stems from Fiji, 1913.

Readers with a quirky mind might consider a line in that *Memoir,* "thrilling," as Brooke says, "with a false simplicity" from "a severe and subtle sonnet in my most modern manner":

I did not think you thought I knew you knew.

Coventry Patmore's (1823-1896) "The Kiss," a quatrain well enough remembered today, closes with the lines:

'He thought me asleep; at least I knew
'He thought I thought he thought I slept.'

It's a pretty little trick. Samuel Hoffenstein performs half of it in winding up a quatrain which I came near to using (*Poems in Praise of Practically Nothing,* Boni & Liveright, 1928, page 108):

I like to think I think I do.

And so on, and so on, I should suppose.

This seems to be the place, in remembering Brooke, to recall Mrs. Cornford's deep and wonderful epigram:

A young Apollo, golden-haired,
Stands dreaming on the verge of strife,

Magnificently unprepared
  For the long littleness of life.

303. *Tim the Dragoon.* Some Gaelic here: *Aroon* is secret,
or a pet name; *Avick* is lad; *Asthore,* my beloved, my
treasure.

Masterful Tim resembles anything but the roaring lad
in "The Irishman and the Lady," included in *The Odoherty Papers,* already quoted from. Philip Hale, the Boston
scholar and music critic, was especially fond of the third
verse:

One of his eyes was bottle-green,
  And the other eye was out, my dear;
And the calves of his wicked-looking legs
  Were more than two feet about, my dear,
    O, the great big Irishman,
    The rattling, battling Irishman—
The stamping, ramping, swaggering, staggering, leathering
  swash of an Irishman.

If Calverley's *Fly Leaves* (1872) is the cornerstone of any
library of light and humorous verse—and most in the craft
will agree that it is—I should like to add a word for another
and largely neglected volume: *Green Bays* (1893), by (Sir)
Arthur Quiller-Couch. It was enlarged and silently reissued
in 1930, but may yet one day come into its own. "Tim the
Dragoon" is in the original; so is "Lady Jane" (page 286).
"The Famous Ballad of the Jubilee Cup" (page 43), and
"The New Ballad of Sir Patrick Spens," from *From a
Cornish Window* (Dutton, 1906) have been included in the
1930 edition.

"The New Ballad of Sir Patrick Spens" begins:

    The King sits in Dumferline town
      Drinking the blude-red wine:
    "O wha will rear me an equilateral triangle
      Upon a given straight line?"

It's pretty long. You will find it also in Sir J. C. Squire's
Apes and Parrots, elsewhere referred to—and with enthusiasm.

305. *A Letter of Advice*. The Aramintas of verse are legion. Laurence McKinney once wrote some stanzas ("The Conning Tower," New York *Herald Tribune*, July 3, 1936) defending this imaginary consistory. He called his verse "In Reply Would State." The first and last four lines:

> "When I write poetry to my Penelope
> Readers inquire: 'Penelope who?'
> If I say 'Phoebe' they ask: 'Who can she be?
> Is there a Phoebe that we never knew?'. . .

> Critics satirical, verse must be lyrical,
> Rhyming is difficult, ponder this well:
> I don't care a thing about names that I sing about
> And if I did I'm the last one to tell."

"A Letter of Advice"—to come back to it—is to me the perfect thing of its kind. The twentieth century reader, unacquainted with Praed, will be rewarded by looking into him. He surely influenced Calverley; and that influence has trickled on down through the years and touched any number of British and American practitioners. Don't look now, but there is evidence of it scattered through this book.

308. *Peadar Og Goes Courting*. Peadar Og—Gaelic for Young Peter.

313. *An Awful Responsibility*. Note to ambitious youth: Get this by heart, and get it quickly.

318. *I Take 'Em and Like 'Em*. Verse, the effectiveness of which depends upon a clever shift of vowels—"I'm fonder of carats than carrots "—has many creative devotees. Harold A. Larrabee balances the change here (itch-etch) against a constant (yearn-earn). All very attractive in result.

THE ITCH TO ETCH

> "Lionel Barrymore yearns to etch . . . delays film."
> Chicago *Tribune*.

> O Lionel has the itch to etch
> While most of us yearn to earn;
> He'd like to be unemployed a stretch
> (These actors have cash to burn).

In order to etch, the idle wretch,
  He's casting his job astern,
For Lionel has the itch to etch,
  Instead of the yearn to earn.

HAROLD A. LARRABEE

And the reader in fortunate possession of a copy of *Spilt Milk* (Putnam, 1942), by Morris Bishop, can turn to "Poetic Five-Finger Exercises." He will find there

Said Hatch the fish-etcher
  To Fitch the fish-hatcher . . . .

Also an impassioned one about "a tutor, Peter Potter"— you can see easily what happens to that—and some other attractive tricks.

319. *Early Rising.* Or, if you prefer,

THE GLORY OF EARLY RISING

Thrice the crested cock has crowed,
  Thrice, and once the lark has sung
His premeditated ode,
  Exercising of his lung.

Chanticleer proclaims, and then
  Scratches with alternate leg;
Partlet,[1] mother, wife, and hen,
  Thinks of laying one more egg.

In the East a glimmer glows
  And a gladsome glamour gleams:
Stops the clamour of the nose,
  Flies the fairyland of dreams.

All the world is waking up,
  Blinking from its nightlong swoon;
And beside the breakfast cup
  Rattles the electro spoon.

This is the poetic fake
  That the poet can compose
Best, when lying half awake,
  Snugly underneath the clothes.

FRANK SIDGWICK

[1] Partlet is a proper name for an English hen.

321. *Abroad and at Home.* For no particular reason, Swift's "A Gentle Echo on Woman" is not included here. You will find it (very amusing) in *The Comic Muse,* compiled by Sir J. C. Squire (W. Collins Sons & Co., Ltd., London, n.d.).

327. *Tobacco & Trout.* Here perhaps is a verse which should rightfully be appended to the section called "Tricky." But it talks of fishing of a sort, and I am not one to carp at any man's joy in a day with hook, line, sinker, a worm, or a little stewed corn.[1] Mr. Newman Levy, as readers of *Gay But Wistful, Opera Guyed,* and *Theatre Guyed* well know, is adroit in the use of internal rhyme and what we shall call reflex rhyme. Anyway, this thing makes a pleasant noise—much better than the hum of mosquitoes nourished in the slow-water ingles of which the author singles—I mean sings.

MIDSUMMER JINGLE

I've an ingle, shady ingle, near a dusky bosky dingle
Where the sighing zephyrs mingle with the purling of the
　　stream.
There I linger in the jungle, and it makes me thrill and
　　tingle,
Far from city's strident jangle as I angle, smoke and dream.

Through the trees I'll hear a single ringing sound, a cow-
　　bell's jingle,
And its ting-a-ling'll mingle with the whispers of the breeze;
So, although I've not a single sou, no potentate or king'll
Make me jealous while I angle in my ingle 'neath the trees.

"When in my pilgrimage I reach." Rupert Brooke's "Heaven" is about a heaven for fish—a private heaven, with "wetter water, slimier slime." "One of the most magically witty poems in the language," says Siegfried Sassoon.

　　　Oh! never fly conceals a hook,
　　　Fish say, in the Eternal Brook. . . .

328. *Ode to Tobacco.* Consider an anonymous quatrain to a vanished member of the Vanishing Race. What a swart figure he cut in the average American town of yesterday!

[1] See reference in Mr. Thompson's rhapsody on rods, page 336.

The painted Indian rides no more,
He stands at a tobacco store;
His cruel face proclaims afar
The Terror of the cheap cigar.

330. *The Bait.* A pleasant turnabout fishing verse is called "To a Fish of the Brooke" by John Wolcot (Peter Pindar), whose dates were 1738-1819. There is no need to quote the first stanza; the second is largely spoiled by the irresistible "tenant of the flood"; but here is the third and last:

Enjoy thy stream, O harmless fish;
And when an angler for his dish,
Through gluttony's vile sin,
Attempts, a wretch, to pull thee *out,*
God give thee strength, O gentle trout,
To pull the raskall *in!*

There is a lot of this sort of thing, though chiefly serious, in John Buchan's beautiful and now hard-to-come-by anthology of fishing, *Musa Piscatrix,* in the Bodley Anthologies (1896). A book for the soul. It is Scotch and English; in some respects more of a hymn to the Tweed than anything else. The only Irish reference I remember is in Kingsley's "Killarney" (*q.v.*), and the collection is untroubled by American streams and rods. I wish that Lord Tweedsmuir in his later Canadian years had reëdited and brought it down to date . . . All of which because none but fishermen will be reading this anyway, and our freemasonry extends beyond the formality of lending flies and borrowing mucilin.

Incidentally, the fact that Buchan in 1896 includes this verse of John Wolcot (Peter Pindar) suggests that years later the name may have given him his fearless and fictional Peter Pienaar, the Dutchman of the Richard Hannay adventures.

And speaking of the Tweed: there is this anonymous verse, which Buchan must have known. I didn't know it, but Morris Bishop does, and I take it gratefully (like a number of other things) from his *A Treasury of British Humor.*

THE RIVERS TILL AND TWEED

Says Tweed to Till:
  "What gars ye rin sae still?"
Says Till to Tweed:
"Though ye rin with speed
  And I rin slaw,
For ae man that ye droon
  I droon twa."

331. *Patience.* To this, an anonymous fragment on what the English call coarse fishing. Do you ever think of a carp as being young? Or tasty?

"Give me some stewed carp,"
  Said Alderman Thorp.
"The roe's dry as pith,"
  Said Alderman Smith.
"Don't cut so far down,"
  Said Alderman Brown;
"But nearer the fin,"
  Said Alderman Glyn . . .

And then what the American angling authority, Mr. Charles E. Goodspeed, once referred to orally as a kind of eeliad. It is taken from the long "Centennial Poem" by William Stark, read at the one hundredth anniversary of Manchester, N. H., October 22, 1851.

From the eels they formed their food in chief,
And the eels were called the *"Derryfield beef."*
And the marks of eels were so plain to trace,
That the children looked like eels in the face;
And before they walked—it is well confirmed,
That the children never crept but *squirmed.*

Such a mighty power did the squirmers wield
O'er the goodly men of old Derryfield,
It was often said that their only care,
And their only wish, and their only prayer,
For the present world and the world to come,
Was *a string of eels and a jug of rum!*

If you care for pike, there is this one, taken from *The Incompleat Angler,* after Master Izaak Walton; edited by F. C. Burnand (Bradbury, Agnew & Co., London, 1887).

> O'er dale and dyke,
> O'er splint and spike,
>   Away! away!
> To catch the Pike!
>
> The Pike, the Pike,
> The fish I like,
> Is worth a dozen cheven;
>   In sooth I mean,
>   He's worth thirteen,
> But that would be uneven.
>
> If upon a bank he lies
> Sixty minutes, then he dies.
> Mourn the Birds, and weeps the shrike,
> All the Fishes go on strike
> At the death of Old King Pike.

Another from the same source, if not the same stream. This time solely—excuse me—just for the sound of it:

> Fish will Nibble
> When you Dibble,
> If you angle in the Ribble.
>   After dining on a Chop
>   'Tis the time to go and Dop,
> Dabble, Dibble, Dop, and Dape,
>   Using these
>   As you please,
> Never will a Fish escape.

Mr. Charles E. Goodspeed, in his masterful book called *Angling in America (Its Early History and Literature;* Houghton, Mifflin, 1939), quotes one stanza from an English verse which appeared in *Punch* some years ago, apparently at a dubious hour when someone threatened to plant the American catfish in English waters. The verse, says Mr. Goodspeed, "ended [*Punch's*] spirited protest against the proposal. . . ." It is doubtful if this old mud

settler would have damaged the chalk-streams of the southern shires, but his possible presence in barge-canals, big
rivers, and the like was assuredly somebody's secret weapon.
What Mr. Goodspeed quoted:

> They say the Catfish climbs the trees,
> And robs the roosts, and down the breeze
>   Prolongs his caterwaul.
> Oh, leave him in his western flood
> Where the Mississippi churns the mud;
>   Don't bring him here at all!

All over these United States, but particularly in the
congested East, stocked water is uppermost in the fisherman's mind and bottommost in the fish's.

Streamlined Stream-Knowledge

> As man and his motor have brought it about,
> The angler must learn, if he hopes to take trout,
> Two dominant factors in fisherman's luck:
> The schedule and route of the hatchery truck.

ARTHUR W. BELL

334. *Fishing in the Australian Alps.* "The muse of fishing
is not an introspective dame: she loves the crust of things
better than the kernel." John Buchan says that.

The undertone of witty rebellion in this fine-grained
verse suggests that Ernest G. Moll is a poet, here on holiday.
He is in fact an Australian poet, now teaching English at
the University of Oregon; the author of a distinguished
and powerful book of Australian poems called *Cut from
Mulga* (Melbourne University Press, 1940).

The Right Way to Fish. Taken from A. E. Bartlett's *The
Ludicrous Experiences of a Humorous Angler* . . . Kala-
mazoo, Mich. (copyright 1884).

And speaking of old books, any fisherman who doesn't
know it, will do well (if he can) to come by a copy of
Historical Sketches of the Angling Literature of All Nations,
by Robert Blakey (John Russell Smith, London, 1856). As
good as a good trout chowder, with lots of onion in it.

Half prose, half verse, some of it amusing; pleasant talk of other lads of other lands of other times in far places —of those who

> deftly wull could *thraw a flee,*
> An' neatly weave the willow wan.

336. *A Song of Satisfaction on Completing an Overhauling of Fishing Tackle.* Mr. Thompson, the painter-fisherman, calls my attention to *Vade Mecum of Fly-Fishing for Trout* by G. P. R. Pulman (1819-1880), who is, "I believe, the first consciously to fish a dry fly and mention it in print. Note the following lines:"

> Armed, cap-a-pie, with basket, bugs, and rods,
> The angler early to the river plods;
> At night his looks the woeful truth announce:
> The luggage half a ton—the fish an ounce.

"Some things," concludes Mr. Thompson, "haven't changed in 100 yrs."

337. *The Microscopic Trout and the Machiavelian Fisherman.* Mr. Carryl liked to spell *Machiavelian* this way.

340. *Tobacco.* When Mr. Graham Hemminger was an undergraduate at Pennsylvania State College in 1915, he was student editor of the Penn State *Froth.* It was in this humorous publication (November, 1915) that one of the most famous of all American humorous verses was born. In *The Saturday Evening Post* for May, 1943, Mr. Ralph Richardson reënacts the scene. "Faced with a publication dead line and two blank inches in the middle of a column, he [Mr. Hemminger] lit his pipe and searched his brain for something two inches long, to woo the student from the cares of the day." One of the college deans "was waging a one-man campaign against smoking, flunking every student he caught in the vile act." Out of this cheerful idea emerged "Tobacco." It was widely reprinted in college publications and in newspapers. It was parodied "to defend everything from horse racing to women." The verse brought various offers of jobs to its author, including one with the firm with which he is still associated.

Pipes in the Sty. Apparently Dum-Dum has never heard the American pronunciation of the name of the Cracker State. His ear is too good to explain his first line otherwise. For that matter, the last line of this informing limerick (which I quote for him) doesn't open with overpowering felicity:

> A funny old lady named Borgia,
> Had a parrot whose nerve would have floored yer;
>   Her mistress would whack her
>   And say, "Have a cracker?"
> And that bird would say, "Fire, Nut, or Georgia?"
>   ANONYMOUS

342. *Tombstone & Twilight.* Which reminds Mr. Philip Hofer of an ancestral headstone, wherefrom the final "e" of the final word has long since weathered away. It now reads simply:

MY GOD SHE IS THIN

'*To me they—drat 'em!—never give.*' From "Adam" in *Rhymes of the East and Re-collected Verses* (Archibald Constable & Co., Ltd., London, 1905).

345. "Here lies Johnny Cuncapod." The codicil to this podicil:

SOLOMON PEASE

> Here under this sod and under these trees
> Is buried the body of Solomon Pease;
> But under this sod lies only his pod:
> His soul is shelled out and gone up to God.
>   ANONYMOUS

People who condemn the *Congressional Record* as a waste of taxpayers' money, according to a *UP* dispatch by Frederick C. Othman in the public press for December 7, 1944, "do not appreciate literature." Apparently the *C. R.* costs the taxpayers $45 a page to print, appendix included. Well enough. Mr. Othman enthusiastically referred his readers to Representative Charles A. Plumley (R) of Vermont, as quoting a speech of [he is now] Governor Mortimer R. Proctor (R) of Vermont which in turn records these coldly chiseled lines about Solomon Pease. Worth $45 in any man's money.

A good variant of Johnny Cuncapod is in Field Marshal Viscount Wavell's *Other Men's Flowers,* elsewhere cited.

347. *"This spot is the sweetest I've seen in my life."* There are many variants of the husband-to-wife, wife-to-husband epitaph. One of the nice ones in the skeptic vein begins familiarly enough:

> As I am now, so you must be,
> Therefore prepare to follow me.

Written under it:

> To follow you I'm not content;
> How do I know which way you went?

Or yet another:

> I laid my wife beneath this stone
> For her repose and for my own.

348. *"Reader, pass on!—don't waste your time".* . . . Mr. Henry Beston, author of *The Outermost House,* assures me that on a certain stone in Topsfield, Mass., this verse is graven with but one or two minor changes—chiefly *cumbrous* for *crumbling.*

349. *"Here lies the body of Jonathan Stout."* In the Jonathan Stout flotilla is Henry Round:

> Here lies the body of Henry Round
> Who went to sea and never was found.

A Brewer. A variant:

> He had his beer
> From year to year
> And then his bier had him.
>   ANONYMOUS

"Underneath this ancient pew." See note against page three-five-two.

351. *ballade* free translation of what the cat who calls

himself francois villon gave forth (a free note from *archy and mehitabel*)

352. *John Bun.* A little sport with any unrhymable surname is meat and drink to Headstoneman Anonymous. Witness again:

ON THOMAS WOODCOCK

Here lie the remains of Thomas Wood*hen,*
The most amiable of husbands and excellent of men.
N.B. His real name was Wood*cock,* but it
Wouldn't come in rhyme.—*His Widow.*

See also the one about Jonathan Blue, page 349.

"Here lies poor stingy Timmy Wyatt." This anonymous fragment apparently has something to do with a cook—not necessarily a good one:

Peace to his hashes.

Also culinary—from Walter D. Edmonds:

Under this crust
There lieth the dust
Of Eleanor Batchellor Shoven,
Well versed in the arts
Of Pies, Custards, and Tarts,
And the lucrative trade of the Oven.

When she'd made enough,
She made her last puff,
A puff by her husband most praised;
And here she doth lie
To make a dirt pie,
In hopes that her crust may be raised.

ANONYMOUS

355. *Sir Roderic's Song.* From *Ruddigore,* ii. To many, this is probably just plain gloomy; yet surely there is *something* ghostly humorous about the line:

With a kiss, perhaps, on her lantern chaps . . .

Again, maybe not, maybe not, maybe not.

At any rate, compare this line with the envoy of the

Don Marquis ballade on page 351. Given suitable ideas, the inventor of archy was a master of the grisly.

360. *Gelett Burgess.* Of the many Kipling parodies, another good one on the same model was "A Ballad," written by Guy Wetmore Carryl. It begins:

As I was walkin' the jungle round, a-killin' of tigers an'
    time;
I seed a kind of an author man a writin' a rousin' rhyme;
'E was writin' a mile a minute an' more, an' I sez to 'im,
    " 'Oo are you?"
Sez 'e, "I'm a poet—'er majesty's poet—soldier an' sailor,
    too!"

There seems no need here to include "The Purple Cow," already in the lucent amber of so many anthologies and indelibly impressed upon so many people's minds; nor Mr. Burgess's almost-as-famous verse which regrets that verse. But:

I can see myself, O Burgess, half a century from now,
Laid to rest among the ghostly, like a broken toy somehow;
All my lovely songs and ballads vanished with your "Purple
    Cow."

BLISS CARMEN (1861-1929)

Hubbub in Hub. Laurence McKinney's knifty verse refers to the Knights of Columbus Games, 1941, in the Boston Garden. J. Walter Mehl won the Prout Mile in 4:09.7, setting a record which still stands for that event (August 4, 1944). In the race, Charles Fenske and Gene Venzke (the only other contestants in whom we appear to be interested) finished fifth and sixth, respectively. Which is probably more than Mr. McKinney knows.

361. *"When Moonlike Ore the Hazure Seas."* Many good nonsense words have been made by accident, as Lewis Carroll says. In proofreading this verse I found *efflugence* for *effulgence* in the second line. What temptation to let it stand! What sonority! Listen:

      When moonlike ore the hazure seas
        In soft efflugence swells . . .

Would Thackeray or Lear have permitted such gold to slip
through their sensitive fingers? I think not, I think not.

> Ah, Prujence!
> If *I* were indulgent,
> Effulgent
> Efflugence . . .

362. *Lay of Ancient Rome.* Macaronic verse used to be
much more fascinating than it is today. Mr. Ybarra's *Lay*
achieved its greatest fame a few decades ago, but I still
think that it belongs in this collection.

He has something amusing to report about its origin in
the following quotation from his popular autobiographical
study, *Young Man of the World:*

I had just enrolled myself in the freshman class at Harvard. One of my closest friends, a youth who had been at
school with me, was now a Harvard junior. Hence he was
prone to remind me that, no matter what my personal
opinion on the subject might be, I was not a human being
but a worm on legs.

I endured this treatment as a well-conducted freshman
should. But now and then I objected. There were times
when I refused to lie flat on the floor and wriggle about
on my belly—the posture and form of locomotion favored
by Harvard juniors for Harvard freshmen. In fact, I even
wrote a set of verses.

I showed them to my friend, the junior. He read them
with an expression on his face which, even among Harvard
men, would have caused comment because of its coldness.

"What are these for?" he asked.

"For the Lampoon," I replied.

He stared at me. His eyes registered disbelief that such
effrontery could continue to exist for a single minute without attracting a whole flock of thunderbolts. He looked at
me for a moment in a way suggesting that he was on the
top of a mountain and I at the bottom of the sea. Then—
when he had finally discovered where he had put his
tongue—he remarked:

"The Harvard Lampoon is a college paper. It is not a

school paper. You are no longer in school. You are in college. Throw your verses away."

"No," said I, bravely—though I was badly upset inside. "I'm going to send them to the Lampoon."

He gave me another look. It implied eloquently that what I needed most was a nice cozy talk with an alienist. Then he walked away majestically in the general direction of the junior class.

I sent my verses to the Harvard Lampoon.

The Harvard Lampoon printed them.

They were also reproduced in several dozen newspapers all over the United States. They were reproduced in England. They were reproduced in Shanghai, China. They were reproduced in Life, which was to New York at that time what the New Yorker is now. In fact, Life reproduced them twice, crediting them the first time to the Lampoon and the next to the Shanghai Times. They were reproduced in various anthologies. They were reproduced, finally, on the program of a low-down dance hall on the Bowery— where Tommy Mett and I gleefully picked them out one night, when we were Bowerying, from among thumb marks and beer stains . . .

363. *To a Thesaurus.* Amen, Frank Adams. Then there is this, taken from *Poems from Life* (Macmillan, 1923), beyond which I have been unable to trace it:

A THESAURUS NIGHTMARE

Drink (ingurgitate, engulph, engorge, gulp) to me only with
    thine eyes (vision, glance, look, gaze, stare, perspicacity)
And I will pledge (toast, salute, do the honors, greet, hob
    and nob) with mine;
Or leave a kiss (buss, smack, osculation) within the cup
    (receptacle, mug, goblet, glass, tumbler),
And I'll not (nowise, on no account, in no respect, by no
    manner of means) ask for (request, beg, sue, pray,
    petition, beseech, adjure, clamour for) wine (spirits,
    liquor, stingo, grog, cup that cheers, Sir John Barley-
    corn).

J. WILLARD RIDINGS

365. *O I C.* Light verse at that hairpin turn of the century, and for some time after, delighted in two-finger exercises of this sordid sort:

Why Not?

If Bet bedecks herself with gems, bestirs herself when bid,
And feels benumbed when very cold—bewails her lot when
　　chid,
Why shouldn't she *bedress* herself with garments, and
　　befeed
Herself with food, and feel *beglad* a nice book to *beread?*
ANONYMOUS

366. *To an Egyptian Boy.* As these pages are being made ready for the press, Mr. Harold A. Larrabee writes me, calling my attention to a fragment of this same sort of thing in *Faces in a Dusty Picture* by Gerald Kersh (Whittlesey House and William Heinemann, Ltd., 1945). A character in the book, who is supposed to know thirty languages, is asked to translate the following presumably Slavonic fragment:

> Svidjanili afromsanit anisi
> Yorlava Veniusi svidjanili
> Idchlitobodi siniginimar-iliol
> Ogatinisatusi svidjanili

The translation, as heard sung in Düsseldorf—complete with commas:

> Sweet Jennie Lee from sunny Tennessee
> You'll love her when you see Sweet Jennie Lee,
> Each little bird is singing merrily, all
> Getting set to see Sweet Jennie Lee.

369. *Aestivation.* While we are still in the happy midst of Latin and learning, let us pause for a brief reference to a goliard translation of "Good King Wenceslaus." Gelid and warm at once: the merry labor of Stephen Hurlbut; *The Classical Outlook*, xx (1942), p. 30.

> Sanctus Wenceslaus rex
> Stephani ad festum,

> Agrum vidit nivibus
>   Gelidis congestum.
> Vidit pauperem sibi
>   Ligna colligentem,
> Qui sub luna splendida
>   Sensit se frigentem. . . .

In the beautiful Century of the Common Man it seems doubtful if much of anything will be translated out of Latin, let alone into it. One of the disciplines which made Calverley and many of his disciples, down to F.P.A., the technicians in verse which they were or are is Latin. Even in a supposedly amusing book it is not a little sad to think that future craftsmen may have small occasion to salute their teachers as Sir Walter Raleigh (the recent one) saluted[1] Professor H. A. Strong, LL.D., on November 24, 1900:

> 'Twas in this toun ye first assayed
> The ancient gerund-grinding trade. . . .

But if Latin survives, by the grace of God, it will be some of the Scotch race (no matter how diluted) who will have a hand in the survival process.

370. *The Axolotl.* This word has haunted me since I was a boy out in Oregon. When at last I came to write a verse about him—her—I thought I was treading entirely original ground. But no. Ten or twelve years later I stumbled on an earlier form of *greatl* (great deal). In volume two, page 330, of *The Odoherty Papers* by William Maginn—I have quoted from it earlier in this section—occurs the sentence: "I'm like St. Paul, I've gone through a gradle o' perils." It is the Irish Dr. John Barrett speaking. Same intent, same sound, different spelling. There's a footnote translating, and the word occurs again. Greetings, *didl* & *fidl*, page 452.

Ah, well, so much for that.

371. *A Play on Words.* In the year of our Mairzy Doatage (1944), Mr. Samuel Hopkins Adams revived in the *Saturday Review of Literature* an ancient example of hog-Latin:

[1] Note the carborundum-Latin sound of *gerund-grinding*.

In pyntarris
In oaknunnis
In mudeelzar
In clainunnis.

Phonetic, but not difficult.

My friend and publisher, Mr. Donald Porter Geddes, reminds me of a mock-Latin verse which I had heard long since and entirely forgotten. Subject to possible variations in spelling, it runs:

Civile, si ergo,
Fortibus es in ero.
Nobile deus trux.
Vatis inem?
Causan dux.

(For the reader unable to begin the translation, the equivalent English is *See, Willy, see her go, Forty busses in a row* . . .)

My learned Dartmouth friend, Mr. Philip Marden, gives me a variant, the pleasantest part of which is the line

Gnoses mari, Thebe trux.

373. *The Up-Set.* You have just read (or it may be you haven't) the longest verse in this book—but wonderfully sustained, you will note. It has seemed wise in general to stay clear of long-term entanglements. Light verse tends to ramble at times; but strictly humorous verse rarely dares to. Thomas Gray, the Elegy man, wrote a pleasant thing called "A Long Story"—thirty-six stanzas by count—in the lightest possible vein. But the only really funny line from one to thirty-six is that in square brackets near the end which says: [*Here 500 Stanzas are lost.*].

384. *The Unfair Sex.* In 1902 Life Publishing Company issued *Rhymes & Roundelays* from the old *Life*—which some of us were pappily nourished on. The current clear-grained, cheerful cynicism which makes our days and nights so much pleasanter was then just round the corner. Or so we say. As a matter of fact, it was well back in the shadows. This

anonymous quatrain is about the meanest verse in the whole collection referred to. Ready?

INVERSE RATIO

Man's inhumanity to man is hard,
　In fact, 'tis scarce in line with aught that's human.
And yet—'tis quite angelic, as compared
　With woman's inhumanity to woman.

385. *In the Days of Crinoline.* What a curious, rugged, elemental, grim humor Hardy has! Not here, perhaps; but he can make a line bite better than almost any poet you can name. Lytton Strachey, in a fine, gloomy essay called "Mr. Hardy's New Poems," somehow fails to be impressed by this obvious fact. I know it, because one of the "new poems" is "In the Days of Crinoline."

390. *Gemini and Virgo.* A fit ending to the book, I think. This, surely, is one of the flawless specimens in the whole shelf of humorous light verse, British or American: human, skilful, amusing, tender, true. One cannot ask, or hope, for more.

Reader, what cheer!
Do you feel queer?
The end is here.

ACKNOWLEDGMENTS

The five-year stretch—what they call a lustrum—which has seen the growth of this volume from an iambic spore to the shiny well-ventilated mushroom in front of you, has been personally rewarding to the editor for a vast correspondence, hours of talk, and a folderful of good suggestions and inspired advice. He is deeply indebted and humbly grateful to many people for many reasons. Not all of the people or reasons can be listed here, but he will do his best. He would acknowledge the patience and purblind trust of his publishers, and the endless, detailed labor and embarrassing intelligence contributed by Miss Rose Dobbs of Coward-McCann. Then, in particular, the careful typing, cataloguing, and first checking of the manuscript and indexes (an arduous task) by Miss Florence W. Earle; proof reading, verifying, and the contribution of useful ideas by Mrs. David E. Humez; the sustaining back-stage interest of Roy Davis; and the vicarious assistance of Miss Marion L. Anderson, whose inspiring struggle with the mechanics of a dozen preceding books made this one possible. And he is grateful to Miss Jane E. Howard for many reasons; and to Miss A. Winnifred Preble for many kindnesses *ex officio*.

He remembers especially the useful suggestion of his friend and teacher, the late George David Birkhoff, the mathematician, that he look into the life of Maxwell—which he did; the insistence of Frank Buxton that he read *The Odoherty Papers* in two volumes—which he delightedly read; the independent kindness of Zechariah Chafee, Jr., and William G. Roelker in reminding him, with evidence, of What Cheer's—the title's—relation to their native Rhode Island; and the thoughtfulness of William B. Cabot who led him by hand to Watkins' *Dictionary of the Cree Language*.

His thanks are due Leonard Bacon for sending him in quest of an observation by the late George Saintsbury; to Tom Boggs for the verses by Robert Clairmont; to Rollo Walter Brown for *The Norsk Nightingale;* to Col. (Chaplain) William D. Cleary, USA, for two anonymous quatrains; to W. G. Constable for a note on Hilton and other British matters; to Robert Frost for help beyond help; to Oliver St. John Gogarty for a verse not in his collected edition; to Henry M. Goodrich for the Cape Cod quotation in the Introduction; to Charles E. Goodspeed for solunar advice on where to fish; to William C. Greene for shaping the note on Evoe; to Robert Hillyer for suggesting Arthur

Waley who might have been overlooked; to Herbert Hitchen for first acquaintance with Wilson MacDonald; to Philip Hofer for first sight of "The Scroobious Pip" by Edward Lear and for a fragment from a headstone; to Earnest A. Hooton for some shards of genuine Hooton; to William A. Jackson for the Gaselee gem; to Harold A. Larrabee for his critical reading of the Introduction, and other friendly acts too numerous to mention; to John H. Bradley, another inspector of the Introduction; to Dr. Fred B. Lund for a medical verse and some research into Horace; to R. L. Marston, editor of *The Fishing Gazette* (England), for the suggestion and clearance of verses by Capt. E. E. Nott-Bower in *Tobacco & Trout;* to John Masefield, the Poet Laureate, for his great kindness in putting an American on the trail of a book that led to a book that led to a discovery; to Hughes Mearns for the sane analysis of his own most insane verses; to Keyes D. Metcalf, Director of the University Library at Harvard, and to other officials of that vast institution, for a hundred courtesies and satisfying investigations; to Ernest G. Moll for the note on "Waltzing Matilda"; to Christopher Morley for advice on Don Marquis and personal counsel; to Nathan Pereles Jr., for delivering Washington Jay McCormick into editorial hands; to E. K. Rand for sponsoring a fragment of Latin —the correct one, if all the others herein are incorrect; to J. Beverley Robinson (encountered on a train for Halifax) for contagiously expanding on the glories of Sidgwick and Dum-Dum; to Theodore Spencer for remembering "The Up-Set"; to Major Stephen H. Stackpole, AC, AUS, then overseas, for the first word about a "Message to General Montgomery"; to John L. Sweeney for suggesting three or four of the briefest and neatest things in the book; to Leslie P. Thompson, N.A., for a brace of rainbows; to Howard Wallingford, who long ago added the unobvious missing line to one's own "Reservation"; to Cpl. John Welsh, III, of the *Stars and Stripes*, for a Mediterranean sheaf; to Harold Wentworth at the eleventh hour for a philological injection; to A. F. Whittem for syntactical morale in the case of *editor vs. the Habitant tongue;* and to the friendly Public Library in Woodstock, Vermont, for all but board and lodging.

And for other editorial or factual assistance his thanks go forth to Rudolph Altrocchi, George P. Anderson, David W. Bailey, the late Arthur W. Bell, Mrs. Margaret R. Baker, Charles B. Blanchard, Charles E. Crane, Dr. John W. Cummin, Albert I. Dickerson, Major P. B. Earle of the British Army, Walter D. Edmonds, Mrs. Walter D. Edmonds, Miss Louella D. Everett, Donald P. Geddes, Harold W. Gleason, Jr., Mrs. Arthur Guiterman, Miss Lois Harned, E. K. Hibshman, Ralph Hodgson, Mark A. DeWolfe Howe, Lt. Eric Larrabee, AUS, Mrs. Edward Levinson, Penn McGrann, Lionel S. Marks, Mrs. Carolyn Pichard, Fred N. Robinson, Roger L. Scaife, Robert Sibley, Miss Ethel Sidery, Vincent Starrett, Louis Untermeyer, Miss Thalia Weston, James N. White, Mrs. Katharine S. White.

Above all he would acknowledge the early inspiration and friendship of his teacher, the late John Livingston Lowes, whose creative mind and kinetic ideals were poetry itself.

The section called *Tombstone & Twilight* owes much of its variety to the scholarship of W. H. Beable whose *Epitaphs: Graveyard Humour & Eulogy* (Thomas Y. Crowell Co., 1925) has been in many cases the editor's authority or source. In this mossy area he is also indebted to a little volume called *Funny Epitaphs*, collected by Arthur Wentworth Eaton (The Mutual Book Co., 1900) ; to other funny books, to several friends who care for this sort of thing, and indirectly to Sir J. C. Squire.

For permission to print or reprint many of the verses in this book, the editor and Coward-McCann, Inc., are grateful to the authors, publishers, literary executors, and estates as listed in the following paragraphs. All possible care has been taken to make full acknowledgment in every case where material is still in copyright. If errors have occurred, they will be corrected with full apology in subsequent editions if notification is sent to the publisher at 2 West 45th Street, New York City, 19.

We thank:

George P. Anderson for three verses by his daughter, Persis Greely Anderson, including "Melodie Grotesque" from *The Poetry World*.

Angus & Robertson, Ltd., Sydney, for "The Intro" and "Pilot Cove" from *The Sentimental Bloke* by C. J. Dennis.

The late Arthur W. Bell for "Case History" and "Streamlined Stream-Knowledge."

William Rose Benét for "Lullaby of the Catfish and the Crab" from *The Flying King of Kurio,* published by George H. Doran.

Boerner Printing Co., Minerva, Ohio, and the author for "The Riddle" by Ralph Hodgson.

The Boston *Herald* and the author for "Unsolved Mystery" by George Ryan.

Bowes & Bowes, London, for the quatrain by Frances Cornford.

Bradbury, Agnew & Co., Ltd., London, the Proprietors of *Punch,* and the author for "I Was a Bustle-Maker Once, Girls," "Here a Nit-Wit Lies," and "Take Me in your Arms, Miss Moneypenny-Wilson" by Patrick Barrington; also for "From a Vigo-Street Eclogue" and "An Ode to Spring in the Metropolis" by Sir Owen Seaman.

Curtis Brown, Ltd., London, and the author for "In Prize" from *Sea Songs and Ballads* by Cecily Fox Smith, published by Methuen & Co., London, and Houghton Mifflin Co.

Curtis Brown, Ltd., New York, and Gerald Duckworth, London, for "On a Great Election," "On a Politician," "On His Books," and "On Lady Poltagrue, A Public Peril" from *Sonnets and Verse* by Hilaire Belloc, published by Sheed and Ward, Inc., New York, and Gerald Duckworth, London.

Gelett Burgess for "I Wish that My Room Had a Floor" from *The Burgess Nonsense Book,* published by Frederick A. Stokes Co., and for "Over the Hills with Nancy" and "I seen a dunce of a poet once," from *A Gage of Youth,* published by Small, Maynard & Co., Boston.

Chapman & Grimes, Inc., and the author for "Black and White Shuffle" from *Mountains & Molehills* by Harry Elmore Hurd, (copyright 1926 by Richard G. Badger), reprinted by permission from Chapman & Grimes, Inc., of Boston.

Robert Clairmont for "A Hero in the Land of Dough" and "The Answers." The former was published in "New Verse" in the Providence *Journal.*

Cobden-Sanderson, London, Messrs. A. P. Watt and Son, London, and the author for "Moan in the Form of a Ballade" by Maurice Baring from *One Hundred & One Ballades.*

Constable & Co., Ltd., London, and the author for the following verses or quotations from verses by Major John Kendall (Dum-Dum): "My Last Illusion" from *The Crackling of Thorns,* "A Soldier of Weight" and four stanzas from "Adam" from *Rhymes of the East and Re-collected Verses,* "Circumstance without Pomp" from *Odd Numbers,* "The Problem of the Poles" and a quotation from *A Fool's Paradise,* "Hug Me Tight" and "Pipes in the Sty" from *Short Doses.* Also for the following verses by Sir Walter Raleigh from *Laughter from a Cloud:* "The Artist," "Ballade of the Goth," "Eating Song," "Ode to Himself," "Stans Puer ad Mensam," and "Wishes of an Elderly Man."

Covici-Friede, Inc., for "Lapsus Linguae," "Warm Babies," "Good Reasons," "The Humorist," "An Awful Responsibility," "An Original Cuss," "Ballad of Barley," and "Marital Tragedy" from *Pot Shots from Pegasus* by Keith Preston, reprinted by permission of Crown Publishers.

Coward-McCann, Inc., and the author for "Perambulator Poems," "Convalescence," and "History of Education" from *And What's More* by David McCord, copyright 1941. Also for "Madeline at Jefferson Market Night Court" from *The Lost Year* by Margaret McGovern, copyright 1929.

The Trustees of Dartmouth College for "Eleazar Wheelock" by Richard Hovey.

The Editor of *The Decachord* for "The Ass" by Edwin Allan.

Demcourier, published by Demco Library Supplies, Madison, Wis., for permission to use material from an article on Louis Untermeyer by David McCord.

The Detroit *News* and the author for "A Geologist's Epitaph" by Jane W. Stedman.

Dodd, Mead & Co., Inc., and the author for "Third Row, Centre" from *Starry Harness* by William Rose Benét.

Dodd, Mead & Co., Messrs. A. P. Watt and Son, and the Executrix of the late G. K. Chesterton, as well as Methuen & Co., Ltd., London, for the following verses from *The Collected Poems of G. K. Chesterton,* copyrighted by Dodd, Mead & Co., Inc.: "Elegy in a Country Churchyard," "Commercial Candour," and "The Englishman." Also Dodd, Mead & Co., Inc. and McClelland & Stewart, Ltd., Canada, for "Dear, They Have Poached the Eyes You Loved So Well—" from *Rupert Brooke: A Memoir* by Edward Marsh, copyright, 1918 by Dodd, Mead & Co., Inc. Also the publishers and the author for "A Grain of Salt" from *Nautical Lays of a Landsman* by Wallace Irwin. Also Dodd, Mead & Co., Inc., for "Sonnet on Stewed Prunes" and two brief quotations from *The Norsk Nightingale* by William F. Kirk. All selections reprinted by permission of Dodd, Mead & Co., Inc.

Doubleday, Doran & Co., Inc., for "Étude Géographique" and part of the "Song of Switzerland" from *What the Queen Said* by Stoddard King, copyright 1926 by Doubleday, Doran & Co., Inc. Also for "Us Potes," "To a Thesaurus," and "Rarae Aves" from *Column Book of F.P.A.* by Franklin P. Adams, copyright 1928 by Doubleday, Doran & Co., Inc. Also for "Mad Dogs and Englishmen" from *Collected Sketches and Lyrics* by Noel Coward, copyright 1931, 1932, by Noel Coward, reprinted by permission of Doubleday, Doran & Co., Inc. Also for "Apex" from *Our Cat* by Baron Ireland, copyright 1931, 1932, 1933, and 1934 by Doubleday, Doran & Co., Inc. Also for "ballade," "prohibition," and "the honey bee," from *archy & mehitabel* and "archygrams," "archy experiences a seizure," and "archy a low brow" from *archys life of mehitabel,* both by Don Marquis,

1932, and "The Question Mark," 1930, by Persis Greely Anderson; "Pillow Cases," 1942, by Richard Armour; "The Anatomy of Humor," 1941, "The Immoral Arctic," 1943, "Merry Old Souls," 1943, "A Salute to the Modern Language Association," 1938, and "Sing a Song of the Cities," 1943, by Morris Bishop; "After Reading the Reviews of Finnegans Wake," 1939, by Melville Cane; "A Little Bow to Books on How To," 1940, by Irwin Edman; "Obit on Parnassus," 1937, by F. Scott Fitzgerald; "On the Vanity of Earthly Greatness," 1930, by Arthur Guiterman; "Enigma in Altman's," 1936, "Recipe for an Evening Musicale," 1936, and "Text for Today," 1935, by Phyllis McGinley; "The Firefly," 1942, "Introspective Reflection," 1930, and "Song of the Open Road," 1932, by Ogden Nash; "Policy," 1928, by Carolyn Wells; "A Classic Waits for Me," 1944, "Commuter," 1925, and "Marble-Top," 1927, by E. B. White.

Faber & Faber, Ltd., London, Curtis Brown, Ltd., London, and the author for "On Some South African Novelists," "The Death of Polybius Jubb," and "On Professor Drennan's Verse" from *Adamastor* by Roy Campbell.

Farrar & Rinehart, Inc., and Leonard Bacon for "Epitaph in Anticipation" and "Tower of Ivory" from *Rhyme and Punishment,* copyright 1936 by Leonard Bacon and reprinted by permission of Farrar & Rinehart, Inc., Publishers.

Farrar & Rinehart, Inc., and Brandt & Brandt for "Unfamiliar Quartet" by Stephen Vincent Benét, from *Ballads and Poems,* published by Farrar & Rinehart, Inc., copyright 1918, 1920, 1923, 1925, 1929, 1930, 1931, by Stephen Vincent Benét.

Richard H. Field for a limerick.

Mitchell D. Follansbee, Jr., and *The [Harvard] Lampoon Fifty Year Book* for a quatrain by Mitchell D. Follansbee.

Robert Frost, George F. Whicher (who owns the letter in which the poem appears), and The Jones Library, Amherst, for "A Correction," by Robert Frost, not previously published.

Strickland Gillilan for his "On the Antiquity of Microbes."

Good Housekeeping and W. E. Farbstein for his "Double Duty," taken from the March, 1942, issue of the magazine.

Al Graham and the *Saturday Evening Post* for "Theme Song for a Songwriters' Union"; also Mr. Graham and *The New York Times Magazine* for "Folks, I Give You Science!"

Richard L. Greene for two verses in Basic English: "Autolycus' Song" and "Song to Imogen." See also a note against page 257.

Hamish Hamilton, Ltd., London, and the author for "Old Dan'l," "A Memory," "From the Greek Anthology," "Sunday Morning," and "The Brewer's Man," from *Selected Poems,* 1931, by L. A. G. Strong.

* Originally published in *The New Yorker*.

Harcourt, Brace & Co., Inc., for "Mia Carlotta" and "The Tides of Love" from *Selected Poems of T. A. Daly,* copyright 1936 by Harcourt, Brace & Co., Inc. Also for the prose passage quoted from *Characters and Commentaries,* pages 271-272, by Lytton Strachey. We thank them and the authors for "Enigma in Altman's," * "Recipe for an Evening Musicale," * and "Text for Today," * from *One More Manhattan* by Phyllis McGinley, copyright 1937 by Harcourt, Brace & Co., Inc. Also for "Einstein Among the Coffee-Cups (by T. S. Eli-t)," two verses from "The Modern Nursery," and "Round (by Alfr-d Kr-ymborg)" from *Collected Parodies of Louis Untermeyer,* copyright 1927 by Harcourt, Brace & Co., Inc.

Harper & Brothers and the author for "The Archaeologist of the Future" from *Lost Buffalo and Other Poems,* by Leonard Bacon, published by Harper & Brothers; the same publisher for "The Microscopic Trout and the Machiavelian Fisherman" from *Fables for the Frivolous* by Guy Wetmore Carryl; also (with Edward Arnold, London) for "Aunt Eliza," "Grandpapa," "Patience," and "Presence of Mind" from *Ruthless Rhymes* by Harry Graham; and for "Commuter," * "I Marvel at the Ways of God," and "Marble-Top" * from *The Lady is Cold,* and "A Father Does His Best" * from *The Fox of Peapack,* both by E. B. White, published by Harper & Brothers.

Louise Dyer Harris for "Review of a Cook Book" and "Crossing Boston Common" from *Pen Grins,* published at 185 Highland Ave., Newtonville, Mass.

Francis Whiting Hatch and *The Old Farmer's Almanack* for "He Laughed Last;" and Mr. Hatch for "So This is Middle Age!"

Leland Hayward, Inc., and the Society of Authors, London, for "When Adam Day by Day" and "Amelia Mixed the Mustard" by A. E. Housman, reprinted from *A.E.H.* by Laurence Housman; permission granted by the Society of Authors as the literary representative of the Trustees of the Estate of the late A. E. Housman.

Messrs. A. P. Watt and Son and the author for "Epitaph on an Unfortunate Artist" from *On English Poetry* by Robert Graves, published by William Heinemann, Ltd., London, and Alfred A. Knopf, Inc.

New York *Herald Tribune,* and the author in each instance, for "Listen, pigeon, bend an ear" by H. W. Haenigsen; "Hub-bub in Hub" by Laurence McKinney; "Miniver Cheevy, Jr." by David Fisher Parry; and "Ludmilla" by Ernest W. Thiele.

* Originally published in *The New Yorker*.

Hodder & Stoughton, Ltd., London, for "Sam" from *The Collected Poems of St. John Adcock*.

Henry Holt and Co., Inc. and also the author, in each instance, for "The Bees' Song" and "The Spectre" from *Collected Poems* of Walter de la Mare; "Brown's Descent" from *The Collected Poems of Robert Frost*, "A Considerable Speck" from *A Witness Tree*, and "The Hardship of Accounting" from *A Further Range*, both by Robert Frost; also for "Table for One" * and a quotation from "Notes for a Mural: Men at Work," both from *Fair Warning* by John Holmes; also for two brief verse quotations from "The Rougherneck" in *Foolish Fiction* by Christopher Ward.

Earnest A. Hooton for "Lines to Homo Somejerktensis" and "Ode to a Dental Hygienist."

Houghton Mifflin Co. and the author for "Sentimental Journey" and "Wednesday" from *Strange Truth* by Elspeth (Bragdon); Houghton Mifflin Co. for "The Walloping Window-blind" from *Davy and the Goblin* by Charles Edward Carryl; for "Jim," "Mrs. Judge Jenkins," and "Plain Language from Truthful James," from Bret Harte's *Poems*.

Houghton Mifflin Co. and the author for "Pocket and Steeple" from *Songs of September* by Mark A. DeWolfe Howe; and Houghton Mifflin Co. and Lionel S. Marks for "Concerning Love" from *The Singing Leaves* by Josephine Preston Peabody.

Mark A. DeWolfe Howe for "Petrillo," not previously published.

Bruce Humphries, Inc., and the author for "Assorted Relishes," "Horses," "Money," "Not a Cloud in the Sky," "One Down," "To a Human Skeleton," and "Transportation" from *Yours for the Asking* by Richard Armour, copyright 1942 by Bruce Humphries, Inc.

Hutchinson & Co., Ltd., London, and the author for two passages by D. B. Wyndham Lewis from *Take It To Bed*, quoted in Part II (*After All*).

Alfred A. Knopf, Inc., Gerald Duckworth & Co., Ltd., London, and the author for "The Dromedary" and "The Hippopotamus" from *Cautionary Verses* by Hilaire Belloc, copyright 1931 by Hilaire Belloc; Alfred A. Knopf, Inc., and the author for "Moo!" and "Epigram" from *The Collected Verse of Robert Hillyer*, copyright 1933 by Robert Hillyer; Alfred A. Knopf, Inc., Pearn, Pollinger & Higham, Ltd., London, and William Heinemann, Ltd., London, for "Fate and the Younger Generation," from *Pansies* by D. H. Lawrence, copyright 1929 by Alfred A.

* Originally published in *The New Yorker*.

Knopf, Inc. Alfred A. Knopf, Inc. and the author for "I Wonder What Became of Rand, McNally," "Midsummer Jingle," "The Scandalous Tale of Percival and Genevieve," and two stanzas from two other verses, all from *Gay But Wistful* by Newman Levy. Alfred A. Knopf, Inc., and Constable & Company, Ltd., London, for "The Philosopher" from *170 Chinese Poems* by Arthur Waley, copyright 1919 by Alfred A. Knopf, Inc.

J. B. Lippincott Co. for "Here Lies Bill" from *The Laughing Willow* and "Stairs" from *Excuse It Please*, both by Oliver Herford.

J. B. Lippincott Co. and the author for "The Grapes of Wrath," "Psychoanalysts," "Thoughts for St. Stephen," and "Unearned Increment," from *Mandarin in Manhattan*, copyright 1933 by Christopher Morley, and "A Rose Is a Rose" from *Streamlines*, copyright, 1933 by Christopher Morley, both published by J. B. Lippincott Co.

Little, Brown & Co. and the author for "The Firefly," * "The Kangaroo," * and "The Termite" from *Good Intentions*, and "The Duck," "Introspective Reflection," "The Japanese," "Kind of an Ode to Duty," "The Kitten," "Song of the Open Road," * and "The Turtle" from *The Face is Familiar*, both by Ogden Nash. All selections reprinted by permission of Little, Brown & Co.

Liveright Publishing Corporation and the author for "You hire a cook," "You work and work," and "Breathes there a man" from *Poems in Praise of Practically Nothing*, and "Come weal, come woe," a couplet from "As the crow flies," and a quotation from "Serenades and Songs for a Pent-House Window" from *Year In, You're Out*, both by Samuel Hoffenstein, copyright, respectively, 1928 and 1930.

Robert Lovett for "Forbidden Drink."

Washington Jay McCormick for "In Montana" and "The Rigger."

Wilson MacDonald for his "Armand Dussault," and "De Baby Show," from *Quintrains of "Callender"*; "Pierre of Timagami in New York," from the *Railroad Workers Journal;* and "Teemothy Hatch" from *Comber Cove* published by Wilson MacDonald in Canada.

Laurence McKinney and F.P.A.'s *The Conning Tower* for a quotation from a verse by Laurence McKinney used in Part II (*After All*).

H. S. Mackintosh, whom our London agent has been unable to trace, for "Il Est Cocu—le Chef de Gare!" from *One Hundred & One Ballades*, published by Cobden-Sanderson, London, 1931.

The Macmillan Company, New York and London (with the Executors of the Estate of T. E. Brown) for "To E. M. O." and quotations from "The Pazons" from *Selected Poems of T. E. Brown;* (with Messrs. A. P. Watt and Son and Executors of the Estate of Lewis Carroll) for "Jabberwocky" from *Through the Looking Glass,* "How Doth the Little Crocodile," "Twinkle, Twinkle, Little Bat," and "You Are Old, Father William," from *Alice in Wonderland,* "Little Birds" from *Sylvie and Bruno,* and a selection from *The Hunting of the Snark* by Lewis Carroll; (with the Trustees of the Hardy Estate) for "In the Days of Crinoline" and "Seventy-four and Twenty" from *Satires of Circumstance* by Thomas Hardy; (with the author in each case) for "On Troy" and "A Parable for Poetasters," from *Selected Poems* by Oliver St. John Gogarty; "A Glass of Beer," "Peadar Og Goes Courting," and "Why Tomas Cam was Grumpy" from the *Collected Poems* of James Stephens. The Macmillian Company, New York (and the author) for "The Fat-buttocked Bushmen" from *Up From the Ape* by Earnest A. Hooton; "New England" from the *Collected Poems* of E. A. Robinson; and "Said Aristotle unto Plato" from *Philosophy 4* by Owen Wister. The Macmillan Company, London, for "In Memory of Edward Wilson" by James Clerk Maxwell, from the *Life of James Clerk Maxwell* by Lewis Campbell and William Garnett.

Miss Bernice Marquis for "A Hot-Weather Song," by Don Marquis.

John Masefield, Thomas W. Lamont, and The Houghton Library, Harvard University, for "Book & Bookplate" by John Masefield, previously unpublished.

Mathewson, Wilson & Smith, Montreal, and the Estate of William Henry Drummond for "The Wreck of the 'Julie Plante'" from *The Habitant,* and one stanza from "Le Vieux Temps" from the same book by William Henry Drummond.

Melbourne University Press, Melbourne, Australia, and the author for "At the Grave of a Land-Shark" from *Cut from Mulga* by Ernest G. Moll.

Methuen & Co., Ltd., Messrs. A. P. Watt and Son, Doubleday, Doran & Co., and the author for permission to reprint the following verses by Sir A. P. Herbert: "Bacon and Eggs," "Come to Britain," "Recipe," and "'Twas at the Pictures, Child, We Met," from *Ballads for Broadbrows;* "Tomato Juice," from *Mild & Bitter,* and "The Bowline" from *Siren Song.* In addition to permission for the foregoing, the following verse, also by A .P. H., is reproduced by permission of the Proprietors of *Punch:* "The Racing-Man" from *Wisdom for the Wise.*

* Originally published in *The New Yorker*.

Ernest G. Moll for his "Fishing in the Australian Alps" and "Undertaker's Advertisement."

Christopher Morley for a couplet from *The Bowling Green* in the New York *Post*; and for a traditional limerick, "There was an old fellow of Trinity," revived in *Thorofare*, Harcourt, Brace & Co., 1942.

William Morrow & Co., Methuen & Co., Ltd., London, and the authors for "How I Brought the Good News from Aix to Ghent" from *Horse Nonsense* by R. J. Yeatman and W. C. Sellar.

John Murray, Ltd., London, for a verse from *Continual Dew* by John Betjeman.

The Nation and the author, in each case, for "To Henry David Thoreau," by Irwin Edman; and for the long quotation from "Homage to Ezra Pound," by Gilbert Highet, which appeared in the issue of February 21, 1942.

Captain Francis Newbolt, Executor, for "Master and Man," taken by permission from *Poems New and Old* by Sir Henry Newbolt, published by Messrs. John Murray, Ltd., London.

New Directions for "A Narrative" from *The Paradox in the Circle*, by Theodore Spencer.

Messrs. A. D. Peters and the author for "Ballade of Charon and the River Girl," by J. B. Morton.

Poetry: A Magazine of Verse and the author for "To an old Tenor," by Oliver St. John Gogarty.

New York *Post* and the author for "The Art of Our Necessities is Strange" by Forrest Izard, copyright 1940 New York *Post*.

The Proprietors of *Punch*, London, for "To an Egyptian Boy," by H. W. Berry, reproduced by their permission; the Proprietors of *Punch*, London, and the author for "A False Gallop of Analogies," by W. St. Leger; the Proprietors of *Punch*, London, Messrs. A. P. Watt and Son, and the author for "Mr. A. E. Housman on the Olympic Games" and "The Stately Homes of England" from *Poems of Impudence* by E. V. Knox.

G. P. Putnam's Sons and the author for the following verses from *Spilt Milk*, 1942, by Morris Bishop: "The Anatomy of Humor," * "Eschatology," * three limericks,* "Lines Written in a Moment of Vibrant Ill-Health," * "Mournful Numbers," "A Tonversation with Baby," "We Have Been Here Before." * G. P. Putnam's Sons and William Heinemann, Ltd., London, for the following verses from *Poems in One Volume*, 1926, by Sir J. C. Squire: "A Fresh Morning," "Lines," and "On Oculists." G. P. Putnam's Sons and Cobden-Sanderson, London, for these verses by Sir J. C. Squire from *One Hundred & One Bal-*

lades: "A Ballade of Any Father to Any Son," "A Ballade of Diminishing Control," "Ballade of the Poetic Life." G. P. Putnam's Sons and Hodder & Stoughton, London, for "If Gray Had Had to Write His Elegy in the Cemetery of Spoon River Instead of in That of Stoke Poges" from *Collected Parodies* by Sir J. C. Squire. G. P. Putnam's Sons and Sally Harrison, agent and editor, for "The Dick Johnson Reel" from *The Bulls of Spring* by Jake Falstaff.

Random House, Inc., and The Modern Library for a quatrain quoted by Lewis Carroll.

Philip H. Rhinelander for "Bathtub Gin" and "Hangover," copyright 1945 by Philip H. Rhinelander; Mr. Rhinelander and *The Tavern Club*, Boston, for his "It's Very Unwise to Kill the Goose."

Wey Robinson for "Horse & Rider."

F. R. Scott, also M. J. M. Smith, editor of *The Book of Canadian Poetry*, University of Chicago Press, 1943, for "The Canadian Authors Meet" and "Tourist Time," by F. R. Scott.

Charles Scribner's Sons for "A Play on Words" from *Poems* by Eugene Field; "The Up-Set" from *The John Riddell Murder Case* by John Riddell, copyright 1930 by Corey Ford, published by Charles Scribner's Sons; "The Axolotl," "Baccalaureate," "Big Chief Wotapotami," "Reservation," and "On a Waiter" from *Bay Window Ballads* by David McCord; "Miniver Cheevy" from *The Town Down the River* by Edwin Arlington Robinson, copyright by Charles Scribner's Sons, by permission of the publishers; "Two Men" from *The Children of the Night*, by Edwin Arlington Robinson, reprinted by permission of Charles Scribner's Sons.

Sheed & Ward and the author for "Though art be on vacation" by Leonard Feeney, S.J.

Stephen Daye Press and the author for "Medical Aid" from *Walter Hard's Vermont*, 1941.

Stevenson's *Home Book of Verse* as the source for "The Modern Hiawatha" from "The Song of Milkanwatha" by George A. Strong, presumably out of copyright.

The New York *Sun* and the author for "The Dignity of Labor" by Robert Bersohn.

Mrs. B. L. Taylor for "The Bards We Quote," "Canopus," "To Lillian Russell," and "To What Base Uses!" from *Motley Measures* by Bert Leston Taylor, published by Alfred A. Knopf, Inc.

The New York *Times* and the author for "Opera in English?" by Benjamin M. Steigman.

The Viking Press, Inc., and the author for "Autobiography"

from *Enough Rope* by Dorothy Parker, copyright 1926 by Dorothy Parker, reprinted by permission of The Viking Press, Inc., New York. Also for "Experience," "Portrait of the Artist," "Résumé," and "Unfortunate Coincidence" from *The Portable Dorothy Parker*, by permission of The Viking Press, Inc., New York.

Ives Washburn and the author for "A Christian is a man who feels," "Lay of Ancient Rome," "Prose and Poesy: A Rural Misadventure," and a prose passage, as well as four lines of verse quoted in *After All*, all from *Young Man of the World*, 1942, by T. R. Ybarra.

Messrs. A. P. Watt and Son, Mrs. George Bambridge, Macmillan Co. of Canada, Ltd., and Doubleday, Doran & Co. for "Pan in Vermont" from *Rudyard Kipling's Verse*: Definitive Edition, and "Municipal" from *Departmental Ditties*.

Capt. William G. Wendell, Jr., USMC, and the Harvard Club of New York City for the quatrain by William G. Wendell.

Werner Laurie, London, Messrs. A. P. Watt and Son, London, and the author for "J. S. Mill," "Lord Clive," and "Sir Christopher Wren" by Edmund Clerihew Bentley.

Whittlesey House, the New York *World*, the New York *Post*, and the author for "Antigonish" and "The Lady with Technique" by Hughes Mearns; and Mr. Mearns for his "The Perfect Reactionary."

Whittlesey House and William Heinemann, Ltd., London, for a quotation from *Faces in a Dusty Picture*, 1945, by Gerald Kersh.

Frederick Winsor for a limerick.

The Yale University Press for a quotation from "Exit God" from *Shadow Verses* by Gamaliel Bradford; and for "And/Or" from *Scenes from the Mesozoic* by Clarence Day.

INDEX OF AUTHORS & TITLES

(With very few exceptions, only verses used in their entirety are indexed. This applies to the section After All as well as to the body of the text. Anonymous verses may be traced through the Index of First Lines.)

INDEX OF FIRST LINES